The Frugal Investor

How to Build a Low-Risk, High-Return Portfolio

Scott Spiering

amacom

American Management Association

New York · Atlanta · Boston · Chicago · Kansas City · San Francisco · Washington, D.C.
Brussels · Mexico City · Tokyo · Toronto

Library of Congress Cataloging-in-Publication Data

Spiering, Scott.
    The frugal investor : how to build a low-risk, high-return portfolio/ by Scott Spiering.
        p.   cm.
    Includes bibliographical references and index.
    ISB0-8144-0270-4
    1. Securities.   2. Investments.   3. Stockbrokers—Salaries, etc.
I. Title.
HG4521.S714   1994
332.63′2—dc 20   94-40052
                                                                    CIP

Printing number

10 9 8 7 6 5 4 3 2 1

To my mother, Aunt Ruth, and Uncle Fred,
whose love and support meant more to me than they will ever know;
and to Nancy, my new bride,
whose love and devotion has renewed my purpose in life.

Contents

PART IV
GROW AND RIGHTSIZE YOUR ASSETS

APPENDIXES: A COMPENDIUM OF FRUGAL INVESTING
TIPS, TRICKS, AND RESOURCES

Why You Can't Afford Any Other Investment Book

Like that other high-rolling era, the Roaring Twenties, that came to a similar crashing halt, the 1980s were a time of excess no matter what your economic station or political persuasion.

Back then, the real estate escalator of the 1970s had passed its upward momentum to an effervescent stock market and, like those margined-to-the-hilt speculators of the 1920s, we rode history's biggest "up-tick" until the clock struck twelve on October 19, 1987, turning a lot of us into pumpkins. In retrospect, we can see now how Black Monday began our long, slow slide into the most serious recession since the Great Depression. And the walls of that deep economic pit, for many, still seem slippery indeed.

The Recovery That Never Was

America is still struggling to free itself from the effects of a decade of both big government *and* deregulation. Mike Milken may have paid his debt to society, but IBM announced its first layoffs ever and the tab for cleaning up the S&L mess just gets bigger and bigger. Congress talks about reducing the national debt but seems capable only of spending more money. A whole new spate of expensive federal programs has been proposed—from crime-busting to health care—but the bill for it all will undoubtedly go where it always does, to the people with the strongest backs and collectively deepest pockets: the American middle class.

Here's what we've got to look forward to ...

1. In 1992, the gap between assets and promised benefits for the largest 50 underfunded pension plans grew by a whopping 31

percent—the fifth straight year such deficits have increased. What can we expect in the year 2002, 2012, or 2022?

2. Around the country, corporate executives and professionals in every field shop for Hondas instead of Mercedes and everyone keeps an eye on unemployment statistics, wondering where the axe is going to fall next. Today, getting ahead often means just holding your own.

3. Club Med vacations are down and "cocooning"—wrapping up in a quilt to watch a favorite video—is in. The good life now means making the most of what you have, not just reaching out for more.

4. Newsletters like the "Tightwad Gazette" and "Downscaling 46510" (no joke—these are *real* publications!) have joined popular books like *Downscaling: Simplify and Enrich Your Lifestyle* (Northfield Publishers/Moody Press) on coffee tables once sporting the *Robb Report* and *Fortune* magazine. Wherever you look, people are trading their costly credit cards for Costco memberships—and the trend has just begun. Saving money used to be the hallmark of the poor; now it's about the only way left to strike it rich.

Bad Times Build Character—and a Little Vigilance

Fortunately, I've estimated that over 25 million fast-track professionals, entrepreneurs, struggling baby boomers, recent retirees, and many who are currently on the lower wrungs of our "post-industrial, service economy" will earn or inherit between $50,000 and $500,000 beyond their current spending needs at some point in their lives. Experience in life's economic trenches has taught these people that despite lavish government promises and seductive stockbroker sales pitches, the financial future *won't* take care of itself. Complicating this is the fact that these same individuals know a lot more about what to do with a $1,000 bonus or tax refund than they do with investing those tens or hundreds of thousands they'll acquire someday in the future. That wake-up call known as the Crash of '87 and the cold-water shower that followed made us focus on, if nothing else, what investment firms and governments do to us under the guise of doing things *for* us:

1. Wrap accounts, still touted as our shield against such abusive stockbroker practices as "churning" (trades that brokers recommend just to pile up commissions) and outrageously high service

costs, have come under fire now for their excessive "hidden" charges, like noncompetitive execution fees that can run as high as 3 to 6 percent of transaction value. Since 1987, the National Association of Securities Dealers, NASD, has arbitrated a growing number of investor-broker disputes, around 7,000 each year, involving churning, misrepresentation, and recommendation of unsuitable investments—a violation of Securities and Exchange Commission (SEC) rules. Customers win *twice* as often as brokers and almost half of the claims are over $100,000: hardly minor-league pickpocketing.

2. Derivatives and repackaged investments, such as zero coupon and STRIP securities (both of which break existing bond investments into new bundles of benefits), hyped by big brokerage firms as new ways of meeting investor needs, turn out mainly to be new ways of building fees and commissions by reselling the same old investments as the hot new "product of the month."

3. Mutual funds, once hailed as the ideal way to diversify or even "buy the market" through broad-based indexing, now vastly outnumber the stocks that comprise them and greatly influence their own market—and the share price of some funds have become as volatile as many individual stocks!

Even active, professional fund management seldom helps the small investor beat the odds. The Top 20 fund managers in any one year often wind up among the bottom 40 the next, and even some no-load funds are now being criticized for excessive "back end" charges. Even worse, some mutual fund companies seem to have caught the "broker's disease" and have been cited by the New York City Department of Consumer Affairs with deceptive advertising involving hidden fees, false guarantees, and misrepresentation of risks. As more and more novice investors turn to such funds as alternatives to low-interest savings accounts and CDs, the possibility of ruined financial lives on a massive scale becomes more than speculation.

The list of investment abuses could go on, but I'm sure you see my point. Whenever an efficient market gets too institutionalized and clogged with too many complicated products and fee-charging intermediaries (many with conflicting interests, such as fiduciaries who also act as product salespeople) something has to give, and it's usually the interests of the small investor. With so many odd-ball "securitized" investments floating around, even good opportunities—to save for a home, pay a child's college tuition, build net worth, or simply finance a comfortable retirement—get lost in the shuffle. A healthy portfolio that manages to return 8-, 10-, or even 15-percent a year can't contribute much to your goals when up to a quarter of its value goes to third-parties, not to mention the steady attrition of ever-increasing state, local, and federal taxes and the silent thief of inflation.

Enter the Frugal Investor

Although I learned about investments as a stockbroker and professional money manager, I began my career on the other side of the counter—as a high-tech entrepreneur. I founded a firm called National Digital Corporation, a pioneer in electronic photoimage processing, and made a profit—and had a ball—leading my own company to national media attention. From this experience in the productive sector, plus the many abuses I saw firsthand among brokerage firms and commission-based money managers, I learned the value of "value orientation." I discovered that it's not just what you make and keep—but *what you don't have to pay*—that counts.

I derived two principles from this experience and coined a term describing anyone who uses them: *the Frugal Investor.* These principles are (1) putting your money into quality securities from at least four basic asset categories and holding those investments for a very long time; and (2) eliminating or minimizing the costs required to do number one.

These principles may sound like common sense, but you'd be surprised how often stockbrokers, investment product/service firms, and financial journalists—especially "tip sheet" newsletter publishers—violate them. Because so much of what you read in investment literature concentrates on the joys of market timing, making a killing in a hot new security, and being sure you don't miss out on the next investment trend, it's important to remember what makes common sense so uncommon.

1. *Frugal Investors put their money in many markets—and stay there for the long haul.* History shows that domestic equities (like U.S. common stocks), fixed income investments (like bonds), cash equivalents (like T-Bills), and international securities (like the stock of foreign companies), as well as mutual funds based on these securities, all tend to react in *different* ways to the same economic events. This means that even a well-diversified portfolio of individual stocks or stock mutual funds can consistently make *or lose* money in certain years while other types of assets go their merry way—marching, as it were, to different drummers. If your

money is invested in only one or two asset categories, even big
gains one year won't save you from big losses the next.

2. *Frugal Investors pay little or nothing to acquire, hold, and liquidate
    their securities.* The Chinese have a saying: "Where there is no
    gain, the loss is obvious." What they mean is that money you
    failed to make is like money stolen from your pocket, and that's
    true as far as it goes. I'm just surprised they didn't go on to add
    what every Frugal Investor knows intuitively: "Where there is no
    loss, the gain is obvious."

For example, $10,000 invested at 10 percent and held for 20 years would
grow to $188,000. If a broker or other investment manager charged as lit-
tle as 25 basis points, or .25 percent, annually (and most charge a lot more)
to manage your account, that return would drop to $158,000—a "loss" of
$30,000. Viewed from this perspective, the penalty for brokerage or
money management fees seem obvious. In reality, costs and returns vary
a lot from quarter to quarter, year to year, and it's easy to lose sight of such
fees—particularly when no two account statements ever look the same.
Ultimately, if total account cost is high enough, a potentially profitable
investment may only break even or could actually lose money.

More Than a Bargain Hunter's Guide: This Book Is Your Lifetime Treasure Map

Some market gurus, financial publishers, and investment tipsters have
written guides for bargain-basement investing—from "being your own
stockbroker" to making millions (they predict) from one or more of Wall
Street's products-of-the-month. Other more technical books, most of them
aimed at institutional investors and professional money managers, present detailed asset allocation strategies and reams of market data—and
that's all well and good. Only *this* book, though, gives you a comprehensive program for getting started in the four major asset categories that I've
found bestow all the benefits of asset allocation *and* shows you how to do
it at the absolute lowest price.

And I'll even go these other value-minded authors one better.

Most investment books tell you a lot about how to choose a security,
but virtually *none* tell you when to sell it—how to draw money down for
any purpose in a way that doesn't threaten your portfolio's safety or
excessively penalize your long-term total return. They also ignore a problem all investors face at one time or another: how to restructure or rebalance a good portfolio cost-effectively as their goals and financial circum-

stances change: how to "fix it," in other words, to ensure you never "go broke."

Best of all, this book will give you the peace of mind you get only when you know you've done everything that can be done to guarantee the safety of your principal while reaching for the returns you need to achieve life's most important goals: buying a first or second home, putting children through college, saving for a comfortable retirement, or simply building the kind of wealth you need to achieve the lifestyle you deserve—money for world travel, starting a business, or helping your community

These are the things that money is really all about. These days, as never before, they begin with Frugal Investing.

Acknowledgments

Like any investment professional, I've received lessons in money husbandry from many people, not all of it intentional. The best guidance was always offered sparingly, judiciously, affectionately, and with good humor—the qualities I've tried to instill in Frugal Investing. To my clients, whose tangible faith in me gave me the confidence to share my ideas with others, and to those precious friends, associates, and advisors who helped me conceptualize, research, organize, and write this book, I can never thank you enough. If your name has been overlooked here, the fault is lack of space and not the value of your irreplaceable advice.

I wish to thank Wayne Rogers for the many years of pleasure his talents as an entertainer have brought us, and for generously sharing with me his insights into fixed-income and cash equivalent investing; Doug Rogers of *Investors Business Daily* for his many good ideas and moral support from the inception of this project; and the staff of Charles Schwab & Company's California Street branch in San Francisco, and Jim Fasth, Manager of Fixed Income Trading for Schwab Institutional for going those many extra miles to assist me and my firm over the past few years.

I thank, too, my friend, Susan Granger, who first got this literary locomotive on the tracks—transcribing my scribbled notes to the computer and putting up with my "brainstorms" when she had plenty of better things to do. Thanks also to Keri Azevedo, another valued friend, who kept the Spiering & Company doors open almost single-handedly while I was learning how to be an author.

But a good book is more than a handful of good ideas. Without Jay Wurts—my editorial colleague and mentor—these ideas would never have seen the light of day, let alone a bookshelf. My thanks to him for helping turn a gleam in my eye into a valuable resource thousands of people will use and benefit from every day.

Finally, I want to thank Laurie Harper and her Sebastian Agency for finding a wonderful publishing home for my brainchild—your unfailing enthusiasm and encouragement made an uphill climb a lot easier; and Tony Vlamis, my editor at AMACOM, for providing that friendly and supportive hearth and a much-needed helping hand at the end of our trek.

Scott Spiering

Part I
What Makes a Frugal Investor?

1

The Four
Cornerstones of
Frugal Investing

When I graduated from Merrill Lynch's three-month course designed to teach rookie stockbrokers the difference between stock and bonds—and to separate the pigeons from the bulls and bears—my wiley old mentor, a broker with decades of experience, told me an amazing fact:

"Well, Scott, you've just received a $100,000 education. Merrill spent the first $30,000. Your new clients will now spend the rest: the $70,000 they'll *lose* bringing you up to speed!"

Why You Shouldn't Buy Securities from a Stockbroker

What he meant was that the training all stockbrokers get to pass the Series 7 NASD exam has less to do with earning money from investments than it does charging commissions from buying and selling them. My new business card said, "Scott Spiering, Financial Consultant." What it should have read, as the cards of commission-happy salespeople in many industries ought to read, is: "Licensed Pickpocket." Here's why:

• Most new stockbrokers have two things in common. First, they have little or no background in investing or professional money management. Second, they're great potential salespeople. Both of these traits are exactly what the big "wire houses," or national brokerage firms—and even many big banks that now sell securitized financial products out of their lobbies—screen applicants for. Professional credentials, investment experience, and freedom from conflicting interests seldom enter the picture.

• Most individual investors also have two things in common. First, they've been conditioned by advertisements, financial journals, and even our regulatory agencies to trust financial intermediaries such as stockbrokers. Second, virtually all of these investors already have twice the money management sense of the typical stockbroker. Why? Because in order to gain investable resources, these people had to succeed in the real world where good ideas, honesty, and true productivity still count.

As a result, the best qualified and most conscientious half of the investor-broker team hands over a sizable portion of the investor's life savings to the one who is the least capable of managing it effectively. In fact, most brokers are highly motivated to put client interests not only second, but third behind their own hunger for commissions and their company's insatiable demand for profits.

To prove this, take a tour through a branch office of a typical brokerage firm. See all those young men and women in the "bull pen"—the low-partitioned common area surrounded by private offices? Each is equipped with the three essentials of the trade: a quotron screen listing securities prices (particularly those the firm is pushing at the moment); a telephone headset just like the 800-number operators use that allows them to make scores of cold-calls each hour without getting tired; and a canned sales pitch tailored to wear down the most resistant prospects— provided they don't hang up.

Most new stockbrokers spend their first two years in the bull pen "building their lists"—selling clients investments made through (and often sponsored by) the firm. They graduate to the private offices when their gross sales—upon which brokerage fees and commissions are based—reach a high enough level. It makes no difference if the security pays off for the client. Stockbrokers make money whether you win, lose, or break even, so increasing the number and size of transactions is the name of their game, even for the honest ones. In the brokerage business, this generation of fees and commissions is called "production." Brokers who achieve high production through gile, half-truths, and outright lies are called "rogues" or "gunslingers." In other industries what they do would be called self-dealing, sharp practice, or worse.

While brokerage firm executives officially condemn such practices, they often promote the worst offenders—keeping their consciences clean by not looking too closely at a high producer's tactics until a client complains. And for a client to even suspect sharp practice, he or she must know the firm's commission policy and commission rates paid for different investment products—impolite questions to ask, and facts your broker won't volunteer.

Unless you've been in the business, for example, it would be almost impossible to know that limited partnerships and annuities pay better commissions than CDs, T-bills, or even stocks. And when your broker assures you there's *no* commission—be even warier. Investment product sponsors have other ways to compensate the sales force. As you'll see shortly, a "commissionless" bond or a Class B share of a bond fund has, in fact, a commission built into the quoted price which never shows up on your statement.

Another favorite broker tactic is to reassure a reluctant client that "no cash" is required to buy a new product since the money will come from selling an old one. What the broker neglects to mention is that you'll be nicked for a commission on *both* ends of the securities' "round trip" (the sell *and* the buy transactions) and that new cash would have been a cheaper way to go, assuming you even wanted the new investment in the first place.

As SEC enforcement official Joseph Goldstein put it in a newspaper interview:

> Consumers have to realize that somebody who is selling you something is doing it for a purpose. And that purpose is to make money on the sale. Be skeptical of what strangers tell you on the phone. They're not your mother, your father, or your friends. They're not going to do something special for you. What they want from you is your money.

A good example of the broker's mentality is reflected in a 1994 "asset gathering" contest (euphemistically called *A Tribute to Excellence*) sponsored by Prudential Securities at a time when that company was being investigated for the use of questionable sales tactics. Under its rules, brokers earned points toward luxury vacations by selling retirement plans and money market accounts to anyone they could talk into buying them.

So, what's wrong with such a contest?

From Prudential's perspective, nothing. Commission-based sales contests aren't new, or even peculiar to stock brokers. And nobody claims that the investment products are fraudulent or too risky. Problems arise, though, when the broker's main incentive is "asset accumulation" rather than client satisfaction and the existence of such contests is not disclosed to prospective customers—to say nothing of the propriety of a firm launching a hard-ball sales contest during a major investigation of its sales practices.

So let's add a third reason why that Series 7 NASD ticket is a virtual license to steal: it connects people with extra money to people who will do

just about anything (short of outright theft, but sometimes that's no bar-
rier) to get it. For the investor, it's a dangerous combination. Here's a true
and all-too-typical example of what I mean.

Never Buy Securities from a Bank

Long after I left the brokerage business, I met a young financial salesperson at a party. She had started out at Dean Whitter but had flunked their
tough "production" standards. Luckily for her, some of our bigger commercial banks draw heavily from this population of stockbroker
wannabes, so she was hired by one right away to sell securities out of
their lobby—and this she did with a vengeance.

Today she was on top of the world: had just put almost all of a new
client's assets into Class B shares of a back-end loaded bond fund with a
12b-1 "trailer" of 1 percent. This meant that, unlike Class A shares where
the broker's 5 percent commission is taken up front and is over and done
with, the fund's sponsor hides the commission by telling customers that
the commission "is saved" if the investor holds the shares for at least six
years. What they *don't* say is that the broker receives the full commission
up front anyway, and the investor reimburses the sponsor a little each
year via the 1 percent fee (which is above and beyond the fund's annual
operating expenses). Even worse, the broker *continues* to receive .25 percent of that trailer annually for as long as the investor holds the shares—
a gold mine for the broker and a strong incentive to sell them to anyone
who can hold a pen long enough to scribble a name. In this case, not only
was the investment substantial—on the order of $400,000—but the sales
commission was enormous: over 4 percent to the broker, or $16,000, just
for making a couple of very persuasive phone calls.

As you would expect, certain alarm bells went off in my head as soon
as I heard this. At the time, interest rates were just beginning to climb after
a long period in the doldrums. Existing bonds with lower coupon rates
were dropping in value and even if her client had escaped the immediate
payment of an exorbitant, if hidden, front-end sales commission, a portfolio concentrated in bonds would undoubtedly look bad at the end of the
year—and like a train wreck after that.

When I asked why she hadn't also put her client into at least one
other asset category, such as stocks, cash equivalents, or, perhaps, an
international fund that would benefit, and not be penalized, from rising
interest rates, she looked at me as if I had two heads. She mumbled something about bonds being a conservative investment and seemed satisfied

with that until I pointed out that even bondholders can lose principal, as well as interest, if they liquidate in a down market. This was news to her—a little fact of life not covered in the Series 7 classes.

"Besides," I said, "the longer your client holds Class B shares, the more money he continues to pay you out of the 1 percent trailer. If he really is a long-term bond investor, he would've been much better off buying Class A shares and getting his sales cost out of the way. Now he can't win for losing: If he has to sell in the next few years, he'll lose principal *and* get dinged for the hidden sales cost. If he rides out the down market, he gets killed with the annual back-end commmission. What kind of investment is that?"

The answer is, obviously, *a lousy one*. What it ultimately came down to was (a) the salesperson really didn't have a clue as to how bond investors made money, and (b) she simply chose an investment that paid the biggest commission and fast-talked her client into a sale. As a result, she became a hero at the office—a "high producer" marked for big things by her boss and, undoubtedly, was given a better list of prospects. The fact that her client would very likely experience an immediate and serious loss didn't merit a second thought in the firm's—and her own—value calculation. When I asked what she would do when the investor noticed his 400K was now worth 350 and called back in a panic, she only laughed.

"Well," she said, "I'll just flip him into something else. We've got some new annuities coming out where the commission is almost as good. I'll have something for him, don't worry."

Sleazy sales practice? Of course. But is it illegal?

No—not according to the SEC. Our guardian of investor rights only protects you from fraud, not from greed or the ignorance of stockbrokers. Even when the securities you buy are appropriate and competitive, the brokerage firm's commissions, fees, and other tariffs on your account will virtually assure that it doesn't stay that way for long. Here's a "what if" example to show you what I mean:

Suppose a typical investor (who hasn't read this book) goes into a local branch of a major brokerage firm—say, my old alma mater, Merrill Lynch—and says she wants to invest $50,000 in the stock market. The first "product" she'll be sold isn't a stock or a mutual fund, but a cash management account (CMA) which features check-writing and VISA-card privileges (which she may or may not want or need) for "only" $125 a year. After an initial discussion of her investment objectives, let's say the broker puts her into five proprietary mutual funds with a sales load of 6.75 percent. Suddenly that $50K has been reduced to $46,500 and not a *dollar* has yet been invested. Suppose, too, that those funds nick each investor 2 percent per year in annual fund operating expenses and the 12B-1 fees (paid directly to your broker) to keep you locked into the investment. This means that our hapless investor will have only $45,500 left to work for her during that all-important first year. If the stock market continues to return the 10.3 percent per year it has over the past 65 years, she'll need almost all of that first year *just to break even*—and if the market is down, it could take even longer.

Now, let's assume this same investor passes a bookstore on the way to Merrill Lynch and a copy of this book catches her eye. Now a Frugal Investor, she marches straight past the full-service firm to a discount broker, say Charles Schwab, armed with the same $50,000 and a list of good equity funds she researched herself, to open a comparable account. This time, her cash management account, checks, and VISA card are *free*, and there is *no* transaction cost or hidden recurring fees to acquire the five no-load mutual funds she selected. Also, because she followed the advice in Part III of this book, her fund managers charge her only 1 percent per year, putting $49,500 to work directly. If the market experiences an average year, this modest cost is earned back in *one month*, not ten or eleven; and if the no-load funds perform even remotely close to the broker-offered load funds, she'll retain this advantage throughout the life of her portfolio.

The first thing all Frugal Investors must learn, then, is how to eliminate or minimize their reliance on such dubious "helpers" as full-service brokers and a high-priced management team.

Two Keys to Financial Freedom: Allocation and Compounding

While greed, sharp practice, fraud, interest rate changes, business slumps and failures, inflation and deflation, illiquidity, and security price fluctuations are risks in all markets, not all markets are prepared to give you the same even break for the risks you take. The key to mastering them is to understand and use appropriately the two fundamental tools available to all investors, with or without brokers or high-priced money managers: (1) time—as an ally, but also a potential enemy; and (2) volatility—the likelihood that your investment will be worth what it should be at any given moment.

Both of these important factors contribute mightily to *return*, the amount you want to make over and above your principal, and *risk*, the chance you have of actually making it. Frugal Investors may have ten thousand or ten million dollars to invest, but they don't have *one single dime* to waste. That's why they confine their allocations to no fewer than four tried-and-true asset categories whose independent responses to the same economic conditions, plus history of long-term price appreciation and ease of no- or low-cost buying and selling give them the best possible chance to achieve their investment goals. I call these primary asset classes the *four cornerstones* of Frugal Investing.

Before we examine their inner workings, though, we need to know how compounded returns—both positive and negative—and the frequency and amount of those fluctuations, or volatility, have made asset allocation the new "conventional wisdom" of investing.

The Double-Edged Sword of Compounding

Figure 1-1 shows the spread of "down years," or years ending with a loss, to the average annual return of portfolios with several different ratios of stocks and bonds over a very long period of time: from 1946 to 1993.

From this period, let's pick the worst year for stocks, 1974. At the end of that year, the S&P 500 closed with a 26 percent loss. In 1975, however, the very next year, the market roared back with a 37 percent gain. The problem is, when such down markets turn around, you don't start building wealth immediately; you must first *earn back* the money you lost. A

Figure 1-1. Down Years vs. Average Annual Returns of Portfolios with Varying Ratios of Stocks and Bonds.

Portfolio	Number of down years	Average loss	1946-93 Worst annual loss	Average annual return
100% stocks	11	−9.4%	−26.5%	11.7%
75% stocks/25% bonds	9	−7.2	−18.4	10.5
50% stocks/50% bonds	8	−4.0	−10.4	9.1
75% bonds/25% stocks	5	−1.5	−2.7	7.6
100% bonds	5	−0.7	−1.3	5.9

Note: Figures are based on Ibbotson Associates' data for the Standard & Poor's 500-stock index and intermediate government bonds.

Source: T. Rowe Price Associates

hundred dollars worth of stock reduced to $74 in 1974's bear market didn't bounce back to a new value of $137 in December, 1975, but only to $101.38—a mere dollar, plus change, over its original value! When price volatility like this works on a portfolio year after year, the compounding effect of incremental losses, as well as gains, can be substantial—and statistics about the "average return" of any one market can be seriously misleading. A more detailed example will show you exactly what I mean.

Two sibling investors, let's call them Jack and Jill, each inherited $15,000 from their favorite Aunt. Jack, a high roller, put it all into aggressive growth stocks except for a few thousand he kept aside for—you guessed it—options and futures. Jill, a steadier sort, diversified her portfolio over stocks, bonds, cash equivalents, and an international mutual fund she saw advertised in the paper, then left her portfolio alone.

After the first year, Jill's portfolio had increased 10 percent in value while Jack's had appreciated 15 percent. The next year the stock market slowed and while Jill still managed 8 percent growth, Jack's portfolio suffered a 4 percent loss. The economic slump got worse in the third year and Jack's holdings plummeted 22 percent while Jill's went down 3 percent. This up-and-down cycle persisted for two more years then ended up with five years of sustained economic growth. Jill's annual returns for these last seven years were consistently positive: 13, 8, 10, 14, 9, 10, and 8 percent. Jack's were more spectacular: 19, –4, 15, 3, 25, 18, and finally a whopping +40 percent. The big question they asked at their family's ten-year reunion, of course, was: Who came out ahead?

Jack and Jill computed their separate average annual returns just the way Jack's stock broker did it, and Jack immediately boasted, "See? What did I tell you? I averaged 10.5 percent to your measly 8.7 percent!"

While Jack reached for the champagne, Jill did another calculation—this one for *compound* annual return—the effect of one year's gains or losses on the previous ending balance, the way investments really work. Using this more realistic measure of performance, Jill's portfolio actually did better, earning 11.55 percent vs. Jack's roller-coaster 10.81 percent—and she suffered no sleepless nights and paid no broker's fees in the process! When Jack added on the costs and commissions resulting from his constant trading, his compound return fell even lower, to 9.37 percent. All that work and worry to do 2.18 percent *worse* than if he had never lifted a finger!

As Jill's strategy shows: What you don't lose, you don't have to recover in order to break even—the first principle of Frugal Investing.

Unfortunately, some people see a different lesson in this story. They decide it's smarter to get out of the stock market altogether and put all their money in a less volatile investment like bonds, or even a low-interest savings account. In fact, the investment industry tends to array its products along a scale based on just this sort of fear of, or tolerance for, price volatility.

Investments that pay no income and whose current price can fluctuate (sometimes a little, sometimes a lot) are called "growth" or if unusually risky, "aggressive growth." Their payoff is not in dividends, but in the capital gain investors receive when the securities are sold for more than they cost. "Income" securities, on the other hand, do just that: pay current income. Income stocks or bonds may appreciate in value, but that's not the main reason people buy them. Many individual portfolios and mutual funds contain some mix of growth and income securities, depending on the investor's overall objectives and tolerance for risk.

As you've already seen, many people are surprised to learn that even Treasury bonds—theoretically the safest investment you can own—can lose principal if you wish to sell them before they mature. If interest rates went up since you bought the bond, the principal will be discounted—that is, the face value of the bond will be effectively *reduced*—by prospective buyers to bring the total return in line with the nominal yield, or the guaranteed interest that gets paid to the owner, rain or shine, year after year.

The main thing to remember here is that compounding is a double-edged sword that cuts *both* ways. It can magnify gains, but it can also turn small, continuous costs and losses into crippling portfolio wounds—and avoiding *that* is what multiasset investing, the frugal way, is really all about. In a multiasset portfolio, nobody cares if the stock component happens to outperform the bond component in a given year. What counts is your total, long-term return—what's available to you when you need it for future spending—and there's simply no better, more reliable way to achieve that return than through long-term, multiasset allocation using the techniques I'll show you in this book.

Cornerstone #1: Cash Is Still King

Unless you've been on Mars since the early 1970s, you'll remember actor Wayne Rogers' charismatic performance as Trapper John on TV's long-running hit series, *M*A*S*H*. What you may not recall is Rogers' equally stellar performance as a world-class money manager. When I asked him how he found success in this unlikely second career, his candid answer surprised me:

"I got into this business buying Treasuries for my wife, who was the original risk-averse investor. Historically, [they] have always provided good cashflow for the investor who wants to sleep at night. For the cash-equivalent portion of your portfolio, nothing can beat short-term treasuries."

If you believe, as Rogers and I do, in the value of a good night's sleep, you'll see that all investment decisions are really *postponed spending* decisions: making sure that the money you want will be there when you need it. This means that (aside from its value as collateral for loans), even the most profitable long-term investment must eventually be converted to cash if it's going to be useful. Although noncash "security swaps" are done every day, one advantage of the four asset categories I recommend are that securities in each can be bought and sold in low-friction, auction-type markets fairly quickly and without excessive costs, commissions, or fees. This is a benefit that many who have invested heavily in such illiquid investments as commercial property, real estate limited partnerships, or closely held small businesses usually come to envy.

However, even though investments in all four basic asset categories can be readily converted to cash, only *one* guarantees cash virtually on demand, without a settlement wait of anywhere from several days to several weeks.

The Magic of Cash Equivalents

Liquid money takes many forms, not just greenbacks in your wallet. Checking (or NOW) accounts from which cash can be instantly produced by the stroke of a pen, passbook savings, money market funds, banker's acceptances, bank or S&L Certificates of Deposit (CDs), commercial and government "paper" (short-term debt floated in anticipation of near-term receipts)—even U.S. Savings Bonds, T-bills, and, if you're willing to wait a couple of extra weeks, certain life insurance policies with cash value—can *all* be used to "park" your money productively while keeping its economic motor running. The one thing all these investment vehicles have in common is that they mature, or reach their full market value, or can otherwise be accessed in 90 days or less—anything longer falls into the fixed-income asset category. With cash like this at your fingertips, you can handle personal emergencies or take advantage of unforeseen investment opportunities.

One way in which many of these cash-equivalent investments differ is their safety. Some products, like bank passbook accounts and CDs, are federally insured up to $100,000 per depositor per institution, whereas money market investments offered by those same banks usually are not.

Figure 1-2. Typical Yields for Consumers. Money Market Funds Yield Is Seven-Day Average. CD Yields Are for Deposits of $50,000 or Less at Major Banks.

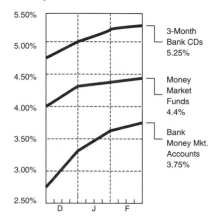

Source: *Banxquote Money Markets; Money Fund Report.*

Of course, even with a wide choice of low-risk vehicles, there is no free lunch—another "sure thing" in investing. As Figure 1-2 shows, the big drawback of cash equivalents is their low return: the penalty for high liquidity. In fact, had it not been for the unforeseen and sustained dip in interest rates in the early 1990s—to levels not approached since the deflation of the Great Depression—low-interest, highly liquid securities like U.S. Savings Bonds, long regarded as the bread and butter of small investors, would probably have dried up altogether.

Nonetheless, I recommend putting an amount equal to three month's income or living expenses into some form of interest-bearing cash equivalents. For many people, this amounts to approximately 10 to 15 percent of their investable assets—probably the minimum you should always hold in this asset category. You may allocate more if you have heavy near-term expenses (such as upcoming medical bills, a big wedding, or college tuition, etc.) or less if you have a very big portfolio, are top-heavy with all kinds of insurance, or simply have a lifestyle that needs less cash.

Don't forget that although 90-day (or shorter) CDs may be redeemed before maturity, regulations allow banks to charge a fee to compensate them for the time they weren't allowed to use your money—the dreaded "penalty for early withdrawal." As a result, make sure your more liquid assets are deep enough to tide you over until these longer-term cash equivalents can mature.

In general, the best return in cash equivalents come from regular money market mutual funds and nonbank money market funds. Less competitive are bank money market accounts and 90-day CDs. However, as you'll see in Parts II and III of this book, a no- or low-cost bank investment deposit account or CD may be preferable to a higher-paying mutual fund if management expenses are high.

I'll give you some suggested allocation percentages at the end of this chapter, and once again in Part IV of this book when we see how changing life circumstances often require you to restructure your assets.

Cornerstone #2: Domestic Equities—Participating in America's Wealth-Creation Process

Equity means ownership. Each share of stock you own gives you a fractional claim against the assets of the business that issued it—although different types of stock have different economic benefits and risks.

Although America's share of global equities has decreased from 75 to 33 percent in the last couple of decades, we still possess the world's biggest industrial and consumer markets. Therefore, most analysts consider U.S. domestic equities (stocks traded on the major exchanges like the New York or American Stock Exchange) to be a major asset category in which almost every investor should participate. This now includes retired people and institutions in charge of public and private pension funds: groups once considered too "risk averse" to take a chance on the stock market's infamous price volatility.

Why Common Stocks Make Uncommonly Good Sense

One reason stocks are now recommended for even these conservative investors is their undisputed, superior long-term performance. Since 1926, the S&P 500 has returned an admirable 10.3 percent, as calculated by Ibbotson Associates, an authority on investment statistics. My own analysis shows that stocks recorded a positive return in 7 out of every 10 years during this period—half the time over 14 percent. Down years in which the market lost more than 15 percent occurred only once every decade and a half, making stocks anything but the "handcart to hell" some critics have claimed.

Another reason for confidence in equities lies in the changing nature of the market itself. It is now possible to economically "buy the market"—that is, to benefit from the long-term appreciation of overall stock values—without personally having to acquire an unwieldy portfolio of hundreds of individual stocks or running the risk that the particular sampling of stocks you choose will accidentally turn out to be losers. These conservative, dollar-wise investment vehicles usually take the form of index funds, so called because the stocks they contain are chosen to statistically reflect the current weighting of a major stock market index, such as the S&P 500, Dow Jones Industrials, or even the broadest possible index, the Wilshire 5,000. But even no-load index funds charge a nominal management fee, and therein lies the rub. Processing transactions and keeping relevant records always costs more when someone else does it for you. As a Frugal Investor, you'll want to consider other ways to "buy the market" using selected, dividend-paying, blue chip stocks that don't charge *any* commissions or fees of any kind. As you'll see in Part II, you can even purchase some of these stocks at a discount from their current market price, realizing an *instant profit of anywhere from 3 to 10 percent!*

Another important factor in equity investing is what analysts call "time diversification": the proven wisdom of holding the stocks you buy for a very long time. Although the price of a typical stock may fluctuate significantly over a period of weeks or months, in the long run its price should grow along with overall market values. Thus, as shown in Figure 1-3, the price volatility of a stock actually *decreases* the longer you own it.

In my view, most investors—including big institutional money managers—are unnecessarily alarmed by the whole issue of "beta," or price volatility. (*Beta* is the ratio of an individual stock's price change to price changes in the overall market: a beta of 1.0 means the stock performs *with* the market; a beta higher than this means the price changes faster; lower means the price changes slower. The bigger the beta in either direction, the more the stock diverges from the market average.) Like all of us, investment experts are creatures of habit and feel comforted by certainty. When things get too unpredictable, especially where money is concerned, they tend to react emotionally. Look at their behavior during and after the infamous Black Monday of October 19, 1987, wherein the NYSE lost 20 percent of its value in a single day. Some pessimists thought the market crash presaged another Great Depression and liquidated large portions of their entire stock portfolios, *guaranteeing* the losses they'd already experienced. Others tried to make up their losses quickly by speculating on short term trades, options, and futures. Most wound up worse than they started. Their problem wasn't the crash but the way they

Figure 1-3. How the Risk on Common Stock Investments Is Reduced by Lengthening Your Investment Period.

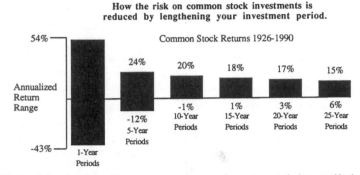

How the risk on common stock investments is
reduced by lengthening your investment period.

This chart displays the highest and lowest average annual returns on large company stocks (represented by the Standard & Poor's 500 Stock Composite Index for six different holding periods during the last 65 years.) Notice that during their best 1-year performance period, stocks produced a 54% gain, and during their worst 1-year performance period, incurred a 43% loss. By contrast, during their best 25-year performance period, stocks produced an average annual gain of 15% and during their worst 25-year performance period, produced an average annual gain of 6%. The average annual return over the entire 65-year period was 10.1%.

Source: *Data from Ibbotson Assoc., Chicago, 1991. All rights reserved.*

reacted to it. *This simply can't happen when you adopt the buy-and-hold, Frugal Investing philosophy.*

The False Threat of Program Trading

Today, big and small price fluctuations are created and magnified by so-called basket trading, or computer program trading by institutional investors who buy and sell great "bundles," or baskets, of index stocks, options, or futures. Conventional investors (namely, the same pessimists who panicked in '87!) view basket trading with alarm, since the trades are triggered by market dynamics rather than any changes to the economic soundness of the businesses underlying the stocks. Smaller investors, used to thinking in terms of such fundamental value, watch the "big boys" jump ship, think the high-priced analysts have seen something they've missed, and do the same, resulting in a stupid and costly market selloff.

My somewhat contrarian view is that program trading, index arbitrage, and the like open windows of opportunities for those same small investors who are most terrified of its effects. My reasoning goes like this:

Stocks owned by conscientious, commonsense private investors almost always have solid fundamental value. Since the smaller buy-and-hold investor also tends to hang onto the stock for a long time (at least one complete market cycle, 5 or 6 years—and often much longer), there's no reason for them to join the lemmings and dump their shares simply because the big guys are doing it, usually for completely different reasons. On the contrary, this particular type of price fluctuation is nature's way of telling small investors that their high-quality stock has suddenly gone on sale. If they can afford it, they should add a few more shares to their portfolio, because the price should eventually bounce back. This is exactly what many smart, more disciplined, and certainly more frugal investors did after the Crash of '87, and their example shouldn't be wasted.

I'll show you more about finding and buying these stocks in Part II. For now, here are the characteristics of individual stocks I consider most appropriate for long-term Frugal Investing:

1. They Should Have a Long History of Paying Dividends

Because you'll enroll in the company's dividend reinvestment plan (or DRP, see below) to help build wealth quickly and at the lowest possible cost, you'll look for corporations that have a long-term policy of consistently paying dividends (not all companies do). This characteristic, once considered a basic requirement for good stocks, was long out of favor on Wall Street and is only now making an overdue comeback. Why are dividends once again so important?

Toward the end of 1987, the last full year before Black Monday, 76 percent of the 2,244 companies listed on the New York Stock Exchange paid an aggregate dividend of $84.4 billon—a lot of money by anyone's yardstick. Since the sale price of a stock is never known precisely in advance, the value of such regular dividends can add significantly to a shareholder's total return, even if the stock must eventually be sold for less than the purchase price. In addition, companies with a history of good dividends go to great lengths to preserve that reputation, since it bolsters the price of their stock. In other words, good dividends breed good management and vice versa. When these dividends are reinvested consistently by shareholders over many years, the growth potential of a portfolio can be astounding.

For example, *Money* magazine recently reported that an investor buying 100 shares of AT&T in 1985 for $1,950 would've seen that investment grow to $4,550 by 1990, even if the dividend yield of 6.2 percent had been taken out in cash. However, if that dividend had been reinvested, the number of shares would've grown to 124 and been worth $5,624—an annual return of 37.6 percent!

This is why I say dividend yield is at least as good a measure of a stock's true value than price-to-earnings or price/book-value ratios commonly used by market analysts. I'll give you some quick but reliable methods for evaluating individual stocks in Part II and in the appendix to this book.

This brings us to one cost-eliminating device that most investors know little or nothing about: the so-called DRIPs, or DRPs—*dividend reinvestment plans* offered to shareholders by over 800 of America's premium companies. Ordinarily, when a typical investor wants to buy a major stock, say 100 shares of BankAmerica, he or she places an order with a broker, pays the price of the stock plus commissions and other costs on settlement day, then sits back and waits to get rich. If the stock does well, the broker calls the investor and talks him or her into buying another hundred shares—and the investor pays the new higher unit price, plus even more transaction and execution expenses.

What the broker never reveals is that BankAmerica, like many other first-rank U.S. companies, has a plan that allows shareholders to automatically purchase *more* stock with the dividends those companies usually pay—a virtually *painless* way to build a portfolio. What's more, many of these companies, BankAmerica included, offer these new shares at a discount of 3 to 10 percent *below market price* to DRP participants; and some even have an optional cash purchase (OCP) provision that permits participants to buy even more new and fractional shares with outside funds. This allows average investors to increase their holdings in a quality stock even faster than with DRP alone—and all without a dime's worth of commissions, fees, or other third-party payments!

For the buy-and-hold Frugal Investor, techniques such as DRP and OCP, even with firms that *don't* offer discounts, are like manna from heaven. What you don't spend to acquire an asset, that asset doesn't have to earn back in extra returns. This gives you an extra margin of profit when positive results are compounded, and an extra margin of safety when prices fall.

After all, where there is no cost, the gain is obvious!

That's why I don't exaggerate when I say that some of the world's top corporations will pay *you*—in dollars you don't spend, in an instant profit you realize the moment you buy the security—to build your wealth through Frugal Investing!

2. THEY MUST BE SHARES IN BLUE CHIP COMPANIES

In poker, blue chips are worth the most and the same is true in domestic stocks. The so-called blue chip firms are the largest and stablest corporations in America. Their consistent earnings and financial strength are long established and, although they're not immune from the effects of recession, inflation, and other economic ills (as witnessed by the dramatic 1993 stock price collapse of the bluest of them all, old "Big Blue" itself—IBM—to a third of its former value) they have demonstrated their ability to survive them with few financial scars. From this elite, Frugal Investors consider only those stocks that pass two additional tests:

1. They must have the dividend history described earlier.
2. They must engage in business operations that enhance the quality of life in America.

Why this last requirement? Because firms that are committed to safe and effective products, consumer satisfaction, and progressive management techniques traditionally enjoy the highest levels of customer, employee, executive, and supplier loyalty. This high level of personal commitment on both sides of the cash register, in turn, translates into long-term financial health for the firm and its securities, it's that simple.

As you can see, these criteria would seem to eliminate many worthwhile stocks, but unless you have very aggressive objectives: you won't miss these riskier alternatives. Also, few of these others offer the collateral programs, such as dividend reinvestment programs, essential to Frugal Investing. The criteria also discourage purchase of OTC (over-the-counter) stocks, or the stocks of smaller companies ("small-cap," or capitalization) and shares in businesses not sold in auction markets. While many high-potential firms can be found in these environments (indeed, risk-tolerant investors with high growth objectives would be crazy to ignore them), your chance of picking losers is much higher than finding winners. When you can both make and save money buying the best, why would the average investor shop the rest?

Of course, if you're one of those investors who are both value-conscious and extremely risk tolerant, you'll probably want to put some money on these higher stakes bets. When one looks at the potential rewards of these investments, it's hard to blame you.

For example, I once calculated that $10,000 invested in common stocks in 1925 at an index rate of return would have grown to over $5.2 million by 1990—a pleasant pipedream by anyone's standards. I then wondered what would happen if, instead of putting the $10K in the S&P 500 (which generated a compounded annual return of 10.1 percent over this period), I had put the entire amount in small-cap stocks, which enjoyed a slightly better 11.6 percent compounded annual return. Would this slightly higher return have been enough to compensate for the well-known risks of small-cap stocks? How much dollar difference would the additional 1.5 percent have made?

The answers are: yes, and plenty. The small-cap portfolio would now be worth a whopping $12.7 million—more than *twice* the value of its indexed counterpart—all for a silly percent and a half's worth of extra growth.

This experiment is more than yet another demonstration of the astonishing power of compounding. It illustrates the hidden potential of one of the equity market's most volatile sectors. Any investor with an aggressive growth objective would be foolish not to consider it. Unfortunately, past performance isn't necessarily a prologue to the future. Will small-cap stocks retain their luster for the rest of the 1990s? Will that all-important extra margin of return persist into the twenty-first century?

Many analysts think it will. They believe that sometime in the early 1990s the torch of big profits passed from giant consumer companies like Wal-Mart, Procter & Gamble, and General Mills to mid-sized and smaller companies in other industries whose profits traditionally come from growing markets.

Why did this happen?

Because the big consumer companies got used to feeding off what economists call "elastic demand." When they wanted bigger profits, all they had to do was raise their products' price. Unfortunately for them, the sharp recession of the early 1990s showed consumer pocketbooks to be anything but bottomless. This doesn't mean the consumer giants are doomed like the dinosaurs, but they'll definitely have to change their feeding habits in order to thrive—and that will take time. If you're one of those hardy investors who can stand the ups and downs of a market in transition, won't need your cash for 10 to 20 years, and would like a sampling of small-cap stocks to turbo-charge your portfolio, you can get them in a number of the no-load index funds I'll recommend in Part III.

Of course, some small-cap investors will ask, "Why choose an index fund? Why not just buy into a no-load fund specializing in small-cap stocks?"

These questions answer themselves if you recall my two basic rules for Frugal Investing: (1) buy and hold securities in four asset categories, and (2) do so at the lowest possible cost. Since index funds buy stocks to mirror a market and not to beat it, they're spared the costs of high-priced analysts and frequent trading—a constant temptation for small-cap funds that feel pressured to discard old losers and pick new winners. As a result, index funds traditionally have the lowest operating expenses of all the equity mutual funds. Since most index funds include a sampling of small-cap stocks, why not use them as a low-cost way to add that extra kick?

3. THEY ARE *NOT* A COMPONENT OF SOME INVESTMENT GIMMICK

Although blue chip common stocks are recommended for Frugal Investing, a surprisingly large number of other securities you'll find on major exchanges are not. Among these are the so-called *derivatives*, covered and naked options (contracts to buy or sell a stock at a certain price in the future), futures themselves (which do the same thing for commodities like soybeans), and hedge funds, which are mutual funds or limited partnerships that specialize in these investments as well as other forms of short-term market timing. These "side bets" on stock performance really have nothing to do with the original conception of equity markets as a place to encourage, sustain, and reward capitalism—the engine that drives our nation's (and much of the world's) wealth creation machinery. The only people who consistently make money in these risky investments are the brokers, who realize a profit on each transaction, win or lose. Everyone else who plays these "millionaire's" games (the minimum account is often $100,000 and an investor's net worth must frequently be more than a million) is really a gambler. As such, these players should observe the gambler's dictum: Never bet more than you're prepared to lose—and "loss" is a word Frugal Investors absolutely refuse to hear!

Unless you have a good reason to change your initial allocation, such as upcoming retirement or other pressing need for near-term cash, equities should comprise around 60 to 70 percent of your total multiasset portfolio. Investors with more ambitious wealth-building objectives will likely allocate more to this potentially most lucrative asset class; while those who have significant spending needs within the next few years (or just get hives with each down-tick of the market) will be happier with less. The key idea, though, is to be neither 100 percent out of, nor 100 percent invested in, the domestic equities market. Unless your crystal ball is perfectly clear, you just can't afford to do otherwise.

Cornerstone #3: Fixed-Income Investments— Lending Money to the World's Best Borrowers

Wayne Rogers' fixed-income expertise extends past cash-equivalent Treasuries to their "big brothers": long-term government bonds. When we talked about what careful investors should do after their cash-equivalent allocation has been made, he answered without hesitation:

"If someone bought Treasuries of any maturity back in the 1980s, when interest rates were extremely high, and kept those investments, they'd be sitting on a gold mine today: investments with excellent cash flow, backed by the full faith and credit of the U.S. Government."

And if you staggered the maturities of those bonds, I added, you'd be sitting even prettier.

"That's right," Rogers concluded, "You buy them, you hold them, and your income is predictable."

Predictable—that's the name of the game in fixed-income investing and you just heard if from one of the biggest names in the business. The wide array of debt-based securities comprising this asset class all have one thing in common: they pay a pre-determined, predictable rate of interest and promise the return of the investor's principal at maturity. Unlike stock dividends that depend on a company's earnings, fixed-income investments pay the same amount for the life of the note—the contract that created the debt. (There are some exceptions, like adjustable-rate mortgages and bond funds that trade assets with different rates and maturities, but the principle is the same: the income received is fixed for a given period.)

All this may sound fine, especially to conservative investors, until you consider the ever present threat of inflation. With a long-term inflation rate of 3 percent a year, a 7½ percent bond paying 5 percent after taxes, would produce a paltry 2 percent real (after inflation) return; and 2 percent a year by itself, even if it's compounded, just isn't good enough—especially when other lower risk investments, like dividend-paying blue chip stocks, can compensate for this loss. Figure 1-4 shows the disproportionate effect of inflation on T-bills versus common stocks for a recent 10-year period.

Of course, the maturities (or term) of fixed-income securities vary and, on occasion, even the interest rate itself can change from time to time, as is the case with adjustable rate mortgages and first mortgage pools that contain large numbers of these notes. Although certain cash equivalents, like 90-day bank CDs, also pay a fixed return, they're not part of the fixed-income asset category because their terms are much shorter than the first and second mortgages, municipal and corporate bonds, treasury notes and bonds, and longer term CDs that comprise this asset class.

Another thing these longer lived instruments have in common is their sensitivity—as "old debt"—to interest rate risk. Because few investors want to hold a 20-year Treasury bond or 30-year mortgage loan for its full term, most are re-sold on a variety of aftermarkets, and therein lies the risk. As shown in Table 1-1, if interest rates go up after a bond is purchased, new bonds become more attractive and the resale price for old bonds must be discounted to lure investors. Unlike stocks, whose price volatility tends to dampen with time, the price of a bond becomes *more* volatile the longer its term. Still, debt investments as a whole tend to be more secure—and less subject to price swings during the holding period—than most equities.

Figure 1-4. Every Year, Inflation Takes a Sizeable Bite Out of Your Investment Returns. And Then You Have to Pay Taxes as Well.

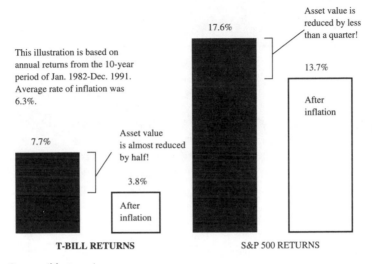

Source: *Ibbotson Assoc.*

Table 1-1. How Changes in Interest Rates Affect Bond Prices. Assuming a $1,000 Bond Paying 8 Percent Interest.

| | If Rates RISE 1% | |
| | Market | Percent |
Bond Maturity	Value	Change
2 years (short-term)	$ 982	−1.8
5 years (intermediate-term)	$ 960	−4.0
20 years (long-term)	$ 908	−9.2

| | If Rates FALL 1% | |
| | Market | Percent |
Bond Maturity	Value	Change
2 years (short-term)	$1,018	+1.8
5 years (intermediate-term)	$1,042	+4.2
20 years (long-term)	$1,107	+10.7

Table 1-2. Diversified Index vs. Major Market Indices

				Boldface Figures = Best Performing Asset			
Year	U.S. Stocks	Int'l Stocks	Cash Equivalents	Real Estate	U.S. Bonds	Int'l Bonds	Diversified Index*
1977	−7.2%	19.4%	5.2%	10.5%	3.0%	**43.7%**	6.2%
1978	6.6%	**34.3%**	7.1%	16.0%	1.2%	23.3%	13.0%
1979	18.6%	6.2%	9.8%	**20.7%**	2.3%	−4.0%	11.5%
1980	**32.5%**	24.4%	11.3%	18.1%	3.1%	5.8%	17.9%
1981	−4.9%	−1.0%	14.1%	**16.9%**	7.3%	−3.6%	6.5%
1982	21.5%	−0.9%	10.9%	9.4%	**31.1%**	7.0%	14.4%
1983	22.6%	**24.6%**	8.6%	11.0%	8.0%	2.8%	15.0%
1984	6.3%	7.9%	9.6%	12.0%	**15.0%**	2.3%	10.2%
1985	31.7%	**56.7%**	7.5%	10.1%	21.3%	35.0%	25.5%
1986	18.7%	**70.0%**	6.1%	6.5%	15.6%	31.4%	23.4%
1987	5.3%	24.9%	5.8%	5.4%	2.3%	**35.1%**	8.7%
1988	16.6%	**28.6%**	6.8%	6.9%	7.6%	2.3%	13.3%
1989	**31.7%**	10.8%	8.2%	5.6%	14.2%	−3.4%	14.1%
1990	−3.1%	−23.3%	7.5%	1.7%	8.3%	**15.3%**	−1.8%
1991	**30.5%**	12.5%	5.4%	−5.7%	16.1%	16.2%	11.8%
1992	**7.6%**	−11.9%	3.5%	−4.9%	**7.6%**	4.8%	0.4%
1993	10.1%	**32.9%**	3.0%	2.3%	11.1%	15.1%	11.9%
Cum Ret	786.5%	1238.4%	249.3%	278.1%	408.9%	647.2%	552.9%
Ann Ret	13.7%	16.5%	7.6%	8.1%	10.0%	12.6%	11.7%
Std Dev	13.1%	23.1%	2.9%	7.4%	7.9%	15.2%	6.9%

Source: *U.S.Stocks = S&P 500; U.S. Bonds = Shearson Govt/Corp Bond; Int'l Stocks = MSCI EAFE; Cash Equiv. = 3 month T-Bill; Real Estate = FRC Property Index; Int'l bonds = 1985-1993 Saloman Bros. (Non U.S.$); 1977-1984 composite consisting of Japan, U.K., Germany, and France.*

*Diversified index (20/20/20/20/20 mix) does not include international bonds.

Used with permission of Bailand, Biehl & Kaiser.

How Fixed-Income Investments Complement a Multiasset Portfolio

Most investors know that stock prices and interest rates tend to work against each other. That is, when interest rates go up, stock investors realize they can receive higher returns from lower-risk bonds, so they tend to move money out of equities and into debt investments, causing stock prices to drop. When interest rates go down, even conservative investors begin to weigh the poor return of bonds against the better return and relative safety of blue chip stocks, which can also pay current income in the form of a dividend, and money begins to flow from bonds to stocks, bidding up stock prices.

This transfer of wealth from one asset category to another is called *disintermediation*, and while it can be significant, it doesn't last forever. The drop in stock prices caused by high interest rates will eventually be reversed when enough bargains—undervalued stocks—flood the market. Similarly, interest rates can only go so high before they begin to stifle economic growth. When this happens, key decision makers like the Federal Reserve Board and major banks eventually lower interest rates, stimulating business. As business earnings increase, stocks again become more attractive. In fact, it was this historical interplay between stocks and bonds that caused researchers to look seriously at the relationships among different asset classes, giving rise to multiasset allocation theory.

In the past, a portfolio was considered "balanced" if it contained only stocks and bonds. Today, such limited diversification is considered quaint—simplistic and subject to economic setbacks that can negatively affect *both* markets, although to different degrees. One such phenomenon is "stagflation," a situation where inflation is high (penalizing fixed-income investments) and economic activity, as reflected in stock prices, is low. If your portfolio is "diversified" over only stocks and bonds, you may suffer staglation's unique but potent double whammy.

But hedging against disinflation or deflation and providing cash for living expenses or new investments are only minor benefits of fixed-income investments. Even when interest rates are low, the regular income from bonds helps compensate for a temporary drop in the prices of your stock, thus stabilizing the value of your overall portfolio at any given moment. And it goes without saying that cash received today brings you that much closer to the amount you need for goal-related spending tomorrow.

Once smaller investors perceive and appreciate this fundamental role of bonds, they become even more aware of the necessity of having different maturities for their different fixed-income investments. If the bonds you hold all mature at the same time, for example, you may be forced to "roll them over" in an adverse debt market—at a time when interest rates are abnormally low. Investment firms respond to this dilemma by offering mutual funds with "laddered" debt investments, or bonds with various maturities paying different rates of interest. When funds like these also maintain a healthy cash reserve, they become active players in fixed-income markets, buying and selling old bonds as well as purchasing new ones, when such trading seems most profitable—a process called "managing for total return." Although you can do it too, it's not a procedure I recommend for Frugal Investors—at least until the spread between old bonds and new is great and the economy is growing at a steady pace. A typical example will show you why.

Suppose a portfolio, such as a mutual fund, holds some bonds paying 9 percent and the market rate for similar bonds is 3 percent. An investor "managing for income" (which is most Frugal Investors) would simply hang onto the 9 percent bond because it pays more current cash. However, other investors desiring that income will happily pay *more* for that old bond than they would for its 3 percent equivalent in new debt. Thus a fund manager interested in total return and committed to staying in the fixed-income market (as asset allocators are) could come out ahead by selling the old bond then buying *more* of the 3 percent bonds with the extra principal earned in the sale.

So far so good, but there are two classic problems with this concept. First, mutual funds (regardless of their market and objectives) *always* charge a management fee, if not commissions. By definition, this further reduces the return on an asset whose value is *already* limited by fixed-income and, because of that, is constantly threatened by inflation. Putting a lot of money in such funds is like betting on a football team that has publicly announced it won't score more than 21 points. That may be fine for low-scoring opponents, but what happens when the opposition gets tough? How many football games have been decided by one or two points? Again, profit—like victory—always resides in the margin.

Second, you don't have to be a rocket scientist to buy and hold a portfolio of good fixed-income investments. Except for their interest rates and maturities, one Treasury investment is much like another. (I say "Treasury" and not "federal" investment because not all debt issued by government agencies is backed by the full faith and credit of the U.S. government—and state- and mortgage-backed securities can be even more problematical.) Since you won't be speculating on interest rate spreads, the securities you choose can have convenient and relatively infrequent rollover periods that will allow you to save commissions and let your bonds do what bonds do best: lie around and pay interest. You can then reinvest that accumulated interest in more debt, or put it into other asset categories that pay a higher return or offer some other benefit.

All this can be done cheaply when you buy the fixed-income component of your portfolio directly from some of the sources for no- or low-cost debt investments I'll describe in Parts II and III.

Cornerstone #4: International Securities— Building Wealth in the Global Village

Believe it or not, there was a time when *foreign-made* meant cheap, unreliable, risky, and—well, un-American. Today, with dynamic economies in Japan, Western Europe—and even among the developing nations of the Pacific Rim and South America—the most adamant "Buy American" investor now realizes that no low-risk, high-performance portfolio is complete without an international component.

What's Un-American about Foreign Securities?

Of course, securities bearing the label "made in Japan" or "a product of Germany" carry with them a few extra risks. For one, products, services, and securities originating in another country must eventually be paid for in that country's currency. This means that customers of, and investors in, those firms (or their financial intermediaries) must convert U.S. dollars to yen or pounds or Deutsch Marks and therein stand to lose money if the currency exchange rate, which is subject to market pressure, goes against them. And even if the currency exchange rate is in your favor, you still face markets in many countries that are far less developed, or regulated, than those in the United States. Although most securities offered by major foreign firms have reasonable business risk, the protection you have as an investor in case of fraud or other irregularities is usually less than for comparable investments in the United States. Therefore, the Frugal Investor's preference for blue chip securities is even *more* important when it comes to foreign stocks.

Still, because foreign economic developments tend to lead or lag those in the United States, it makes good sense to keep a portion of your total portfolio in high-quality international securities, especially those denominated in U.S. dollars and offered conveniently to American investors on our own securities markets.

Components of Your International Portfolio

Aside from domestic mutual funds that trade in foreign securities, a number of high-quality foreign investments are available for U.S. dollars on domestic markets, minimizing both the risk of foreign exchange and the need to pay mutual fund managers.

Among these alternatives are American Depositary Receipts, or ADRs, featured on all major American stock exchanges. These certificates show your fractional ownership of specific international stocks held by U.S. banks that have branches in those particular countries. Although your ownership rights are legally confined to the ADR, the value of your ADR varies directly with the value of the underlying foreign stocks.

You can also use U.S. dollars to buy shares in certain premium foreign companies whose stock is listed on American exchanges, such as Switzerland's Nestle Corporation, Britain's Phillips Petroleum, and Germany's Mercedes. Although these stocks are more closely linked to the U.S. economy than some other foreign issues you could buy, they still give you a measure of diversity into the international asset class.

You can also buy the foreign equivalent of the other three major asset classes, too, although, according to the rules of multi-asset allocation, they're all considered part of your International Securities portfolio.

For example, since Eurodollars are nothing more than U.S. dollars on deposit in foreign banks, you can invest in that bank's cash equivalents, or Euro-CDs, denominated in our currency. Because they're not liable to U.S. regulation and insurance requirements, the interest paid on these riskier near-money investments is often higher than comparable cash equivalents in the United States. Unfortunately, Euro-CDs are available exclusively through brokers, so their higher returns are often offset by the commission.

In the fixed-income category, you can invest in just about every type of long-term debt available on domestic markets, but beware. Most foreign laws are very lax regarding private debt. Therefore, if you want the protection we customarily enjoy with such investments, be sure your international bonds are issued by foreign governments rather than private firms. When they're purchased, serviced, and redeemed in U. S. dollars held overseas, such notes are called Euro Bonds. Because interest rate structures can vary significantly among countries in the short term, Euro Bonds can have both additional advantages and risks. Nondollar bonds, denominated in foreign currency, are also available in the United States, but the foreign exchange risk (along with a variety of other business and political risks) makes them less attractive. Like Euro-CDs, both Euro and nondollar bonds also come with a hefty broker's commission, so they're not for the average Frugal Investor.

If you're willing to pay a management fee for third-party expertise in selecting foreign securities, international mutual funds are now available on major U.S. exchanges with a wide range of objectives (such as aggressive growth, current income, and so on) with securities from many, rather than just a few, foreign countries.

No matter how you acquire the international portion of your multi-asset portfolio, or which individual securities you choose, never forget that the main reason for doing so is *to complement your other holdings*. This means you want to make sure your international securities will perform more or less *out of phase* with their American counterparts. That is, when domestic equities are down, your international stocks should be up—at least a little. Since you'll be using dollar-cost averaging to add to your holdings in every asset category, this will allow you to buy more domestics at lower prices while buying fewer internationals at inflated prices. Overall, these self-dampening forces create the major benefit of multiasset investing. You don't want to undermine it by giving your domestic and international holdings too close a family resemblance.

Three Asset Classes You Don't Want to Hold

Experienced investors will notice I've omitted certain well-known asset categories that many other advisors, even those with years of experience in asset allocation, consider basic categories. The reason for this is obvious: they just don't fit my criteria for Frugal Investing—an approach wherein a significant portion of the return is based upon savings derived from the method used to acquire, hold, and dispose of the asset.

Here are some well-known examples of investments that may be okay for other investors, but are not recommended by me.

Getting Bogged Down in Real Estate

Real property ownership is a venerable investment field. Few high net worth individuals don't have some portion of their holdings in commercial real estate, either as direct owners of income property or as shareholders in group investments like real estate investment trusts (REITs) or real estate limited partnerships (RELPs), although these latter investments were generally marketed more for their tax-shelter benefits than their intrinsic economic worth. Indeed, some people make a fetish of real estate as the basis of all true wealth. John Paul Getty was supposed to have advised prospective billionaires to simply "Get there first and buy up all the land!"

Because of these and other fictions, including the notion that a dollar saved in tax deductions is somehow as productive as one earned through business operations, group real estate investors suffered greatly when the tax benefits justifying their purchases dried up, beginning with the 1986 Tax Reform Act. REIT and RELP organizers were then left with income properties that couldn't pay their way, often because of heavy debt service. Most investors bailed out, taking significant losses, while most organizers and intermediaries continued to earn fees and commissions while they "rolled up" troubled properties and resold them as "new" investment vehicles.

This underscores the main problem I see with real estate for Frugal Investors. Most income property is terribly illiquid (it takes months for even good properties to sell) and the underlying asset is very inflexible economically. While factory owners can sometimes switch to other products, an office building has only office space to rent. Families needing homes can't live in retail storefronts, and shopping malls become so much glass and mortar when consumers can't buy goods. If the business sector to which an income property is tied experiences hard times, or if properties serving that sector are overbuilt, there is little a property manager can do about the resulting lack of tenants. And, because commercial property is literally cemented to the ground, it is—and always has been—a local business, and local economic conditions can differ drastically from region to region, or even among districts within the same city.

Because of this, and because it takes a lot of money and expertise to get into such investments, and a lot of time, patience, and expense to get out, I consider any real estate beyond your personal residence (and, perhaps, a vacation house) to be unsuitable for Frugal Investing.

Tripped Up by Collectibles; Burned by Precious Metals

Using the same logic they apply to real estate, some advisors tout old coins, rare stamps, antiques, precious gems, gold and silver bullion, fine art, and other so-called collectibles and precious substances for their intrinsic, tangible value. The problem with such commodities, aside from the lack of a ready market (auctions don't count—they're not held frequently enough for true liquidity and not all auction houses deal in every type of artifact), is that there are many ways to get such investments wrong and only a few ways to get them right. When personal taste is involved, for example, most people have trouble telling the merely appealing from the truly valuable, and unscrupulous dealers know it. And even if you have the expertise and self-discipline to treat such purchases as investments, you still have the problem of determining a fair price, then finding a suitable investor when the holding period (however *that's* determined!) is over. In short, if you want to go antiquing, do it for fun, not to build a nest egg.

Similarly, ever since currencies went off the gold standard, precious metals and jewels derive their worth mostly from cultural, rather than economic forces. True, there is only so much gold, silver, and diamonds to go around, and bullion has been conveniently securitized in mining stocks, mutual funds, and limited partnerships. Unfortunately, investments like these tie up your cash without producing income, and because prices can change radically (or hover in a stagnant state for many years) they're poor choices even for growth. Just ask the Hunt brothers, who made a fortune cornering the silver market, then lost it all just as quickly.

Again, because such assets are costly and full of hidden risks, they're unsuitable for Frugal Investors.

Exotic and Special Situation Investments

Other investments variously touted as "sure winners" or tax and inflation hedges—investments like oil income and drilling, equipment leasing, farms, entertainment ventures (such as movies and sports teams), and self-storage operations—all have one thing in common: they depend on tax laws and the competency of people in very esoteric fields to make money. So, unless you're already knowledgeable about motion picture production, tuna fishing, airline operations, or oil exploration, leave them to the experts. If you believe transportation or energy companies are a good bet, why not just invest in airline stock or public utilities directly and (like a good Frugal Investor!) eliminate the middle man altogether?

How to Weight Your Allocations

In an episode of that old TV series, *Suspense Theatre,* an experienced Las Vegas gambler, played by Jack Kelly, is asked by a thrill-seeking million-aire played by Pat Hingle, to help him "beat" the craps table at a fancy casino. Kelly's character agrees, but tells the Hingle character, "You won't like how I do it."

He was right.

The rich amateur expected lots of fancy footwork, brilliant bets, and instant millions. The professional's approach, however, was to beat the casino at its own game. He "invested" a huge amount of money, steadily and over a period of many days, simply to ride out the odds and let the same probabilities that worked for the house make money for his mil-lionaire backer. In other words, he forced the high-rolling gambler to think like an investor and, in the story at least, it paid off.

Asset allocation theory begins with a similar notion: Since individual markets are so difficult to beat consistently in the short term, investors can do better by allocating a fixed percentage to each asset category then sit-ting back and letting "irresistible" economic forces do the heavy lifting.

One pioneer of multiple asset allocation, Bailard, Biehl & Kaiser, Inc., a prominent investment advisory firm, actually constructed a hypotheti-cal portfolio spread evenly over six asset classes with an equal percentage of total asset value maintained in each, then painstakingly computed its aggregate, compounded performance from 1977 through the end of 1993. The portfolio realized a positive return for all but one of its sixteen years for an annual return of 11.7 percent—an amazing record when you con-sider the economic ups and downs of the era and the fact that the portfo-lio had absolutely nothing special going for it other than asset allocation. But that's not the end of the story. (See Table 1-2.)

BB&K then compared the standard deviation, or variability, of that portfolio return to the individual standard deviations of the six asset classes (U.S. and international stocks, cash equivalents, real estate, U.S. and international bonds) that comprised it, and discovered that only T-bills did better. In other words, although better returns were possible in three of the individual asset classes, only one—short-term U.S. Treasuries—did so with comparable predictability.

The lesson from this is clear: The whole is more than the sum of its parts. A superior, predictable return *really is* achievable through multias-set allocation and the last bit of marginal profit every Frugal Investor counts on *really does* make a difference to total return!

As a result, I advise clients to use a modified form of the passive allocation strategy. Because, as shown in the accompanying chart, equities are the real engine of growth in a portfolio, I like to see between 60 and 70 percent of a client's assets allocated to stocks—both foreign and domestic. This leaves 30 to 40 percent for foreign and domestic fixed-income investments, which would include a cash-equivalents component equal to about three times your average monthly income. This margin for liquid assets is mainly a buffer for emergencies, but it can also be used as a pool for instant cash when bargains appear in other asset categories.

Remember, though, that these allocations are just a starting point. Investors at various stages of their financial life cycle will need slightly different allocations—advice I'll give you in Part IV of this book. The important thing to understand now is that your near- and long-term goals, financial situation, and tolerance for risk will determine the allocation strategy that feels intuitively right for you.

The only two hard and fast allocation rules I insist upon are:

1. Always have *some* money in each of the four basic asset categories (a house can't stand with one of its cornerstones missing).
2. Never reallocate in an attempt to beat a particular market.

This last rule is especially important, because some allocation experts will tell you to skew your holdings slightly—quarterly, annually, or at some other regular interval—in an attempt to anticipate future economic developments. Not surprisingly, most of these "strategic reallocators" also sell expensive newsletters telling you when and how to fix what may never be broken.

No matter what it is called, though, "flipping" securities with an intent to beat the market is still market timing. To the Frugal Investor, reallocating for reasons other than to correct a portfolio's imbalance or to accommodate new financial goals only increases marginal costs and the risk of losses. Besides, as you'll see shortly, making new purchases beyond those called for by dollar-cost averaging usually works against the very benefits you're trying to achieve with that technique.

Notice that I said "usually," not "always." Like all good rules, this one has an exception, and it applies even to Frugal Investors.

Occasionally, a good stock or other security may "go on sale" and if it does, you should buy more of it if you can.

By "going on sale" I mean that a normally high-priced and stable blue chip, for example, experiences a short-term and wholly uncharacteristic drop in price—from $60 per share, say, to $30 or $40—for reasons unrelated to the stock's (or the company's) underlying value. The reasons for such a price drop may range from the "basket trading" I've already discussed to a new government regulation or an adverse verdict in a high-visibility lawsuit. Sometimes simple bad publicity, such as an unantici-pated earnings drop (even though dividends remain constant), seasonal layoffs, a plant closing in an already depressed area, or a scandal involv-ing a prominent executive can temporarily put a big market leader in media cross-hairs. Whatever the cause, though, institutional investors sometimes take out their anxiety (or simply strip their portfolios of sud-denly unfashionable holdings) by dumping their shares, creating a won-derful buying opportunity for you—provided you already own the stock.

This strategy doesn't mean you must constantly shop for bargains, but it does mean you should stay informed about assets you hold and be able to recognize opportunities when they occur. Frugal Investors are con-trarian enough to know that the best time to increase their holdings (over and above their normal dividend reinvestment and dollar-cost averaging purchases) is when the good securities they already own become happily undervalued.

No matter how you allocate your resources, though, you still must buy specific, high-quality securities at the absolute minimum cost within each of the four basic asset categories, then reinvest in them regularly from dividends, interest, and the surplus from your occupation or profes-sion. And oh yes—you must also know how and when to draw down a portion of your portfolio for periodic restructuring and goal-related spending: to harvest the fruit of your labor without endangering next year's crop.

In Chapter 2, I'll give you an overview of precisely that: a roadmap for navigating the entire Frugal Investing process.

To Remember Before Going On

- Stockbrokers and other fee- and commission-charging intermedi-aries, such as bank lobby brokers, are often poor investment advi-sors: people motivated by *their* profit, not yours.
- Time (the power of compounding) and volatility (the magnitude and frequency of price changes) are the two factors primarily determining risk and return. Frugal Investors put *both* to work by buying and holding quality securities in four basic asset categories then using dividend reinvestment programs (DRPs) and optional cash purchase (OCP) plans to keep their portfolios growing at lit-tle or no additional cost.

- Frugal Investors *always* allocate funds to cash equivalents, domestic equities, fixed-income investments, and international securities while avoiding real estate, collectibles and precious metals, and special situation investments.
- Specific allocations depend on your stage of life, investment goals, financial situation, and tolerance for risk.

2

The Five
Commandments of
Frugal Investing

One successful investor I know was fond of clipping ads and sending away for free brochures, pamphlets, booklets, prospectuses—sales literature that described all kinds of financial products and services. And he did this not once, when assembling his initial multiasset portfolio, but as a kind of annual rite. I finally asked him:

"Look, every year you collect all this stuff and never buy a thing. What's the point?"

He only grinned, "I'm always amazed at just how many new things there are that I don't need!"

It's Not Just What You Make and Keep,
But What You Don't Have to Make at All

When I was a stockbroker, I laughed at my friend for passing up lots of good opportunities simply because he was too cheap to "spend money to make money." What I didn't realize was that he already had a leg up on my clients whose investments, even before the ink was dry on the purchase agreement, were in the hole for my commission, execution fees, future management fee deductions, and capital gains liability on the frequent trades my company would recommend. When he pored over all those product and service brochures, it wasn't just to chuckle about all the money he was saving. He was educating himself on what investment professionals thought about the changing economy. He wasn't so much trying to figure out where the "smart money" was going as he was evaluating where the tons and tons of "dumb money" was being diverted. It started as kind of a hobby for him, but it gradually turned him into the canny, consistent value-hunter I admire very much. Soon, I began looking for these traits among my other clients—people from all walks of life who had become the most successful investors. These frugal people, I discovered

- *Have good memories.* They remember good as well as bad experiences and learn from them.
- *Know not only what they need, but what they* don't *need.* This not only saves money, but time and effort.
- *Consciously avoid waste.* This starts as a chore, then becomes a habit, then a profitable way of life.
- *Are flexible, open, and resourceful.* They know their limits and boundaries, which is why they so often succeed at what they do.
- *Have patience.* Impulsiveness and self-indulgence are expensive luxuries. Occasional splurging is fun and good therapy, but in investing, it can be ruinous.

After awhile, I distilled these traits into five commandments, or general principles, for successful no- or low-cost investing:

Commandment 1. Let Somebody Else Do Your Homework—But Be Careful Who You Ask

This runs contrary to most advice you'll hear, and the sense of guilt and responsibility that's drilled into us by parents and in school, but it really works. Knowledge is not just power, it's a commodity. That's why people buy books like this, pay tuition for college, and hire advisors such as lawyers and CPAs.

Most brokers, though, and virtually all financial salespeople—even many investment newsletters—want to keep investors ignorant, at least of the things that count. In their view, investors should be just smart enough to grasp the hook (and take the bait) of this month's new investment product, but not know enough to really see the big picture. The truth is, you only need to learn the truth *once* about investing. The rest is simply planting the seeds of that knowledge, pulling weeds periodically from your financial garden, and raking in the harvest. It doesn't take a library of financial textbooks or manuals by investment gurus to make money reliably from investments. Much of what you *do* need to know will be provided free by the people who expect to benefit from your decisions. You'd be surprised how many experts, entrepreneurs, bureaucrats, and sales-people are willing to educate you on their nickel—or even in casual con-versation. And they don't even have to be in the investment business to make you a better investor.

Use What You Already Know

Take, for example, the experience of Claude Rosenberg, founder and principal partner of RCM Capital Management, a venerable San Francisco money-management firm. For years, RCM played the research game using typical Wall Street methods, poring over reams of statistics and technical analyses that would have done NASA scientists proud. The day of reckoning for Rosenberg and this method came in the early 1980s when Warner Communications stock, buoyed by sky-high expectations for its chief profit center, Atari, hit the brickwall known as the Reagan-Volker recession. Until then, few conventional analysts had understood the real-world sensitivity of consumer electronics to swings in the business cycle. It was one of those forehead-slapping revelations that looks obvious in retrospect, but was completely beyond the grasp of traditional research at the time. RCM's (and a lot of other financial advisory) clients were not happy after this highly visible breakdown in a system they'd learned to respect. A lot of people clamored for change. What did the investment gurus do about it?

Most of them did nothing. Rosenberg, however, created what RCM called Grassroots Research, an in-house market intelligence arm that bypassed the expensive pseudo-science of conventional investment analysis and went directly to the real world of consumers, suppliers, pur-chasing agents, and field managers—people on the economic front lines where trends begin, not in the air-conditioned back offices of the big bro-kerage and advisory firms where those same trends, at best, might be detected months later. Unlike traditional research groups, Grassroots was organized like a news service, with "editors and reporters" rather than research associates and analysts. After a decade of operation, Grassroots has saved RCM clients millions through trip-wire alerts unavailable from technical analysis alone (they anticipated before anyone else the big Philip Morris "Marlboro Friday" sell-off and Nike's embarassing toe-stub in Europe) and made millions more by spotting new opportunities (such as the 1993 renaissance of the U.S. furniture industry) as they begin to emerge from the pack.

Does this mean Frugal Investors must shell out thousands to sub-scribe to the newsletters of clever market researchers—assuming the best of such studies are even available outside the trade?

Not at all. RCM's experience shows mainly how most conventional brokerage-style analyses (even those that are not biased in favor of house products) are not only overpriced and unreliable but are also out-of-date by the time they reach the printer, let alone the mailbox of investors like you. A fad is not a trend, and the real investment picture comes into focus only from *a variety* of angles, viewed over a reasonable period of time, and not just from one hot tip or another. Fortunately, most of the information you'll need to acquire an initial, buy-and-hold multiasset portfolio can be had for a lot less than the slick, expensive, jargon-filled reports the "dumb money" usually follows. And you can't get much cheaper than free: from the public library, from broadcast, public, and cable TV news, and from the newspapers and magazines you probably already read.

Rating the So-Called Experts: What the Pros Don't Want You to Know

Of course, old habits die hard. If you're one of those who are convinced that investment wisdom is the exclusive province of the pros, you'll be interested in the 1994 results of the *San Francisco Chronicle's* annual stock-picking contest. Each year, the *Chronicle* asks a panel of prominent brokers, researchers, and money managers to choose the stocks they think will do best over the next 12 months, then publishes the results. For 1993, the panel's cumulative forty stocks and mutual funds appreciated 25.2 percent compared to a 10.8 percent return for the S&P 500. Sounds great, right? How much would you be willing to pay to have regular access to such expertise?

For one of the contest's top "analysts," the advisement fee is a couple of bananas and admission price to a wildlife amusement park. You see, third-place winner Jolyn is an orangutan at Marine World/Africa USA, who picked her investments by jabbing darts into the newspaper's stock quotations. Armed with neither a Series 7 license nor stacks of computerized research, Jolyn finished with a respectable 18.6 percent return: third in a field of eight.

In another widely reported and not so tongue-in-cheek experiment documented in his book, *Beating the Street*, ace fund manager Peter Lynch asked a bunch of seventh graders to pick a portfolio of stocks based on what they knew—liked and disliked—about candidate companies' products. Combining Jolyn's charming naivete with Grassroot's focus on shopping-mall economics, the schoolkids "beat the street" (the S&P 500) by 26 percent over a two-year period.

Lynch's dictum, "Never invest in any idea you can't illustrate with a crayon," was validated again in a second *Chronicle* contest, this one for investment outsiders. The 1993 winner, a Berkeley botany student, and the two runners up who had never invested a dime, attributed their success to "gut feel" and a bit of leg work to see if their intuitive choices—companies they were familiar with from general reading and personal experience—were not about to fall off any financial cliffs.

Need more proof? A study by Hulbert Financial Digest, which regularly tracks investment newsletter performance, discovered that newsletters attempting to pick short-term winners and losers (in other words, that gave market timing advice) generally did worse than the market average—sometimes, considerably worse. According to Hulbert, an investor following the advice of one popular and highly touted eighties guru, the Granville Market Letter, over the last 10 years would have lost 96 percent of the original principal. Even Jolyn could have done better.

Now, I am not recommending you take a completely random walk through the aisles of the multiasset supermarket, or buy only securities that teenagers and great apes like. My point is that by saving money you don't *have* to spend—on useless, costly, and often biased advice—then holding the commonsense selections you've made for a long time, you'll put Mother Nature (the law of large numbers and the power of compounding) on your side from the beginning, instead of letting her work against you.

In Parts II and III of this book, and later in the appendix, I'll list sources of free or low-cost information for every type of security you'll need to establish and manage your multiasset portfolio. Instead of buying the latest financial bestseller and subscribing to expensive market-timing newsletters (then paying even more in fees and commissions to implement their bad advice), you'll be able to put that money where it will do the most good: directly into your investments.

Commandment 2. Go Directly to the Source for Your Securities

Capitalism has always been a contract between two parties: the person who supplies the cash and the entrepreneur who uses it productively. In the old days, wealthy individuals (usually aristocrats or bankers) were approached by entrepreneurs who cut a deal unique to each opportunity. Interest rates were not set by committees but were whatever you could negotiate, and nobody policed equity or debt agreements except the parties themselves—and, of course, their lawyers.

Once the shares were issued or loans were made, the capitalists met in coffee houses and swapped securities, as well as war stories, like a genteel parlor game. The whole idea of commissioned intermediaries and standardized "investment products" came relatively late to modern economies and, far from making those markets more efficient, only gummed up the works by rationing critical information and virtually eliminating any sense of personal commitment between capital supplier and capital user—the key ingredient that made the whole system work. Eventually, a growing host of self-important middlemen obtained legislation making it even more difficult for capitalists and entrepreneurs, lenders and borrowers, to get together directly and cut the commission-charging intermediaries out of the loop. After a few generations, specialists such as stockbrokers came to be regarded as wondrous, respected professionals, like the family doctor, even though the elaborate and costly "investment distribution system" they invented was modeled more on retail merchandising than science or even basic capitalism. The only skills these "professionals" really needed, then or now, were persuasiveness and persistence and, in the age of telephones, faxes, and modems, they are once again superfluous.

Alternatives to the Licensed Pickpockets

More and more large-scale investors, for example, are bypassing floor traders altogether and making computerized deals through private stock exchanges. This burgeoning new industry, based on proprietary software, a network of established investors, and a handshake between responsible people, comes close to resurrecting the kind of old-style "coffee house capitalism" that made the Western economies great—despite its use of twenty-first century technology. Taking their lead from these trend setters, smaller investors, too, can now execute their trades through PCs and modems on almost any exchange in the world, cutting out the middlemen almost completely. And this does not include the many Treasury securities and common stocks that are available to individuals directly from the issuer, avoiding any exchange at all!

In Part II, I'll show you how to bypass—with or without a computer—the current cast of expensive and not-so-helpful helpers to connect directly with literally hundreds of securities issuers, cutting a legion of overpaid middlemen completely out of the loop. The money you *don't* spend on them you'll use to buy more of the security itself and otherwise accelerate the achievement of your financial goals. Eventually, these savings will represent a sizeable cash reserve that your investments simply will not have to make.

Commandment 3. "Settle" for the Deepest Discount

When Charles Schwab revolutionized the investment industry with his long overdue concept of discount brokerage services, he probably didn't realize he had started a trend whose end still is not in sight. A few years after the first discount houses opened their doors, "deep discount" services appeared, some in the form of brokerages, some in the form of "at-cost" service extras laid on by securities issuers or institutions that didn't depend on securities sales for their primary profit.

Of course, no-load mutual funds have also long been a resource for value-oriented investors; and if you're willing to pay the nominal fees and expenses *all* these investment companies charge in one form or another, they too can be the "next best thing" to direct-from-the-source securities.

Since your custom portfolio may require products that simply can't be acquired directly, you may have to "settle" for the minimal costs these deep discounters and no-load mutual fund companies charge. If a direct source isn't available, I'll tell you in Part III which deep discounters and funds to turn to, and how to tell if you're getting the absolute best price available.

Commandment 4. Build Your Portfolio Steadily Through Dollar-Cost Averaging

When I give investing seminars, I am always amazed at how many experienced investors have never heard of DCA, or *dollar-cost averaging*—a technique some market observers have called "Wall Street's best-kept secret," although it has been described in virtually every investment handbook I've seen.

In a nutshell, DCA is a kind of investment ju-jitsu: it uses a market's own volatility to your advantage and allows you to purchase securities regularly at the best possible unit price. When it's used as part of an overall Frugal Investing strategy—with the optional cash purchase (OCP) plan on shares you already own—virtually *all* of your new principal goes directly into the investment, with no brokerage fees or commissions at all. The method is startlingly simple.

First, select a regular time period for contributing a fixed amount of new cash to your portfolio. Obviously, putting more money into your investments more frequently will payoff faster than putting less money in less frequently, but the key words here are *regular* and *fixed amount*. If once a month takes too much money away from current spending, contribute quarterly or twice a year. Just make sure you put in the same amount each time, no matter what the economy or the markets appear to be doing. That takes discipline at first, but once it becomes a habit, you'll see the technique pay off and kick yourself for not starting it earlier. Here is an example of how DCA works:

Suppose you buy $300 worth of stock directly from the issuing company at a price of $6 a share, giving you an initial portfolio of fifty shares. You then begin a monthly DCA program using this same amount through the company's optional cash purchase plan. Let us say that for the first three months, the stock price increases. In the second month, the price of $8 allows you to buy only 37.5 shares for your $300 (instead of the original 50) and only 30 in the third month when the price has risen to $10 per share.

Now you'll undoubtedly think, "What a great investment!" and be tempted to violate DCAs hard-and-fast rule of investing a constant dollar amount, rain *or* shine. Reluctantly, you decide not to raid your other liquid assets for funds and limit yourself to buying only the thirty shares your fixed allotment of $300 will allow.

Now suppose it's month five and some economic calamity has caused investors to lose confidence in the market. Your stock has fallen back to $8 a share, the unit price you paid in month two. You're only human, so your first impulse is to "sell this turkey" and put your money into bonds, where interest rates are rising. Still, your DCA discipline has now become a habit, so you plunk down your $300 and walk away with 37.5 shares—more than you could afford when the price was $10 per share, but less than when you started back in the first month.

Now let us assume the stock's price continues to fall the rest of the year, bottoming out at $2 per share before climbing again to $4 in month ten and $6 per share in month eleven, right back where you started. At the end of the year, you evaluate your DCA results, which are plotted in Figure 2-1, and summarized as follows.

Month	Amount	Price	Shares
1	300	6	50
2	300	8	37.5
3	300	10	30
4	300	10	30
5	300	8	37.5
6	300	6	50
7	300	4	75

Month	Amount	Price	Shares
8	300	2	150
9	300	2	150
10	300	4	75
11	300	6	50
12	300	6	50
Totals:	3,600	72	785

Average Cost per Share: 3,600 / 785 = $4.59
Average Price per Share: 72 / 12 = $6

By sticking with your game plan and letting DCA work its magic, you notice that you now own 785 shares which, at a current price of $6 per share, gives you a portfolio value of $4,710—a profit of $1,110, or a return of 30 percent on your DCA investment of $3,600. Not bad! And a lot better than you would have done if you had followed your instinct and "bought high" at $10 per share and "sold low" when the stock price hit $8, $6, or lower.

Now, a clever stockbroker might point to this same example and say, "Look, I would've told you to sell everything in month four as soon as the price hit the plateau of $10, giving you a profit of $275 and a healthy 22 percent return without all the aggravation of waiting out the downside of the cycle!"

That's always possible, but who's to say the broker wouldn't have told you to sell when the price first moved up to $8, or buy even more than your original dollar amount at that newer, higher price? It's far more likely, too, that he or she would have advised you to bail out as soon as the stock dropped back to $8 and put your battered principal into his firm's hot new "product of the month"—costing you the potential returns achievable through DCA, and fattening the broker's commissions!

The point is, DCA allows you to profit not from beating the market, but from putting its irresistible (and often imponderable!) forces to work for you. You *always* bought your new shares at the lowest possible cost basis, and even if you didn't market-time and "sell high," you at least avoided excessive buying at those high prices and didn't lock-in big losses, like the rest of the herd, when the price dropped below what you paid. With DCA, instead of paying expensive intermediaries to guess what you should or shouldn't do with *your* money, you use those same short-term

Figure 2-1. Dollar-Cost Averaging–Illustration of Investment of $300 Per Month.

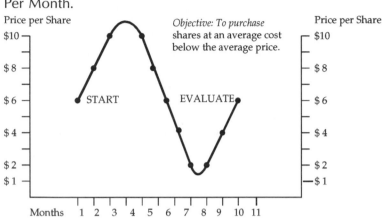

price cycles to steadily build your holdings, augmenting your profit by the amount you *didn't* have to spend on bad advice.

Of course, DCA works best over several complete market cycles (10 years or longer) and assumes the security has sound fundamental value. As you'll recall from our discussion in Chapter 1, "time diversification" theory suggests that an adequate holding period is at least as important as traditional securities selection to the success of any portfolio.

In Part IV of this book, I'll show you how to apply dollar-cost averaging as a wealth-building device in all four basic asset categories, and how to use DCA as a means of rebalancing a multiasset portfolio unbalanced by actual investment results.

Commandment 5: Decide When and How to Cash Out

As you've seen, plenty of smart people have done a lot of heavy thinking about when and how to get into investments—from sophisticated technical analysis of individidual stocks and grassroots market analysis, to surprisingly simple techniques like dollar-cost averaging. Relatively few, however, say much about when and how to get *out* of those investments, profitably and efficiently, so that your nest egg is not cracked, fried, or scambled when you draw down money to meet your long-term spending goals.

Three Rules for Low-Risk, Cost-Efficient Liquidation

Since our motto as Frugal Investors is: "What you don't lose, you make," you'll plan well ahead for any securities liquidation, moving money earmarked for near-term spending *gradually* out of longer term, more volatile markets and into those that are more stable and liquid. In a sense, invested funds needed for approaching goals like college tuition or a home down payment become another asset category demanding special attention. Here are the rules of thumb I've developed for efficient, low-risk securities liquidation:

RULE #1: PAY OUT ALL PLANNED DISBURSEMENTS FROM YOUR CASH EQUIVALENTS ACCOUNTS

Since this is a liquid asset anyway, and since many cash equivalents (like money market funds) have check-writing privileges, it makes sense to use this as the "last stop" for money withdrawn from other assets, such as stocks or bonds, that you intend to use for significant near-term spending. Although parking your earmarked funds in such vehicles means you'll be accepting lower returns than you might have made by leaving the money until the last minute in their less-liquid or higher risk cousins, you have, in transferring them to cash equivalents, inoculated yourself against the chance that some unforeseen circumstance, in either a particular market or your specific securities, could severely devalue your holdings just when you need them most.

If you don't think this can happen, look at investors who held blue chip IBM from its go-go days in the 1960s through its huge price drop in the otherwise booming stock market of early 1993. If the money in those shares was needed for important goal-related spending, it should have been shifted to bonds no later than the winter of 1991. This leads us to ...

RULE #2: DOWNSIZE EQUITIES TWO TO THREE YEARS BEFORE YOU'LL NEED THE FUNDS

Put them into fixed-income investments with appropriate maturities. Speculators used to thinking of price changes in terms of days, weeks, or months are astonished by this advice, but history shows it's one of Frugal Investing's most important rules. Since growing evidence supports the idea that most return is gained over the course of one complete market cycle (that is, four to six years), you should wait no longer than half that period to take out the profit you've made from previous cycles. To do otherwise puts you at risk of being caught at the bottom of a particular market cycle—a foolish thing to do considering the variety of lower risk, productive alternatives for your money.

Since international equities are considered slightly riskier than their domestic counterparts, you should add another six months to a year to your liquidation timetable if foreign stocks are involved. This means you would reallocate any earmarked amount *out* of your international securities and into your domestic equities three to four years before the date of your planned spending.

RULE #3: CASH OUT OF FIXED-INCOME INVESTMENTS SIX MONTHS TO ONE YEAR BEFORE YOU'LL NEED THE FUNDS

Fixed-income securities earmarked for goal-related spending should mature (and funds transferred to cash equivalents) no later than six months before you'll need the money. This helps guard your funds from last-minute fluctuations in interest rates as well as that "penalty for early withdrawal." If inflation is high or is climbing rapidly, you also want to minimize the time your money is locked into longer term rates—particularly if short-term interest rates have temporarily risen above them, a situation that, while rare, is not completely unknown.

Part IV of this book will give you specific tips on how to draw down funds most cost-efficiently from unique or unusual securities in each of the four basic asset classes—those that may require special handling and advanced planning.

For now, roll up your sleeves, sharpen your pencil, and put fresh batteries in that trusty calculator. You're about to design and acquire your own multiasset portfolio: the Frugal Investing way.

To Remember Before Going On

Frugal Investors ...

- Learn from experience and know what they *don't* need. They conserve resources, know their limits, and have patience.

- Let the right people do their homework for them—get needed information from no- or low-cost public sources—and trust their own common sense above self-styled experts.
- Go directly to the source for securities whenever possible, avoiding brokers and other intermediaries.
- Settle for the deepest discount or most cost-effective mutual funds when necessary.
- Build their portfolios steadily through dollar-cost averaging.
- Draw down needed funds intelligently to preserve allocated capital and keep their portfolio working.

Part II
Buying Securities Direct from the Source

3

Cashing In on Cash Equivalents

Legendary writer Ben Hecht made a lot of money in the late 1920s, most of it by promoting Florida land. He was so successful, in fact, that his friends began joking about the "few extra pounds" he seemed to be carrying around his waist because of his new prosperity.

They didn't know the half of it.

Hecht never trusted banks or brokers. He kept all his cash in pockets sewn into his garments. When the stock market crashed in 1929 and the deflation of the Great Depression followed, the buying power of Hecht's "stuffed shirt" made him one of the most successful noninvestors in history—and all because he put his faith in cash.

Of course, you don't have to wear your wealth on your sleeve like Hecht to benefit from the liquidity and safety of cash, or to benefit from its next best thing: cash-equivalent investments. Better still, you don't have to pay an arm and a leg to acquire them.

In this chapter I'll show you how and where to acquire the cash equivalent portion of your multiasset portfolio without losing a dime in sales commissions or other intermediary fees. To do that, I'll focus on two of the very best: Treasury debt and short-term bank and thrift CDs.

Tapping the U.S. Treasury

The first mistake many people make is to go to their bank for money. That may sound odd, since in advertisements, banks like to depict themselves as "money stores." It's especially strange since banks have tried in recent years to become veritable supermarkets of financial products, blurring the line between bankers and brokers, white-glove money managers and suede-shoe super salespeople.

Unfortunately, their favorite cash equivalent, the typical bank money market fund, has yields so low that only one other cash equivalent investment—any sort of bank savings account—pays a worse return. Neither keeps up with inflation and even the miniscule interest they pay is taxable on both your state and federal return, so the highly touted "security" of bank investments (savings accounts are insured; most money market accounts aren't) becomes a meaningless sales gesture.

As a result, my first rule of cash-equivalent investing is: Once you have a balance in an interest-bearing checking account (such as a "negotiable order of withrawal," or NOW account) sufficient for paying your bills, stay away from banks.

Where then should you go?

The first stop for any Frugal Investor, and the economic engine that drives almost any cash-equivalent account—either directly as an underlying asset or by comparison to the rates it pays—is the U.S. Treasury. Unlike bank accounts where only the principal is federally insured, the principal *and* interest of U.S. Treasury securities are guaranteed, and you don't pay a dime for the premiums. Even better (and also unlike bank-paid interest), the interest on Treasuries aren't taxed at the state and local level. For these and other benefits (such as their ease of acquisition, safety, and liquidity) shorter term Treasury securities are the chief underlying asset for most money market funds. Since that's what gives most of these funds their value, why not do what the fund managers themselves do and "buy them wholesale"?

WHERE TO GO

Any investor can buy U.S. Treasury securities directly from any Federal Reserve Bank—also known as the fed, the "bankers' bank" whose network of twelve district and thirty-seven branch offices forms the basis of our central banking system. Appendix A gives you a complete listing of both "walk in" and mailing addresses for not only the fed branch banks themselves, but the more convenient Treasury Servicing Offices in almost all metropolitan areas. If you want more free information on how Treasury securities of any type work, contact:

Bureau of Public Debt
Division of Customer Services 1300 C Street, S.W. Washington DC 20239
(202) 287-4113

WHAT YOU'LL SAVE

If you bought Treasury securities through a bank or stockbroker, you'd pay a minimum of $30 to $50, or even more (I've seen them as high as $75) for commissions on each purchase transaction—and pay the same amount again should you sell your securities before maturity. This cost is completely avoided when you buy direct from the Treasury Department or its agent, the Federal Reserve Bank.

So why doesn't everyone go directly to the source for cash equivalents? Why are expensive and low-return bank and mutual fund money market funds so popular?

Most financial salespeople will tell you it's because their customers like the convenience of a personal banker or broker who'll "scour the market" for the best products and do all the paperwork, but that's nonsense. About the same amount of paperwork is required to buy securities directly from the fed as it takes to open and maintain a brokerage account, and every brokerage firm I know adds an increment to their statements of at least four to five dollars for "mailing expense"—well above the price of the single first-class stamp you'll need to mail off your tender. Besides, as you'll see in the following, once you've opened a Treasury account, you can rollover your allocation automatically without lifting a finger and order new T-bills with minimum effort and *zero* additional expense.

TAX IMPLICATIONS

The interest paid on Treasury securities is exempt from state and local taxes, although (like almost any U.S. government payout) Uncle Sam still gets his share. Interest paid on your Treasuries will be reported to the IRS on a Form 1099-INT. Payments you receive may be subject to backup withholding of 20 percent if you don't provide a valid taxpayer identification number, fail to certify that you aren't subject to backup withholding, or the IRS turns you in for underreporting interest income.

WHAT TO BUY

The shortest term Treasury securities are called Treasury bills, or T-bills, whose maturities are thirteen, twenty-six, or fifty-two weeks (three-months, six-months, and one year respectively). I recommend you buy the shortest term (3-month) bills first, if you can afford the rather high minimum purchase, since they better allow you to keep up with changes in short-term rates. If you'd like extra stability in your short-term portfolio or have a fairly large sum to invest, add a few six-month T-bills but stay away from the year-long commitment, since this encroaches on fixed-income terrority—a totally different asset class.

WHEN TO BUY

Since the money raised through the sale of Treasury securities goes directly to paying the expenses of our massive federal government, the fed's T-bill counter opens at regular, frequent intervals advertised in the financial pages of most major newspapers. Three- and six-month T-bills are offered each week. Offerings are announced on a Tuesday, auctioned the following Monday, and issued on the Thursday after the auction. Twelve-month T-bills are offered every four weeks. Offerings are announced every fourth Friday, auctioned the following Thursday, and issued a week later. When some calamity occurs and the U.S. government needs a little extra cash, additional offerings are made. Similarly, the debt window may be closed temporarily, as when the annual debt ceiling has been reached and Congress has not yet authorized the Treasury Department to go beyond it. But these unscheduled events are rare. For all intents and purposes, the fed is ready to do business when you are. Auction dates for Treasury debt are published in the Money & Finance section of the *The Wall Street Journal* and in most major metropolitan newspapers.

HOW TO BUY

T-bills are sold in a minimum denomination of $10,000 and in $1,000 increments after that. If this initial minimum is too high for your present investable resources, go directly to the discussion of CDs later in this chapter, or to Chap. 7 where I'll show you how to trade a high minimum investment for the minimal fees charged by the deep-discount money market mutual funds I've selected.

If you *can* afford the Treasury's minimum investment, you'll purchase your T-bill at a percentage discount from the face value—rather like buying an item "on sale" at a retail store. The difference between the price you paid and the face value of the T-bill at maturity is your profit, or the equivalent of interest paid. Expressed as percentage, this is known as *discount yield* and may be computed using the formula:

Yield = (Discount ÷ Face Value) × (360 ÷ Days until maturity)

For example, if you buy a 91-day (3-month) $10,000 Treasury bill for $9,850, the discount yield would be:

Yield = (150 ÷ 10,000) × (360 ÷ 91) = .059 (just under 6%)

This $150 difference is what the Treasury Department pays you for the use of that $9,850 for the three-month maturity period. Obviously, a sum borrowed for a longer period would pay more, so fifty-two-week T-bills are more steeply discounted than those maturing in a quarter of that time.

A lot of people are confused about how this discount amount, or discount yield, is set. They figure that a powerful borrower like the U.S. government simply names the rate and lenders line up, checkbooks in hand, grateful for the opportunity to make such a safe investment. In fact, nothing is further from the truth.

You may have heard the sale of Treasuries referred to as "auctions"; and for the big players—large institutional investors and money managers with tens of millions in assets—it is. These high rollers participate by what the fed refers to as the *competitive bidder* list, much the same way as "highly qualified" or "sophisticated" investors participate in stock market games like options and futures. In a nutshell, these big institutions submit bids in competition with one another that are just low enough to interest the borrower (the U.S. Treasury Department) yet are high enough to motivate their investors, the lenders, who expect a reasonable return for the maturity period. The fed then takes the weighted average of each auction's bids and that becomes the discount rate that the *noncompetitive bidders* (the rest of us) pay. Thus we smaller investors benefit from the judgment of experienced institutional money managers without having to pay a dime for that advice or assume the risk some very highly competitive bidders do of being shut out of the process because they got too greedy.

The only downside to this process is that we smaller investors won't know the interest we'll receive until after we've purchased our bills, but this isn't as bad as it seems. T-bill rates don't change much between auctions (although they can change significantly over several months) and the results of last Monday's auction (widely published in newspaper financial sections) plus a general sense of the direction interest rates are going will give you a good idea of what to expect. Besides, it's hard to go wrong when what is already the world's safest investment is constantly pressured by experts to yield the absolute best return.

After you've purchased your bill, you'll not receive the nifty engraved certificate typical of private stocks and bonds. Instead, your account is a simple bookkeeping entry in Treasury Department records. Because of this, there is no "aftermarket" in old T-bills: The original investor must hold them to maturity. Of course, as cash equivalents, the maturity dates are quite short, so you probably wouldn't want to sell them anyway. If you have the minimum T-bill amount and like the idea of investing in Treasuries but can't afford to tie up such a relatively large sum for even these short periods, go directly to Chap. 7. For the minimal fees I've screened these companies for, a money market mutual fund or deep-discount bank or broker will buy T-bills for you while guaranteeing redemption virtually on demand.

To purchase T-bills directly, ask the nearest fed branch or Treasury servicing office for a book-entry "Treasury Direct" account tender form. Fill it out and return it at the time you wish to make your first direct purchase. You probably won't have an existing 11-digit Treasury Direct Account Number, so simply indicate "create new account" next to the account number boxes at the top of the form. Soon after your book-entry securities are issued, you'll receive a statement of account reflecting your new number and a description of your current holdings.

On the tender form, you'll be asked for the amount of tender (how much you want to invest: the sum of the minimum and any incremental amounts), if you want your bid to be competitive or noncompetitive (you want "noncompetitive"), your name, address, social security number or employer identification number, daytime and home phone, and, if you've purchased Treasuries before, your Treasury Direct account number. Don't worry about using the wrong form: all forms are color-coded depending on which maturity you want—red for thirteen weeks, yellow for twenty-six weeks, and blue for fifty-two weeks. Among the most important data on the form is your direct deposit account information, which I'll come back to shortly.

As with other investments, you can register ownership of your bill in a variety of ways, depending on your needs and financial situation. For example, if you don't want to hold the bill in your name as a single owner, you can name a spouse, child, or anyone else as joint owner with or without the right of survivorship. You can also name someone as beneficiary of the bill in case you die before it matures. If the bill is for a trust or part of an estate, you can register it to a trustee or custodian, or a court-appointed guardian—all of which can have different tax consequences, so consult your CPA before you decide.

A sample of a typical thirteen-week maturity tender form is shown in Appendix D.

Return the form along with a cashier's check or certified personal check obtained from your bank. Tenders submitted by mail must be postmarked by midnight the day before the auction and received by the issue date. Tenders delivered in person (over-the-counter) or to the lock box at the fed/Treasury office must be received by 9 AM on the auction date (West Coast) or by noon if you live in the East. As you'll see, the Treasury Department now offers an automatic reinvestment (rollover) service which can save you further time and money when your T-bill matures and you want to reinvest your principal.

HOW YOU'LL BE PAID

The discount rate you've received is disclosed on the statement sent to you after the auction closes. As a first-time investor, you'll receive a Treasury Department check for the discounted amount (the $125 from my previous example) approximately three weeks after the bill is issued. Your principal will be refunded (redeemed) at maturity in the form of a direct deposit to the bank, thrift, or brokerage account you designated on your direct account form. That's why this data is among the most important information on the form: *It's now the only way direct-purchase principal is redeemed.* This saves the government the cost and headaches of cutting, posting, and tracing checks; and you the risk of having your check get lost or stolen, not to mention the trouble of depositing it on receipt. If you don't have a direct deposit account, you'll have to open one before you can participate. It's a simple procedure that takes only a few minutes at your local bank or discount broker's office, but the benefits last a lifetime.

Some investors don't like the fact that T-bill repayments are made in two lump sums—the first (your profit) three weeks after purchase, the other (your principal) at maturity. While this may be a disadvantage for income-oriented investors who prefer steady monthly checks, it can help others since the federal tax liability doesn't occur until the maturity date, which may not fall in the current tax year, even when you've already received your check. In essence, the IRS lets you use the interest on a "tax deferred" basis until the following year—quite the opposite of its usual "imputed tax" requirement. If you are retired or otherwise prefer monthly payments, go to my discussion of CDs at the end of this chapter or directly to Chap. 7, where you'll find a variety of low-cost money market mutual funds which, because of their laddered T-bill portfolios, can distribute monthly income to their investors.

Since your money will be invested in cash equivalents permanently, I recommend that you select the automatic reinvestment, or rollover option, on your Treasury Direct tender form when you first purchase your bills. This option lasts for two years, after which you must renew it through a new tender form. (New tender forms aren't necessary under the automatic reinvestment plan unless you wish to add new cash.) If you don't select the rollover option at first but wish to do so later, notify the fed at least twenty days prior to the maturity of your bill. (Have no worry, if you forget about this option, the Treasury Department will remind you forty-five days before maturity—like any investment sponsor, they don't want to let a buck out of the house!) The number of reinvestments you'll get is based on the maturity of the bill you've purchased. For example, a thirteen-week T-bill can rollover eight times during the two-year period. After that, you'll have to submit a new reinvestment request to renew the service. Subsequent discount payments will be wired to the direct deposit account listed on your form. On the other hand, if you want to take your money out of T-bills, you can cancel the reinvestment service at any time—provided you notify a fed branch or servicing office at least twenty days before your bill matures.

What if a really big emergency hits and you need your principal before the maturity date?

The fed will cooperate and return your principal provided the withdrawal is *not* made during the first or last twenty days of the holding period. (This isn't stinginess—just the time it takes to get into and out of the government's accounting system.) Naturally, the government rebates to itself from your principal a pro rata portion of the previous discount and interest payment to compensate them for the early withdrawal.

Banking on Short-Term CDs

Believe it or not, banks used to give away toasters and actually *compete* to get new business. Checking accounts were free and financial institutions made their profit by lending money to productive people with good credit—not by nickel-and-diming customers for every conceivable service, lending fabulous sums to South American dictators, or pretending to be stockbrokers, the way things seem to be now.

Although banks are among the absolute *worst* sources for investments, one venerable bank product that offers good value is the short-term certificate of deposit, or CD: a tried-and-true interest-paying investment offered without commission by banks and thrift institutions for various terms and at various competitive rates—although that competition is sometimes purely nominal. The principal of a CD is federally insured up to $100,000 for each account, so the only people who run any real risk of loss are those wealthy individuals and institutions who invest in so-called Jumbo CDs, or single accounts in excess of this amount. However, these bigger operators manage their debt portfolios to maximize total return and so offset that extra risk by profiting from capital gains and interest fluctuations.

As a Frugal Investor, though, your main objective in cash-equivalents is to find a safe and reasonably productive place to "park" your cash reserves—not to maximize income or play interest rate arbitrage when you reinvest your short-term securities. As a result, give the Jumbos and other speculative CDs (including those with very long terms) a wide berth, even if you can afford them.

WHERE TO GO

CD terms and rates for various commercial banks and S&Ls are sometimes published in the financial section of major newspapers, and regularly in *The Wall Street Journal* under the "Banxquote Money

Markets" masthead. (Wilmington, Delaware-based Banxquote is a registered trade- and service-mark of Masterfund, Inc, an FDIC-registered deposit broker who may be contacted at [800] 666-2000.) The Banxquote survey publishes the average yields and other data concerning major bank and brokerage CDs.

If a newspaper or *Journal* aren't handy, CD rates for local banks and S&Ls are always available over the phone when you call the institution directly. Be sure to get a good sampling of rates and maturities from a variety of institutions and don't automatically buy CDs from the bank where you do your checking. Blind loyalty is fine for patriots, dogs, and spouses, but everyone else must earn your trust! Some of the best CD rates come from small institutions (they're more aggressive marketers) with few branches (they pass the savings on to you) and *all* can be reached by phone. Use the Yellow Pages of your phone directory to generate your list and you'll come up with plenty of choices.

CDs are also offered by institutions in other states. These can be purchased through the mail or by wire transfer, so if you see them mentioned in articles and ads in national publications such as *The Wall Street Journal*, *Money* magazine, and the *Donoghue* newsletter (and even many major metropolitan newspapers) they may be worth pursuing if local rates are unattractive. However, even if the out-of-state rates look great, the banks issuing them may be in, or on the verge of, financial difficulty. Since CD rates seldom vary more than a percent or two among institutions and you'll rollover your cash equivalents fairly frequently anyway, the extra risk and trouble you'll take with these investments may not be worth the extra return.

On any selection of CDs, though, be sure to compare apples to apples. A quoted rate that's compounded daily will always yield more than the same rate that's compounded less frequently, such as monthly or annually.

WHAT YOU'LL SAVE

Brokerage firms typically acquire their CD products from smaller or aggressively managed banks or institutions already in, or on the verge of, financial difficulties, such as a liquidity crisis. Why do they deal with such high-risk suppliers? Because these nonrated CDs must tout a higher than usual interest rate to lure investors while still paying enough to deliver a handsome broker commission. Of course, once the CD has been sold to the firm's customer (you, the hapless investor) and has been removed from the broker's inventory, the extra risk goes exclusively to you. Once again, the brokerage firm makes the killing (typically $50 to $60 for each $1,000 of the client's money invested) while *you* get stuck with the corpse!

TAX IMPLICATIONS

Regardless of the maturity or institution, all CD interest is taxed as ordinary income by the IRS, state, and (if applicable) local government. Unlike the discount on T-bills, this interest is taxable when you receive it.

WHAT TO BUY

Although you can buy longer term CDs (indeed, banks tend to push these products harder and you may acquire some for the fixed-income portion of your portfolio) you'll want only CDs with a maturity of ninety days or less (some may be bought for so short a time as seven days) to serve as cash equivalents. The only exception to this would be when two special conditions exist: (1) when six-month CD rates are for some reason extraordinarily attractive over their shorter term cousins, and (2) when buying those longer term CDs wouldn't put you at risk of illiquidity.

Although CDs are almost always sold in fixed and affordable amounts (sometimes for as little as $100) some institutions offer "designer" CDs for odd amounts, but these are usually confined to bigger or longer-term investments. Similarly, variable and "rising rate" CDs are sometimes available, too, but with the lower than usual initial rate they offer and longer terms, they're seldom suitable for the cash equivalent function.

WHEN TO BUY

CDs are staple products of the financial industry and are always available, although interest rates can and do fluctuate—sometimes from day to day. So if a rate is competitive and you aren't fully allocated yet to cash equivalents, make your purchase without delay. Remember, this is a short-term investment (most CDs are sold with thirty-one- or ninety-one-day maturities). Like a bad haircut, no mistake is so terrible that it can't be fixed in a matter of weeks, or months.

HOW TO BUY

Buying a CD at a bank is like opening a checking or savings account and can be done even faster if you already have such accounts at the institution.

HOW YOU'LL BE PAID

The yield on most one- and three-month (and many six-month) CDs is tied to the thirteen-week T-bill rate, reduced by the offering institution's own markup. As a result, you'll never make as much with a CD as you would investing in T-bills directly. If you withdraw your funds before the maturity date, the bank will deduct a penalty that can wipe out your interest, so be sure to invest no more than you can afford for the time period in question. However, since you'll always have some money in cash equivalents—10 to 15 percent of your total portfolio or the equivalent of three month's income or living expenses—your main concern will be rolling over your principal productively rather than taking money out too soon. On the other hand, some institutions offer "pullout" CDs wherein you may withdraw a small portion of your principal (seldom more than 15 percent) ahead of time should interest rates rise and you are willing to reinvest that amount immediately in a new, higher rate CD at that same institution. Again, the lower rates paid initially for this flexibility and the short time any marginally higher rate has to operate on the comparatively small amount involved negates any real economic advantage to this scheme.

Direct-Marketed Cash Equivalents You Don't Want to Buy

Experienced investors will notice I've not mentioned certain other cash equivalents: from commercial paper (short-term corporate debt) and banker's acceptances to U.S. Savings Bonds (the latter being available at no cost to investors). Why omit what some people consider bread-and-butter investments in this asset category?

THE SCAM OF INVISIBLE INTEREST

With the advent of higher paying, fairly liquid cash equivalents like short-term CDs and money market funds, the staples of low-end consumer investing (such as passbook savings, some credit union accounts, and U.S. savings bonds) should be avoided. The only people who value them these days (besides the institutions who receive your money as a virtual gift) are parents teaching little kids the "habit of thrift" and adults too gullible, conservative, or set in their ways to realize it's no longer 1956. There will always be egregiously unfair and noncompetitive investments tailored exactly for such people. Fortunately you, as a Frugal Investor, aren't among them.

THE HIGH COST OF SOPHISTICATION

At the other end of the cash-equivalents spectrum are the more sophisticated tools for securitized short-term borrowing, such as commercial paper (discounted notes issued by corporations and state or local governments), banker's acceptances (notes held by banks to finance commercial exports), and repurchase agreements, or "repos" (an institutional securities portfolio "loaned" to another institution in exchange for short-term cash).

The main problem with all of these higher yielding opportunities aren't their complexity (remember, investment sponsors are usually happy to educate you on their nickel if they think you can afford the investment) or even their higher risk (most require investment by high-income, high net-worth "qualified" or "sophisticated" investors), but the fact that they're still, for the most part, monopolized by commission- or fee-charging intermediaries or otherwise violate my basic rules for Frugal Investing.

For example, even though commercial paper may be purchased directly from the issuer (the corporation, financial company or governmental agency) its high minimum investment (usually $100,000) makes it suitable only for investors who *already* have substantial (perhaps 80 to 90 percent of their cash-equivalent) allocation in T-bills. If this is the case, any individual to whom $100,000 represents 10 percent of a 10 to 15 percent asset category (that is, $100,000 represents 1 *percent* of his or her total investable assets!) probably won't be using this book—he or she has already broken the code of Frugal Investing or has a professional money manager to look after the store.

Banker's acceptances, too, present a unique set of problems for the average individual investor. First, not all banks "accept" acceptances and those that do have fees all over the map. Even worse, there is no common system of denomination for securitized exporter assets or an auction-type market for setting or comparing the interest rates (really a discount rate, like T-bills) they pay. As a result, Frugal Investors interested in participating in the higher yields available from acceptances will almost always save money by letting a low-cost money market mutual fund manager do this specialized function for them.

Finally, repos are even more esoteric and costly to acquire on an individual or direct-from-the-source basis. Conceptually, a repurchase agreement is used as collateral by a firm needing short-term financing. The borrowing company doesn't want to liquidate a portion of its long-term common stock holdings, say, just to raise short-term cash, so it pledges to the lender that it will "buy back," or repurchase, the securities offered at a slightly higher guaranteed price a few days (or weeks, or months) later. The obvious question for the Frugal Investor here is: Why buy the repo, even directly, when you can buy the underlying stocks that provide its value?

Again, repos, like acceptances, are tools developed primarily to help particular businesses solve specific financial problems. Their usefulness as securities in a secondary market are therefore problematical to the average individual investor, even one whose full-time occupation is managing his or her assets. As long as better direct-from-the-source cash equivalents are available, Frugal Investors shouldn't bother with these.

In the next chapter, I'll show you how to make direct-buy investments in a much more substantial and fundamental asset class—domestic stocks—and how to keep the benefits of those direct purchases working over the entire life of your portfolio.

To Remember Before Going On

- Treasury bills are the principal asset underlying most cash-equivalent investments, including money market funds, so if you can afford the $10,000 minimum purchase you should always buy them direct.
- Although you should avoid virtually all bank investment products, short-term CDs can offer good value as direct-buy cash equivalents—but be prepared to do a little shopping.
- Because of noncompetitive low returns, avoid bank passbook accounts and U.S. savings bonds. Because of high minimums and other costs, avoid direct-buy commercial paper, banker's acceptances, and repurchase agreements and consider them only if they're part of a competently managed, nonbank money market fund.

4

"Buy the Dow"— On Your Own

Stop me if you've heard this one:

After a lot of procrastinating, a first-time investor finally calls his stockbroker brother-in-law and asks him to recommend a portfolio of "sure winner" common stocks. The brother-in-law, of course, is happy to oblige. A few months later, the investor calls in a panic.

"Those stocks you sold me went right into the toilet—lost half their value before my check cleared the bank! I want you to sell all those losers and put me into some nice, safe government bonds!"

"That's fine for you," the broker replied indignantly, "but what do I know about government bonds?"

This little morality tale has been brought to you by all those stockbrokers out there who think they know more about what is best for your money than you do. They earn fine livings trading off not just your ignorance, but their own. As a Frugal Investor, you can't afford the luxury of educating brokers on your dime *or* experimenting with the raft of do-it-yourself get-rich-quick schemes floating around in investment literature. What you want and need is a no-nonsense method for selecting high-quality U.S. stocks to buy without commissions and hold without headaches as the core of your multiasset portfolio.

Where Do Value-Conscious Stock Investors Begin?

Since this part of my book is dedicated solely to no-commission, no-fee investing, and since *all* mutual funds—even passive index funds—charge at least a nominal management fee, I'll confine my discussion here to:

- Quality individual U.S. common stocks that can be purchased initially *without a broker*,
- Quality stocks which can be purchased *without a commission* after you already own the first share, and
- Quality stocks that mirror a major stock market index but with only a fraction of the companies that comprise that index. This allows you, in essence, to "buy the market" and enjoy its long-term performance without paying a fund manager to do that job for you.

Best of all, the stocks I'll recommend here all feature automatic dividend reinvestment (DRP) and optional cash purchase (OCP) plans—the two most powerful ways I know to boost your portfolio's growth.

Which Index Should I Mirror?

Although market indexes have sprouted like weeds over the decades, the two most venerable indexes are still the best. Their long histories give you the best measure of past market performance in almost any economic climate, and thereby provide the most reasonable guide to the future. Nothing is guaranteed of course, in life or investing, but if you don't know where you've been, it's a lot tougher to see where you might be going.

This narrows the choices to the two most-often quoted favorites: the Dow Jones Industrial Average (DJIA, or Dow), and Standard & Poor's (S&P) 500. The Dow charts the general price movement of 30 widely held NYSE stocks by adding their prices and dividing the sum by an adjusted denominator. The demoninator began as thirty, but over the years has been adjusted for stock splits, dividends, substitute stocks, and so on, and is now about 1.3. (The stocks comprising the index and the current denominator are published in the footnotes accompanying the DJIA chart as published in *The Wall Street Journal*.)

Although the S&P 500 contains a larger selection of stocks, that isn't necessarily an advantage to smaller direct-buy investors. Since your goal is to mirror the index with as few individual stocks as possible, a smaller index makes that task easier. Consequently, I recommend a portfolio that reflects the DJIA.

As Figure 4-1 shows, this index also gives you a slightly better historical return than the S&P 500 (just over 1 percent better in the last ten years; a half-a-percent better over the last twenty), making more in up years and losing less when the market turns down. When you couple these advantages to the benefits of dividend reinvesting, OCP contributions made using dollar-cost averaging, and the power of compounding, your portfolio will begin its life with the proverbial silver spoon in its mouth.

Figure 4-1. DJIA–S&P 500, Total Returns—1983 Initial Investment of $10,000.

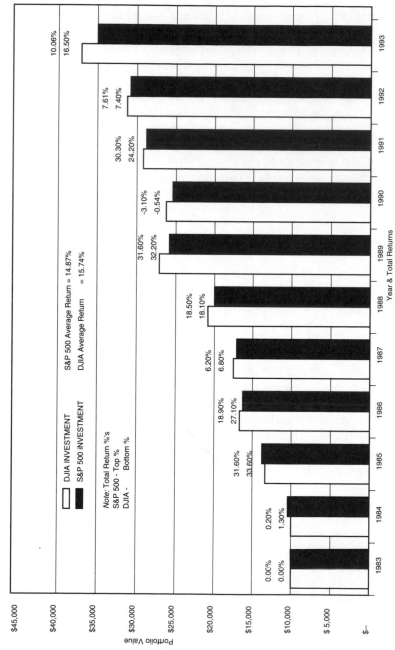

Source: Spiering & Company Inc.

How Do I Mirror the Dow?

Most analysts categorize all stocks in at least two ways. The first category reflects the stock's economic sector: those "sister firms" that are more or less sensitive to the same economic pressures. The second category reflects the stock's market action: how it has performed over time and how investors have responded to that action. Naturally, you can find companies of any particular market category in any given economic sector, so you have to consider *both* classifications if you really want to understand the stock you intend to purchase. Because I'll come back to these concepts from time to time, it's important to take a moment now and see what makes them tick.

Economic Sector

Although the stock market in aggregate tends to move one way or another as the economy changes, all stocks don't make these moves at the same time. This makes sense because when interest rates go up, for example, firms that must borrow frequently, such as utilities, and firms dealing with customers who are dependent on financing to make their purchases (such as new car buyers, home buyers, and real estate developers) feel the heat first. These leading edge firms are then followed later by their suppliers as production slows and demand for the steel, glass, building materials, etc., these primary industries use also slows down. Similarly, companies dependent on seasonal consumer spending, such as toy manufacturers and retailers (that do well at Christmas) and travel/leisure-time companies like airlines and resorts (that do well during the summer months and holidays) respond to factors that affect transportation and fun, such as bad weather and high gasoline prices. Companies sharing such common attributes are grouped in the same "economic sectors." Here (in alphabetical order) are the sectors used in the Dow Jones industrial groups:

Basic materials:	These are firms that harvest raw materials from the earth and sea, such as mining and forest product companies.
Conglomerate:	Giant firms doing business in many economic sectors.
Consumer, cyclical:	These are the companies that tend to reflect our "lifestyle" habits and choices, and as such are sensitive to swings in annual spending or changes in the busi-

	ness cycle: from airlines and lodging to fashions and toys—even broadcasting and the burgeoning leisure-time industries like theme parks.
Consumer, noncyclical:	These firms provide products and services steadily to other firms as well as to consumers: from packaged food and beverages, drugs and cosmetics, to health care.
Energy:	These companies explore for, secure, and process the oil, gas, and coal our economy needs for productive activity.
Financial:	These firms provide the capital needed to make capitalism work, from regional banks and thrifts to insurance and secondary investment markets.
Industrial:	This is the heavy industry that provides the "produced goods needed to produce other goods"—from factory and farm machinery to railroads, shipping, trucking.
Technology:	These are the companies that make high-tech equipment such as computers, scientific instruments, aircraft and military weapons, and so forth.
Utilities:	These giant firms deliver gas and electricity to businesses and consumers.

Economists and other analysts interested in indexes track stocks within these sectors that perform in a way that's typical of each sector. If you can find a stock that does the same consistently, you've essentially "bought that sector." When you buy such stocks in the handful of sectors that are most instrumental in determining the direction, rate of change, and value of a given index (you don't really need *every* sector since some are much smaller than others and some indexes, like the Dow, don't contain every sector anyway) you've "bought that index." That's the strategy you'll use as a Frugal Investor to mirror the Dow without having to buy all thirty stocks or pay a fund manager to do that for you.

However, we are still not finished. Although we've satisfied our requirement for a representative sampling of stocks, the companies *within* each sector will have different stock trading histories and characteristics. For example, some firms may be relatively new while others are more mature with seasoned management and decades of experience. Some may be the darlings of institutional investors, who take large positions in the stock, while others, for many reasons, may be shunned by the big portfolios. To attempt to mirror a desired index, we must select from among our candidate stocks those with the appropriate market characteristics.

MARKET CHARACTERISTICS

Stocks are traditionally growth- or income-oriented. Growth stocks seek appreciation of share value while income stocks put a premium on paying dividends year after year. The key difference is that a growth-oriented (and often younger) company tends to reinvest its earnings and not pay them out to investors. Mature companies can still grow too, and are often very profitable, but that rate of growth is slower. Their steady, significant dividends contribute more to their investors' total return than their slow appreciation in stock price. Still other stocks yo-yo from one extreme to the other: sometimes growing quickly, at other times stagnating or losing value, depending on the economic tides. Individual investors can either chart these histories themselves or let the big institutions, mutual funds, and certain select analytical publications do that for them. As a Frugal Investor who prefers to let other, more qualified people do your homework *without additional cost to you,* you'll give a lot of weight to what institutional investors say. The market categories I use are similar to those used by Lipper Analytical Services, a respected source of market (and particularly mutual fund) data:

Capital appreciation:	These companies seek to maximize the market value of their stock. This means all earnings are retained (and the company often goes into debt) to finance its productive operations. Some are large cap companies whose earnings have increased 10 percent or more over the last business cycle. They're favored by more aggressive, risk tolerant investors and may not appeal to many institutions.
Growth:	These are companies whose earnings are expected to grow faster than the market indexes, but not as fast as capital appreciation stock. These stocks appeal to more moderate investors, including many institutions who may hold from one quarter to one third of the outstanding shares.
Mid-cap:	These are the great majority of common stocks: firms whose capitalization and

	revenues solidly bracket the market average. Their long-term histories show that they're not particularly strong candidates for high income or high growth, but can be dependable performers or, on occasion, offer a quick capital gain when outside forces affect them favorably. Mutual funds tend to like these stocks better than the big institutions.
Small company growth:	These are companies that are smaller in terms of capitalization and revenue than the market average. Institutional investors generally shun them but they can be found in certain mutual funds betting on their growth potential.
Growth and income:	These are mature companies boasting a good record of earnings growth and a history of paying regular dividends. The institutions love these stocks and *all* the "Frugal Ten" stocks I've picked below to approximate this Dow possess this market characteristic.

Which Stocks Should I Choose?

Frugal Investors primarily want growth, stabilized by income, in their equity investments. They're not adverse to "value" (as undervalued stocks are often referred to) but they're not contrarians who seek out-of-favor stocks as a principal means of making money. In other words, Frugal Investors are willing to pay for quality, because in the long-run, quality pays.

For all practical purposes, then, you'll need only growth and income stocks for a good portfolio of individual issues, and perhaps a couple of growth stocks for their slightly better value if you're young and have ambitious financial goals. If your investment goals are very aggressive, you might include some capital appreciation, mid-cap, or small-cap stocks such as those I described in Part I, to get that extra kick—but don't go overboard. Targeting anything other than index-type growth is a perilous undertaking, even for the pros, the most successful of which only beat the market averages for a few years at a time. If you're interested in anything other than participating in the general rise of stock market prices over time, I'll give you ways in Chap. 8 and the appendix to find some of the better managed mutual funds who have more aggressive objectives.

WHERE TO GO

Information about a stock's economic sector, market characteristics, and historical performance/objectives is available from a variety of sources—many of them free at your local library or sent with the compliments of the security's issuer or financial salespeople (such as stock brokers) hoping to make some money from your decision.

The best source of not only good objective data but unbiased technical interpretation, in my opinion, is the *Value Line Investment Survey*. Although a typical Value Line data page (one page for each stock) looks intimidating, you'll need to check only a few key numbers for Frugal Investing. Appendix C shows you just what to look for in a typical Value Line listing and other stock-related publications.

If Value Line isn't available or isn't your cup of tea, try the *Standard & Poor Stock Reports* or *Moody's Handbook of Common Stock*. Directions for interpreting the listings are given in the front of each book. Use them as a guide for determining information similar to the information I recommend you use in Value Line.

If you don't want to deal with the data but still want to buy individual stocks yourself, stay tuned. I'll shortly recommend some specific stocks whose initial shares you can buy directly from the issuer without commission, as well as a relative handful of stocks which, in my opinion, will give you the best chance of approximating the Dow without buying all thirty stocks.

WHAT YOU'LL SAVE

You already know that the sales commission charged by stockbrokers hits you coming and going (buying and selling) and that the bill only gets bigger as the purchase price goes up and more and more fees and administration costs, not all of them announced, are added to your tab. I first discovered this "death by a thousand cuts" several years before I became a stockbroker when I tried to do what you're doing now: build a portfolio of hand-selected individual stocks. My first purchase was 100 shares of a stock priced at $20 per share. As a novice, though, I was so thrilled to see the price appreciate almost at once (to $23—an instant 15 percent profit!) that, a mere three weeks later, I gave my broker the order to sell. You can guess the rest of the story. When I got my account statement, I was stunned. The commissions for buying, then selling, my $2,000 worth of stock was a total of $215 (roughly 10 percent of asset value), reducing my "handsome" 15 percent profit instantly to a mere 5 percent; and I didn't even want to *think* about what inflation and taxes would do to that!

The point of my story is that even honest stockbrokers *do* discriminate against small investors—the mathematics of fees and commissions make this inescapable. *Round lots*, or multiples of 100 shares, are sold at a lower commission, while for *odd lots*, or less than 100 shares, the commission is higher. Thus as a percentage of your investment, round lots are always cheaper. Fortunately, as a Frugal Investor, you'll minimize this penalty by buying only one share of each particular stock through a broker—and that only to become enrolled in the stock-issuing company's dividend reinvestment and optional cash purchase plans, after which you can buy literally thousands of shares, bypassing the broker altogether. Here is an example of what you'll save using DRP once you've acquired your initial share:

Suppose you've purchased through a broker one share of a good stock and this month's $500 dollar-cost averaging investment allows you to purchase fifty additional shares at $10 each. If you went through a traditional stockbroker, the total commission (remember, you eventually will have to sell what you buy to benefit from growth) would be $50 in and $50 out, or $100 from a full-service broker—a cost of 20 percent of asset value. This means you'd have to invest *an additional* 20 percent ($100) of principal, or $600, each time you went through a broker just to compensate for the round-trip commission and put your full allocation to work. That extra $100 per month adds up to $1,200 per year; to $12,000 after ten years; and to $24,000 after twenty. Even more significantly, if you assume that first $1,200 had been invested and reinvested at the same rate each year, compounded annually at even a nominal 7 percent with 4 percent inflation, the money your broker *prevented* you from making balloons to a whopping $4,643! With losses like that, you should at least be able to claim your broker as an IRS dependent!

Now let us look at the same transaction (a $500 per month purchase) made through the OCP provisions of the company's DRP—a series of monthly, brokerless transactions. Your commission going in will be zero, and the cost to sell (all companies charge for share liquidition to cover transfer agent fees and other minor administrative costs) is insignificant: seldom more than three to five dollars. Thus to recoup your transaction costs, you'd need to add not 20 percent more principal, but a mere 1 percent. If you multiply this margin for the 120 transactions you'd be making as part of your DCA-OCP program over ten years, you'll save $6,000 in broker's commissions—money that goes directly into increasing the earning power of your investment. And the margin only gets bigger as your contributions increase and DRP–OCP works its magic on your entire portfolio.

TAX IMPLICATIONS

Stock dividends are taxed as ordinary income in the year they're received, even if they're immediately and automatically plowed back into your investment through DRP. If there is a capital gain portion to your distribution (normally you won't experience this with individual stocks until you sell your shares) it will be separately identified on the Form 1099 the company gives you at tax time. Traditionally, capital gains are taxed at a lower rate than ordinary income.

WHAT TO BUY

The only catch in DRP–OCP programs is that you must already own at least one share to participate. If you're a stickler for frugal investing and absolutely refuse to pay any broker any sort of commission whatsoever, this limits your universe of direct-buy stocks to companies that will sell you that first share directly: a precious few. Still, such companies do exist. With the exception of Central Vermont Public Service and DQE corporations (see the following note), any investor in any state can purchase these common stocks directly from the companies (minimum purchases, if any, are listed in parentheses after the firm's telephone number):

Arrow Financial Corp.
(518) 793-4121 (No Minimum)

Atlantic Energy
(609) 645-4100 ($250)

Barnett Banks
(800) 446-2617 ($250)

Central Vermont Public Service
(802) 747-5406 ($50)
Note: Available to residents of 22 states.

COMSAT Corp.
(800) 524-4458 ($250)

DQE Corp.
(800) 247-0400 ($100)
Note: Not available to non-U.S. residents or residents of AZ, FL, NE, NC, ND, OH, OK, and VT.

Dial Corp.
(800) 453-2235 ($100)

Exxon Corp.
(800) 252-1700 ($250)

Interchange Financial Services Corp.
(201) 703-2265 ($100)

Johnson Controls
(414) 276-3737 ($50)

Kellwood Co.
(314) 241-4002 ($100)

Kerr-McGee Corp.
(405) 231-6711 ($750)

Mobil Corp.
(800) 648-9291 ($250)

Regions Financial
(800) 638-6431 ($20)

SCANA Corp.
(800) 763-5891 ($250)

Texaco, Inc.
(800) 283-9785 ($250)

US West
(800) 537-0222 ($300)

The following companies permit direct purchases of stock for the corporation's customers and/or residents of the state in which the company is headquartered (check with the issuer to see if a particular stock is available to you). Minimum purchases are shown in parentheses behind each stock:

Bankcorp Hawaii, Inc. ($250)
P.O. Box 2900
Honolulu, HI 96846-6000
(808) 537-8239

Centerior Energy Corp. ($10)
P.O. Box 94661
Cleveland, OH 44101-4661
(800) 433-7794

Central Maine Power Co. ($25)
Edison Drive
Augusta, ME 04336
(800) 695-4267

Duke Power Co. ($25)
Attn: Investor Relations Dept.
P.O. Box 1005
Charlotte, NC 28201-1005
(800) 488-3853

Hawaiian Electric Industries, Inc. ($100)
P.O. Box 730
Honolulu, HI 96808-0730
(808) 543-4605

Minnesota Power & Light Co. ($10)
30 West Superior Street
Duluth, MN 55802-2093
(218) 723-3974 or (218) 722-2641

National Community Banks, Inc. ($100)
113 West Essex Street
Maywood, NJ 07607
(210) 845-1000

Nevada Power Co. ($25)
P.O. Box 230
Las Vegas, NV 89151
(702) 367-5000 or (800) 344-9239

Philadelphia Electric Co. ($250)
Shareholder Relations
P.O. Box 8487
Philadelphia, PA 19101
(800) 626-8729

Puget Sound Power & Light Co. ($25)
P.O. Box 96010
Bellevue, WA 98009-9610
(206) 462-3719

Southwest Gas Corp. ($10)
Attn: Shareholder Relations Dept.
P.O. Box 98510
Las Vegas, NV 89193-8510
(702) 876-7280

Union Electric Co. (no minimum)
P.O. Box 149
St. Louis, MO 63166
(800) 255-2237

While these stocks are absolutely the least expensive to obtain in terms of fees and commissions (there are *none*), as investments they may not be the best for your individual goals or risk tolerance—and certainly shouldn't be considered in aggregate a diverse portfolio or in any way representative of a market index. One reason for this is obvious: most of these stocks are from the finance and utility sectors—important economic players, to be sure, but still only two sectors in a much broader market. Another and more important reason is that not all are seasoned stocks with good dividend paying histories—prime criteria for Frugal Investing. If you're serious about investing in any of them, refer to Value Line and evaluate them according to the methods I give in Appendix C.

A better choice for most cost-sensitive Frugal Investors are high quality blue chips that *do* approximate the Dow, provided you don't mind paying the minimal commission a discount broker will charge to buy that first share. All of the following stocks I recommend are traded on the NYSE, all are mature-growth companies with good dividend-paying histories, and all offer some form of DRP and OCP programs, although the frequency and amounts of allowable OCP contributions will vary. A couple will even allow you to reinvest at a 3 percent discount from market price: offering you an *instant* profit unavailable to *any* brokerage customer. Even better, as a portfolio, these stocks outperformed the Dow by over 3 percent and the S&P 500 by more than 4.5 percent to return an impressive 19.06 percent for the 10-year period ending in December, 1993. (See Figure 4-2.) Although past results are no guarantee for the future, I believe these *Frugal Ten* are absolutely the least expensive way you can "lock in the Dow" and build your asset base year to year without commissions. The economic sector of each stock is shown in parentheses after each listing:

General Electric Co. Reinvestment Plan Services
P.O. Box 120063 Stamford, CT 06912
(203) 373-2816 (203) 326-4040
(Conglomerate)

The Coca-Cola Company
P.O. Box 1734
Atlanta, GA 30301
(404) 676-2777 (800) 446-2617
(Consumer, Non-cyclical)

Figure 4-2. Mature Growth Blue Chip Companies.

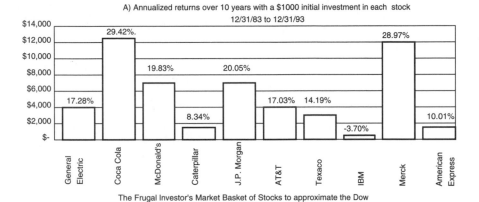

A) Annualized returns over 10 years with a $1000 initial investment in each stock
12/31/83 to 12/31/93

The Frugal Investor's Market Basket of Stocks to approximate the Dow

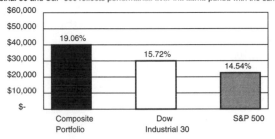

B) Composite portfolio contains the "Frugal Ten" with an initial investment of $1000 in each stock, or a total of $10,000.
Dow Industrial 30 and S&P 500 reflects performance over the same period with the same initial investment.

Source: Spiering & Company Inc.

McDonald's Corp.
c/o First Chicago Trust-NY
P.O. Box 3506, Church St. Station
New York, NY 10008-3591
(Consumer, Noncyclical)

Caterpillar, Inc.
100 NE Adams St.
Peoria, IL 61629-7310
(309) 675-4619
(Industrial)

J.P. Morgan & Co., Inc.
c/o First Chicago Trust,-NY
P.O. Box 3506, Church St. Station
New York, NY 10008-3506
(212) 791-6422
(Financial)

Texaco, Inc.
2000 Westchester Ave
White Plains, NY 10650
(914) 253-6084
(Energy)

American Telephone & Telegraph Co.
c/o American Transtech
P.O. Box 45048
Jacksonville, FL 32232
(800) 348-8288
(Technology)

International Business Machines Corp.
590 Madison Ave.
New York, NY 10022
(212) 735-7000
(Technology)

Merck & Co., Inc.
P.O. Box 2000
Rahway, NJ 07065-0909
(908) 594-6627
(Consumer, Non-cyclical)

American Express Co.
American Express Tower
World Financial Center
New York, NY 10285-4775
(212) 640-5693
(Financial)

Of course, there is still no free lunch, even in direct-buy, no-commission investing. Although this is the minimum number of stocks I've found
that are capable of mirroring the Dow, this smaller selection will necessarily be a bit more volatile than the Dow itself. This means that over the
long haul, you'll likely experience slightly higher highs and slightly lower

lows than the DJIA itself, but these stocks should track the index's overall movements quite faithfully—and one of them (Texaco) can be purchased initially with no broker at all!

If you don't like one or a few of the stocks I've selected, you can still customize or fine-tune your portfolio by making your own substitutions using the analytical and screening guidelines in Appendix C. These methods can also be used to skew your portfolio toward more aggressive growth stocks, or stocks offering more predictable income, depending on your investment goals. In any case, if you decide to replace any stock I've recommended with a choice of your own, try to stay within the same economic sector and market type and *most importantly*, make sure the company offers DRP and OCP programs. To find out which candidates qualify in this regard, and for more information about the quality of your choices, check the current year's edition of *Standard & Poor's Directory of Dividend Reinvestment Plans*. A sample data page is shown in Figure 4-3.

If you want to add new stocks to my list, begin with others on the Dow until you've, essentially, "bought the Dow." However, I think these extra funds would be better spent making regular DCA contributions to the core stocks I've selected. After all, what counts is your long-term compound return, not which companies you've blessed with your patronage.

A final note on which individual stocks to buy: Many people already own shares in leading companies and just don't know it. They may have inherited those shares from a relative's estate, own them through an employer's profit-sharing plan, or hold them through the activities of an investment club—even if they have not been active with that club for many years. Like any good Frugal Investor, make sure you really *need* something new before you go shopping for it!

WHEN TO BUY

Stocks are among the most liquid investments around. You can buy or sell them any time the market is open. However, you won't receive your cash until settlement occurs, which is five business days at a brokerage firm, or up to several weeks if you're dealing with the transfer agent administering your DRP account (they do all transactions once per month). If you're buying that initial share through a broker (hopefully one offering deep discounts), you may have to visit the firm in person to open an account and deposit a check as a condition for making your purchase. If you do so, your buy order will be executed on the spot. If you open your

Figure 4-3. Sample Page from Standard & Poor's Directory of Dividend Reinvestment Plans.

STANDARD & POOR'S DIRECTORY OF DIVIDEND REINVESTMENT PLANS

COMPANY/SYMBOL ADDRESS/PHONE PLAN AGENT; PHONE COMPANY DESCRIPTION	SPECIAL FEATURES (SEE PAGE 93)	OPTIONAL CASH PURCHASE ($)	CASH DIVD. PAID SINCE	CURRENT INDICATED ANNUAL DIVIDEND ($)	% DIVD. INCREASE (1989-1993)	S&P QUALITY RANKING	$1,000 INVESTED ON 12/31/83 WORTH ON 12/31/93
CMS ENERGY/CMS 212 W. MICHIGAN AVE. JACKSON, MI 49203 (517) 788-1867 *COMPANY ITSELF; (517) 788-1867.* *ELECTRIC AND GAS UTILITY, MICHIGAN.*	Δ⁴,AW	25 MONTHLY; 60,000 ANNUALLY M	ª1989	0.72	500	B	2,408
CNB BANCSHARES/CNBE 20 N.W. THIRD ST. EVANSVILLE, IN 47739 (812) 464-3400 *CITIZENS NATIONAL BANK OF EVANSVILLE; (1-800) 779-3949.* *COMMERCIAL BANKING, INDIANA, KENTUCKY.*	†, E	25-2,000 MONTHLY M	1936	0.88	20	A	N/A
COCA-COLA BOTTLING CONS./COKE 1900 REXFORD ROAD CHARLOTTE, NC 28211 (704) 551-4400 *FIRST UNION NATIONAL BANK; (1-800) 829-8432.* *BOTTLES AND DISTRIBUTES COCA-COLA SOFT DRINKS.*		10-1,000 MONTHLY M	1967	1.00	0	B-	2,166
COCA-COLA CO./KO ONE COCA-COLA PLAZA N.W. ATLANTA, GA 30313 (404) 676-2121 *FIRST CHICAGO TRUST OF NEW YORK; (1-800) 446-2617.* *WORLD'S LARGEST SOFT DRINK COMPANY AND MAJOR PRODUCER OF JUICE.*	†	10-60,000 ANNUALLY M	1893	0.78	100	A+	12,685
COCA-COLA ENTERPRISES/CCE ONE COCA-COLA PLAZA, N.W. ATLANTA, GA 30313-2499 (404) 676-2100 *FIRST CHICATGO TRUST OF NEW YORK; (1-800) 446-2617.* *WORLD'S LARGEST BOTTLER OF COCA-COLA PRODUCTS.*	†	10-60,000 ANNUALLY M	1986	0.05	0	NR	N/A
COLGATE-PALMOLIVE/CL 300 PARK AVENUE NEW YORK, NY 10022 (212) 310-2000 *FIRST CHICAGO TRUST OF NEW YORK; (1-800) 446-2617.* *PRODUCES HOUSEHOLD AND PERSONAL GOODS.*	†	20 MONTHLY; 60,000 ANNUALLY M	1895	1.44	72	B+	7,835
COLONIAL BANCGROUP 'A'/CLBGA P.O. BOX 1108 MONTOGOMERY, AL 36101 (205) 240-5182 *TRUST CO. BANK, ATLANTA; (1-800) 568-3476.* *COMMERCIAL BANKING, ALABAMA.*	†	10-3,000 QUARTERLY Q	1982	0.82	18	B	N/A
COLONIAL GAS/CGES 40 MARKET STREET LOWELL, MA 01852 (508) 458-3171 *FIRST NATIONAL BANK OF BOSTON; (1-800) 442-2001; IN MA (1-800) 827-1446.* *GAS UTILITY SERVING MASSACHUSETTS.*	†, K	10-5,000 QUARTERLY M	1937	1.24	8	B+	5,969

1994 EDITION

21

account by mail, you'll have to confirm by phone that your deposit has been received before a purchase will be permitted. If you already have an account, you may give your buy order anytime during the firm's business hours, although if the market is closed, the order won't be executed until the beginning of the next business day.

Above all, remember that although portfolio building can be fun, it's also a serious, disciplined activity. Don't overallocate to stocks or otherwise fill your "market basket" with unneeded issues simply because you read that the Dow has had a good day or you hear that somebody *else's* stock is mysteriously undervalued.

Chapter 8 gives you complete instructions on how to set up and use both traditional and discount brokerage accounts.

How to Buy

If you're purchasing shares from one of the direct-buy companies listed earlier, simply write a query letter to the address shown, and you'll receive order materials. Send a check for your desired purchase amount when you return your form. Be sure to indicate on the form that you wish to participate in the DRP and OCP plans offered by the company so that an appropriate account can be opened for you with the company's *transfer agent*—an independent firm that acts as administrative liaison between the company and its shareholders.

If you buy your shares through a stockbroker, make sure the stock is registered in *your* name and not *street name*: the broker's shorthand for customer shares held in the brokerage firm's own inventory. Not only will this allow you to escape the broker's fee for holding your certificate, it will enable you to participate in the stock's DRP–OCP program, which normally excludes shares held by brokers. To do this, you must state *at the time you place your order* that you want "good delivery" of the stock certificate, with the stock registered in your name. This is called a *DTC* or *direct-to-client* order in broker parlance, but it's just common sense in Frugal Investing.

Sadly, major brokerage firms, as well as the bigger discounters, have gotten wind of this and are now charging, or raising, fees for good delivery. Brokers would like you to think they're doing this because DTC is requested by fairly few clients and is an administrative headache for which they ought to be better compensated. They hope that value-oriented investors will, at most, compare the street-name fee to the DTC fee and forget about good delivery. Their real agenda, though, is to lock you into the brokerage system—to deny you access to DRP–OCP plans that mean better returns for you and lower profits for them.

Once your DRP account has been established with your selected companies, all your shareholder distributions from a given corporation will be sent once a month to that account, which is operated by that company's transfer agent. These distributions will be used to buy additional whole and fractional shares of the company's stock—you won't have to lift a finger. However, you'll want to purchase additional shares through the company's OCP plan on a regular basis, using dollar-cost averaging. I'll show you how to do this in Chap. 11. The transfer agent's quarterly statements will report how many shares you've accumulated—painlessly, through DRP activity—and how many have been added by your OCP contributions.

If at some point your financial goals change and you want current income from your dividends, simply notify the transfer agent at the address shown on your records and you'll begin receiving checks on a quarterly basis. Similarly, if you instruct the agent to liquidate a portion of your shares (as may be necessary to rebalance your multiasset portfolio) or want to sell all your shares and close your account, you'll receive a check within two to three weeks of your request.

Equity Products You Don't Want to Buy

Like the other investment markets, the market for domestic equities has been muddied with a variety of specialized, securitized, derivative products that *may* benefit certain investors, but are *guaranteed* to enrich the people who sell them. Frugal Investors, beware.

Over-the-Counter (OTC) Stocks

There was a time when OTC stocks were considered orphans of the big exchanges. The name itself comes from those bucolic days of the nineteenth century when there were no supermarkets and general stores sold merchandise to customers "over-the-counter." Early OTC transactions followed this model closely and for "pink sheet" transactions, where buyer and seller of thinly traded issues must be matched manually, it still does. (Indeed, in the summer of 1994, this folksy image was enhanced when a squirrel, gnawing at some critical wiring, shut down the OTC's entire trading system for a day!)

Today trades of most OTC stocks are virtually indistinguishable from those on the major exchanges. In fact, such impressive companies as

Microsoft and Apple Computer can *only* be purchased over-the-counter. So why is this active, vibrant, and growing market generally off limits to most Frugal Investors?

The main problem with the OTC market isn't what it offers, but what it doesn't. Although many companies are perfectly happy to be traded over-the-counter, most would prefer to be listed on the (so-called) major exchanges but don't meet those more stringent requirements regarding capitalization and track record. This by itself isn't bad: lots of small- and mid-cap companies on the NYSE are indistinguishable from their OTC brethren and frequently lead the pack when the markets turn bullish. But it *does* mean you won't find on the OTC the mature, large-cap growth & income stocks that's the core of Frugal Investing. Since there are plenty of opportunities to save and make money on the major exchanges, including a chance to invest in the aggressive growth companies OTC backers sometimes claim as their special province, there is no real need to go bargain hunting "over-the-counter."

Initial Public Offerings (IPOs)

When a company decides to "go public," it offers a specific amount of stock to an investment banker, who then brings it to market through a participating brokerage firm. In these days of acquisitions and mergers, the investment banker and broker are often the same. Obviously, the first public offering of a relatively new firm—even one that has operated as a private or closely held company for many years—is a risky proposition because the price has been set by intermediaries with a stake in its success, and not by market action. Because most IPOs soon fizzle (their market price drops back to, or below, their initial offering price within a few weeks or months), smaller investors should avoid them. However, like any good rule, this one has its exceptions.

The first exceptions are new issues released by long-established companies. Although this event is rare (existing shareholders don't like to see their holdings "diluted" by new stock—it makes everybody's slice of the pie smaller) it happens occasionally. If it does and you're *already* a shareholder of that company, you may benefit from the opportunity to buy more of a good thing. Unfortunately, the best new issues are usually snapped up by the big institutions and other favored brokerage customers, so your chance as a smaller fish of getting a taste ranges from slim to none.

The second exception is for equities issued by foreign companies— virtually the only way to buy international stock without paying a broker's commission. If this option interests you (and beware, it's for bold investors only!), you'll learn all about it in Chap. 6.

PREFERRED STOCK

To the uninitiated, "preferred stock" has a nice ring to it; but you have to ask, "Preferred to what?"

Preferred stock gets its name because, under SEC rules, its holders get a guaranteed yield whenever the company declares a dividend, even if common stockholders don't receive one. With *cumulative preferreds*, that guaranteed yield is accumulated from one quarter to another if, for any reason, the company suspends its dividends. The key word here, though, isn't preferred, but yield. Here is why:

In general, the value of preferreds runs contrary to interest rates. This makes sense, because if interest rates go down, more investors turn away from bonds and buy preferreds for income which drives up the price of preferreds. Unfortunately, the guaranteed yield of these preferreds is based on the ratio of the preferred stock's initial offering price to the dividend in effect when that offering was made. Thus, the higher the preferred's price climbs, the *lower* its yield becomes. That is: The fixed amount paid to the investor in dividends becomes a smaller and smaller fraction of the cost of the asset. Even worse, all preferred stock is callable: It can be repurchased by the issuer for a predetermined price if interest rates go down and the company doesn't want to get stuck paying over-generous dividends. Consequently, the only time preferreds make economic sense is when they're first offered or when their price drops back to, or below, their IPO price. If the company is any good, this will be never; so either way, Frugal Investors should steer clear of them.

Similarly, convertible preferred stock is an old product that our hoary ancestors developed to overcome complaints about the poor growth prospects of preferreds when compared to the same company's common stock. In theory, *convertible* preferred stock, which allows the shareholder to convert preferred stock to common stock under certain conditions, enhances the preferred's growth potential while retaining the preferred dividend policy. Such a security has always been a "financial camel" (a horse designed by committee) and today is justifiably rare. Since your multiasset portfolio will give you the benefits of both the growth and income to which convertible preferreds aspire, you certainly don't need to look for them in the same equity investment.

In the next chapter, I'll show you a much better way to achieve your income objectives through direct-buy bonds and other fixed-income investments that won't leave your financial hands tied.

To Remember Before Going On

- You can buy certain stocks direct from the issuing company, avoiding any commission whatsoever, but a portfolio consisting *only* of those stocks won't mirror an index nor will it be adequately diversified and may not meet your other investment goals.
- If you want to buy individual stocks to mirror an index, be sure to choose stocks from the same economic sectors and with the same mix of market characteristics as the index you select. If you buy the stocks listed in my "Frugal Ten," I'll have done this planning for you.
- The best reference for evaluating individual stocks is the *Value Line Investment Survey*, available free at most libraries. *Standard & Poor's Directory of Dividend Reinvestment Plans* presents all stocks offering DRP-OCP plans and gives additional evaluation information.
- If you buy the first share of a stock through any broker, be sure to say you want "good delivery" of the stock certificate at the time you place your order. Don't be fooled by the extra fee some brokers charge for good delivery—you'll more than make up for it in saved commissions through your future DRP–OCP purchases.
- Avoid OTC stocks because of their high volatility, and preferred stocks because they usually underperform the other income and growth securities.
- Buy domestic IPOs only if you already own the stock.

Bonds Without
the Bondage

"Neither a borrower, nor a lender be," says Polonius in Shakespeare's *Hamlet*—then again, Polonius didn't live in America on the verge of the twenty-first century!

Although our glorious English language is filled with references to the evils of debt ("Don't mortgage your future," "He's operating on borrowed time"), the art and science of borrowing money happens to be the U.S. economy's primary source of productive funds, and is therefore a leading source of investor income. According to the Securities Industry Association, the few thousand publicly traded U.S. stocks have a market value of about $4 trillion whereas the over 1.5 *million* fixed-income issues are worth almost *twice* as much: around $7 trillion. Any way you look at it, we've given debt a bad name and tapping into that lucrative income stream—directly from the borrower and without paying commissions or fees of any kind—is an important part of any Frugal Investor's portfolio.

Before you can break free of old ideas about debt and the traditional expenses that go with them, though, you'll have to accept two important truths about time and money.

First, the interest rate offered on any fixed-income security is directly related to time: The longer the maturity period, all other things being equal, the higher the rate. This makes sense to borrowers, because the longer they have the money, the more alternative uses for that money the lender will have to forego and the greater the chances are that something may happen to prevent the principal from being repaid—although there is a limit to how much any borrower will pay, no matter how long they hold your money. Figure 5-1 shows these two relationships in a typical, hypothetical yield curve.

Second, it's essential to know that yield and total return are generally the same *only* when the fixed -income security, such as a bond, is held to

Figure 5-1. Hypothetical Yield Curve—The Longer the Maturity, the Higher the Yield.

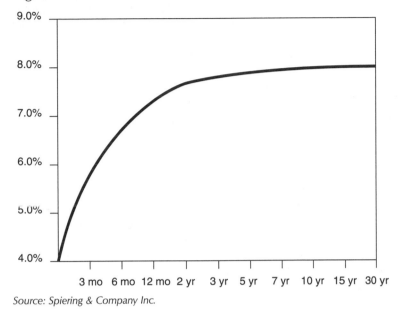

Source: Spiering & Company Inc.

maturity. As you learned in Part I, this is unlikely for very long-term debt or debt purchased by investors who seek capital gains by actively trading their bonds: that is, who manage their bond portfolios for total return. Since price can vary in the secondary market, the best way for any investor to compare bonds is by their yield rather than their quoted or discounted dollar price.

So much for the science of fixed-income investing. Now for the art.

Beyond maturity and yield, fixed-income return is affected by the issuer's creditworthiness (that is, the borrower's ability to service the debt), the demand for the security (which potentially affects your liquidity), and special features, such as "callability" (the option of the borrower to payoff the debt before maturity) and the security's tax status. Virtually all of these are subjective matters that require good judgment as well as a hand calculator to assess. Inflation, too, affects all investments, but fixed-income investments get hardest hit because they're unable to increase payouts as inflation goes up. When inflation is low, however, or if prices actually fall as they did in the Great Depression, bonds and notes can become increasingly valuable with time.

Treasury Notes and Bonds

Just as T-bills form the core of the Frugal Investor's direct-buy cash equivalents, so do longer term Treasuries (Treasury notes, or T-notes; and Treasury bonds, or T-bonds) provide the foundation for your fixed-income portfolio—and for the same reasons:

- *They're the safest investment in the country.* Both principal and interest are backed by the full faith and credit of the U.S. government, including its power to tax. No other type of government security, let alone private sector debt, offers this guarantee. Banks and other private sector lenders consider these securities so safe, they will often lend you up to 90 percent of your Treasuries' face value.

- *Their rates are competitive.* Although you'll find fixed-income opportunities that pay more, none have the favorable risk-return ratio of Treasuries. Remember, it's not just what a bond or CD *promises* to pay, but what it actually delivers—and costs—that counts. The U.S. government has never defaulted on a Treasury issue in history, and the auction process by which its rates are established guarantees *all* investors a fair return. For these reasons and more, Treasury notes and bonds have become the standard by which other investments are judged.

- *They're relatively liquid.* Unlike CDs and certain other popular forms of fixed-income investments, Treasuries are always welcomed in secondary markets. You won't be stuck if you ever want to reallocate or need cash for unexpected emergencies.

- *Minimum face value is low.* With medium- and long-term maturities selling for as little as $1,000, T-notes and T-bonds are among the most affordable securities in their class.

WHERE TO GO

Appendix A shows the address and phone numbers of Federal Reserve Banks and Treasury Servicing Offices where Treasury Notes and Bonds may be purchased directly, without any commissions or fees whatsoever.

WHAT YOU'LL SAVE

Brokerage firms typically charge as much as $60 (half going to the firm, half to the individual broker) for every Treasury issue transaction. This is paid not only when you buy the note or bond, but again if and when you sell it in the secondary market. On the other hand, if you have the minimum T-note or T-bond principal in hand and can afford a couple of first-class postage stamps and envelopes, you can do it all yourself.

TAX IMPLICATIONS

Interest on T-notes and T-bonds is exempt from state and local taxes but is taxed as ordinary income by the IRS. Also, bonds sold before maturity in the secondary market for more than you paid produce a capital gain, which is also taxable, although at a lower rate. Bonds sold for less than their cost basis produce a capital loss, which can offset other income.

WHAT TO BUY

T-notes have maturities of from two to ten years. T-bonds run from ten to thirty years. Thus an ample range of Treasuries exists to intelligently ladder your fixed-income portfolio so that your longer term debt can be rolled over at reasonable and convenient intervals, minimizing interest rate and inflation risk. I'll tell you more about laddering your fixed-income securities in Chap. 11.

In general, your fixed-income Treasury portfolio should be roughly:

- 60 percent invested in three- and five-year T-notes.
- 20 percent in seven- and ten-year T-notes.
- 10 percent in T-bonds longer than ten years.

This will allow you to rollover a substantial portion of your fixed-income assets during a given market cycle while maintaining a substantial amount in longer term reserves. This means that, while you won't catch the peak of a particular interest rate cycle for all your Treasuries, you certainly won't be stuck at the bottom or run excessive interest rate risk. Paradoxically, "aggressive" bond investors are those with portfolios full of long-term bonds, the prices of which become more volatile over time. (Remember, yield and return are the same *only* if you hold the bond to maturity. If you decide to sell, return can go either way.) Conservative investors prefer fixed-income securities with a mix of shorter maturities.

Caution: Although it's rare, some T-bonds may have a "callable premium" which means the Treasury Department can redeem them before maturity (return your principal before the bond has run its full term) provided certain conditions are met. Typically, these conditions include a minimum period before the call feature can be evoked (usually five to ten years) and the payment of slightly more than the bond's face value as partial compensation for lost interest.

Naturally, callability is used mostly for longer term bonds issued during times of unusually high interest rates, when the issuer (in this case, the Treasury) needs a safety valve for getting out from under what would otherwise be decades of crushing debt service. Callable bonds aren't necessarily bad, since their interest rate is usually higher than noncallable bonds. And, because the quoted yield is based on the call date rather than the date of maturity, you're still able to compare their economic potential with other investments.

The only real problem callable bonds present is with the laddering of your maturities: a twenty-year T-bond called at five years performs like a T-note, not a bond. If you decide to buy a callable T-bond, plan on rolling it over at the call date, and not the date of maturity.

Finally, many new investors ask: "Why not just buy an old bond in the secondary market, particularly since T-notes and T-bonds with higher interest are almost always available?"

Such questions sound reasonable, particularly for those people still fighting the "free lunch" mentality. In this case, the tab for your lunch comes in the form of a premium existing owners charge to persuade them to part with what, in a lower interest rate environment, is a clearly superior investment. In other words, while a new twenty-year, $1,000 T-bond paying 8 percent costs $1,000 when purchased from the fed, an *old* $1,000 bond paying 9 percent for the same duration would cost $1,107, or 10.7 percent more, on the secondary market. Figure 5-2 shows the effect this 1 percent change in interest rates can have on the prices of old bonds, not to mention the commissions.

WHEN TO BUY

Figure 5-3 shows the auction schedule for T-notes and T-bonds of various maturities. As with private debt, the longer term securities are sold less frequently because the market is smaller and interest rates change less often than with shorter term issues. Depending on interest rate trends when you begin purchasing your notes and bonds, you should plan on having your entire fixed-income portfolio in place within six months to a year after you start.

If interest rates are stagnant or declining, buy your T-bonds first since it will pay you to lock in these better rates. If interest rates are increasing, focus on short-term T-notes and "go long" on T-bonds when the rates appear to have hit a plateau (two or three months with little or no increase). This is the last "market timing" you'll ever do with bonds. All your future decisions will simply involve reinvesting your principal when the securities mature.

Figure 5-2. How the Market Value of 8 Percent Bonds with Different Maturities Changes With a 1 Percent Change in Interest Rates.

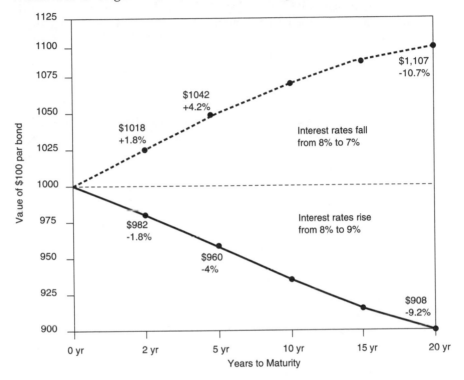

Figure 5-3. Auction Schedule for T-Notes and T-Bonds.

	Maturities	Auction Schedule	Minimum Face Value
		Auction Schedule for Newly Issued Treasury Securities	
T-Notes	2 year	Monthly: 3rd or 4th Wednesday	5,000
	3 year	Qrtrly: February, May, August, November	5,000
	5 year	Monthly: 3rd Week	1,000
	7 year	Qrtrly: January, April, July, October	1,000
	10 year	Qrtrly: February, May, August, November	1,000
T-Bonds	11 to 30 years	Qrtrly: February, May, August, November	1,000

How to Buy

The same procedure you used in Chap. 3 to buy T-bills applies to T-notes and T-bonds. In this case, though, the fed will also accept a check drawn on a money market account or mutual fund as well as a cashier's check or personal check (bank certification isn't required). When you rollover your Treasuries, you may also pay with matured Treasury securities/coupons or the Treasury (or fed) check issued to you for a matured security.

If you hold more than one class of Treasuries (that is, bills as well as notes and bonds) you can set up a "master account" provided all the securities therein are registered to the same owner. This simplifies record-keeping for both you and the government.

Tender forms for T-notes and T-bonds are a little different from the form used for T-bills. Examples are shown in Appendix D.

How You'll Be Paid

Unlike T-bills, T-notes and T-bonds feature a periodic payment "coupon"—so called because bond holders used to be given actual coupon books to claim the interest that was owed them. Longer term Teasuries pay their "coupon" twice each year in the form of an automatic deposit at your bank—the same way your T-bill principal is refunded. Unless you instruct the government to rollover your principal in a similar bond at maturity, your principal will be returned in a like manner.

As with T-bills, the interest rate is determined by the competitive bids of the biggest investment players so, although you won't know your exact rate until you receive your Treasury statement, you can be assured it will be the best possible for such a safe investment in the prevailing economic conditions.

If you want to sell your note or bond before maturity, the Treasury Department must first transfer your security to their commercial book entry system after receiving your request, provided you don't make such a request within the first or last twenty days of the holding period. If you buy a bond, they do the reverse, and transfer the security you've purchased out of the commerical book entry system and into your Treasury Direct account. Remember, though, Frugal Investors are in the fixed-income market for the long-haul, not to speculate on interest rates. By laddering your Treasuries by maturity dates, you can participate in favorable interest rate changes without risking loss of principal by selling your bonds early in a down market.

As with T-bills, T-notes and T-bonds are bookkeeping entries only, so don't expect to receive a handsome, engraved certificate from Uncle Sam—and be sure your account information, including mailing address, is always up to date.

Longer Term Certificates of Deposit

You already know that shorter term (six months or less) direct-buy CDs offer good value as cash equivalents. Longer (intermediate) term CDs can be advantageous, too, in your fixed-income portfolio provided they meet certain tests.

- *The CD must pay at least 2 to 3 percent over a T-note of comparable maturity.* Since intermediate term T-notes are considerably safer, you should demand a reasonable premium for dealing with a bank or S&L.
- *The issuing institution must be solvent.* Since the S&L crisis, small investors have become much more knowledgeable about the risks of dealing with financial institutions. Although you'll never put more than $100,000 (the FDIC and FSLIC insurance limit) into CDs at one institution, a guarantee of principal isn't the same as a guarantee of principal *and* interest. Since Frugal Investors believe that "where there is no gain, the loss is obvious," even return of principal under such conditions means the loss of that one irreplaceable ingredient to successful investing: time.

WHERE TO GO

The same institutions described in Chap. 3 also sell longer term CDs. Usually, institutions offering competitive rates on short-term CDs will be even more competitive on longer maturities—but beware. Business risk increases with time and bad news can hit fast. Unless the institution has a stainless operating record and excellent credit rating, give its longer term CDs a pass.

Two convenient sources of information for the best CD rates around the country are the *Wall Street Journal* and *Investor's Business Daily*—free at your local library. Also, the financial section of newspapers in major metropolitan areas usually print a weekly table of money market and CD rates available in that location and often out-of-state as well. These more aggressive CD marketers occasionally buy advertising space and provide a toll-free number for prospective investors. Finally, if you have access to cable TV, you can tune into "Moneyline" on CNN and the daily and week-ly summaries of financial activity on CNBC—all carry timely information about current CD rates. Obviously all the words of caution I gave you in Chap. 3 about such higher risk investments apply here, too, and to a greater extent, since your money will be at risk for a longer term.

What You'll Save

Longer term CDs are even more expensive when you buy them from a brokerage firm because markup is a function of price and longer term investments are usually more substantial. Since brokered CDs tend to be riskier as well as more expensive, never buy one from a stockbroker.

Tax Implications

Interest from CDs is taxed as ordinary income by federal, state, and local authorities. Even if you immediately reinvest the paid interest into a tax-exempt security, such as a tax-exempt money market fund, those orig-inal taxes will still be due.

What to Buy

Because business and interest rate risk increase with time, I recom-mend that you buy daily compounding CDs, if available (if not, the more often the interest is compounded, the better) with maturities no longer than one year. This means you may have to forego some intriguing hybrids cooked up by clever bank marketers, such as "bitter end" CDs that offer premiums (a cash bonus or kicker of one or two extra percent-age points) if you hold a five-year CD to maturity. If an institution needs your money that much, there must be a reason.

Rising-rate and "bump-up" CDs may be a better option, provided the maturity is three years or less. Under this plan, the bank increases your rate at some regular interval (annually or semiannually), guaranteeing your rate will never go down. If the rising rate is predetermined, a favorite marketing scam is to advertise the final, highest rate—operative only for the last year or six months rather than the entire holding period—instead of the initial rate which may be well below the competition. Needless to say, compare yields and be sure to read the fine print as well as the big, bold advertising headlines.

Least desirable of all are the so-called adjustable rate or market index CDs that tie your return to some outside standard, such as six-month T-bills or even the S&P 500. Invariably, these schemes involve complicated formulas for computing what you'll make, depending on which way the markets jump and whether or not certain nominal fixed-income alternatives you've selected as your "escape valve" kick in. This hybrid is a poor choice for several reasons.

First, it completely defeats the purpose of fixed-income investing by trying to incorporate aspects of other markets. If you want to enjoy equity-sized returns (and risks) or take advantage of changes in T-bill rates, *just invest in those vehicles* rather than gumming up what should be one of the most straightforward and dependable assets in your portfolio. Again, these sorts of gimmicks are designed to keep your cash with one institution, or in one type of market, rather than satisfy a legitimate investor need. In the age of multiasset allocation, they just aren't necessary.

WHEN TO BUY

CDs are marketed continuously by banks and thrifts. It's far more important for your long-term fixed-income portfolio's health to be fully invested within a few weeks or months than to keep your money in cash equivalents (or under your mattress!) indefinitely until interest rates rise to your liking. This is especially true if you're in one of those rare situations when short-term yields exceed those of longer term CDs. This condition occurs precisely because people expect long-term rates to drop, and so are hesitant to commit themselves to longer maturities.

By now, the fallacy of this reasoning should be apparent. If interest rates *are* going to fall, the best thing to do is to lock-in existing rates before that drop occurs. That's far more likely to happen than the opposite (which is what all those hesitant investors are hoping for), namely that long-term rates will be somehow bid up to exceed short-term yield by the usual margin. It just doesn't happen that way. If you must invest under such unusual circumstances, let your general knowledge of the prevailing economic climate and current trends in business be your guide rather than the herd's wishful thinking.

In short, a fixed-income portfolio is a lot like an airliner. The plane has only so many seats, so the airline wants to fill them all before the plane takes off to maximize its income. However, if the pilot sits around indefinitely waiting for those last three rows to fill, the airline won't make a dime and the passengers will never get to their destination! Similarly, cash earmarked for your fixed-income allocation has one powerful and irreplaceable ally: time. If you squander even a few months of it, you'll never get it back; and the only way to make up for it is with riskier, more expensive securities. Would you want your loved ones to fly to Europe on a nice, comfortable 747 or in the nose cone of an experimental rocket?

The procedure for buying short-term CDs, outlined in Chap. 3, is the same for acquiring their longer term cousins.

CDs with maturities longer than nine months typically pay interest annually or semiannually, often as a direct credit to your checking, savings, or money market account, provided you have one at that institution. Some institutions require you to open one of these accounts as a condition of receiving CD interest. As long as such accounts pay competitive interest, give you immediate access to your money, and don't charge for the service, I have no objection to them. Others will mail you a check for the amount that's due.

If you need your money before maturity, you'll pay a substantial penalty in foregone interest, although by law your principal can't be reduced. In this respect, CDs not held to maturity are a bit safer than comparable bonds and notes sold in the secondary market where principal itself can suffer. Don't forget, though, that some banks simply prohibit early withdrawal. This preserves your interest but denies you use of funds you may urgently need, and would be willing to sacrifice interest to obtain. Again, check the terms of your account before you invest.

Initial-Issue, Investment-Grade Corporate Bonds and "Munis"

Highly rated corporate and municipal bonds (debt securities issued by private companies and state or local governments) can be suitable for Frugal Investors *only* when they're first offered by the issuing institution or government agency. Why? Because in these cases, the broker (even a full-service brokerage firm) is essentially a "glass intermediary." The fee charged for launching the bonds is paid by the issuer to an investment banker, whose compensation, as it is with an initial public offering (IPO) for stock, is built into the initial offering price that everybody has to pay, no matter how the security is acquired.

Initial-issue corporate or municipal bonds must be purchased through a licensed broker, but since there is no commmission or broker-added fees, the net effect is the same as buying them direct from the issuer or the issuer's investment banker. In other words, the yield quoted by the coupon is the true yield you'll receive—just as it is with a T-note or T-bond purchased directly from the fed. Chapter 9 contains a list of the deep-discount brokerage firms I recommend for initial issue, fixed-income securities—although you may use a full-service house if that's more convenient and you're willing to put up with the inevitable sales pitch for other securities.

To find out when new-issue corporates and munis will be available during any given week, check *The Wall Street Journal*'s "Money & Finance" section each Monday. It will tell you which institutions are issuing which bonds and what investment bank is underwriting the issue.

What You'll Save

Because the rules governing new bond issues apply throughout the investment industry, you'll experience no special savings beyond avoiding the markups and commissions with initial-issue corporate bonds and munis. Thus, it's even more important for you to evaluate the economic viability of these products in terms of the risks and return they offer.

Tax Implications

Interest from corporate bonds are taxed as ordinary income by the IRS and state and local governments. Interest on municipal bonds will be exempt from state and local taxes but may be subject to federal tax (particularly the alternative minimum tax, even if they're exempt from normal tax computations!) so make sure you know the rules applying to the securities you select. Figure 5-4 shows how taxation decreases the yield on taxable bond income and makes munis and Treasuries more attractive.

Although I discourage premature selling of corporates or munis on the aftermarket, capital appreciation is possible if interest rates have gone down since your purchase. In that case, your profit will be taxed as ordinary income rather than capital gain—an oddity of the 1986 Tax Reform Act.

What to Buy

The corporate bonds you'll buy are technically known as debentures, or unsecured loans backed by the company's general credit, rather than mortgages that are backed by specific assets. Even debenture holders, though, have a claim superior to stockholders against company assets in case of business failure and liquidation. Munis can be either general

Figure 5-4. Taxable Equivalent Yield Table.

	HIGHEST MARGINAL TAX RATES							
	Federal	*CA*	*CT*	*MA*	*NJ*	*NY*	*NYC*	*OH*
State Rate		11.0%	4.5%	12.0%	7.0%	7.6%	11.5%	6.9%
Combined State and Local Rate	31.00%	38.6%	34.1%	39.3%	35.8%	36.2%	38.9%	35.8%

TAX EXEMPT YIELDS

	TAXABLE EQUIVALENT YIELDS							
	Exempt from Federal Tax Only	*Exempt from Federal, State and Local Taxes*						
4.00%	5.80%	6.51%	6.07%	6.59%	6.23%	6.27%	6.55%	6.23%
4.50%	6.52%	7.33%	6.83%	7.41%	7.01%	7.06%	7.37%	7.01%
5.00%	7.25%	8.14%	7.59%	8.23%	7.79%	7.84%	8.19%	7.78%
5.50%	7.97%	8.96%	8.35%	9.06%	8.57%	8.63%	9.01%	8.56%
6.00%	8.70%	9.77%	9.11%	9.68%	9.35%	9.41%	9.83%	9.34%
6.50%	9.42%	10.58%	9.86%	10.70%	10.13%	10.19%	10.64%	10.12%
7.00%	10.14%	11.40%	10.52%	11.53%	10.91%	10.98%	11.46%	10.90%
7.50%	10.87%	12.21%	11.38%	12.36%	11.69%	11.76%	12.28%	11.68%
8.00%	11.59%	13.03%	12.14%	13.18%	12.47%	12.55%	13.10%	12.45%

Notes: Taxable Equivalent yields apply to investors subject to the highest marginal tax brackets. State tax rates given were effective as of January 1, 1992 and are subject to change. The combined federal and state tax rate reflects the deduction of state and local taxes on federal returns.

Effective federal tax rates may be higher than 31% for taxpayers with adjusted gross incomes over $100,000. The required phaseout in personal exemptions and itemized deductions increased taxable income, and therefore effective marginal tax rates increase.

The information provided here should not be construed as tax advice. Please consult your advisor to determine your marginal tax rate and other relevant tax considerations of investing in municipal bonds. Although the information contained in this chart is based on sources that we believe are reliable, Charles Schwab & Co., Inc. assumes no responsibility for its completeness or accuracy.

obligation bonds (backed by the municipality's power to tax) or a specific purpose bond, repaid as revenues are generated from projects (such as a toll bridge, power plant, or airport) constructed by the borrowed funds. General obligation bonds are usually more liquid and of higher quality.

As a Frugal Investor, you're interested only in high quality (also called investment or institutional grade) bonds of either type. Such bonds are identified by their rating, the most common being those supplied by Moody's Investor Services or Standard & Poor's. Although these two popular systems aren't identical, they're roughly equivalent. Figure 5-5 shows the meaning of their respective codes. Expect the highest rated investment grade bonds to offer less interest, with interest rates and risk (including liquidity risk) increasing as you go down the scale. Buy only intermediate term (three- to seven-year) issues to help minimize interest rate and business risk.

Figure 5-5. Moody's and Standard & Poor's Rating Codes.

These rating systems are similar, although not identical.
The chart is a key to reading the ratings:

	Moody's	S&P's	Meaning
Investment Grade Bonds	Aaa	AAA	Highest quality bonds. Issuers are considered extremely stable and dependable.
	Aa	AA	High quality bonds. Long-term investment risk is slightly higher than on bonds above.
	A	A	Bond with many favorable investment attributes.
	Baa	BBB	Medium grade bonds. Quality is adequate at present; but long-term stability may be doubtful.
High Yield Bonds	Ba-B	BB-B	Bonds with speculative element. Security of payments is not well safeguarded.
	Caa-c	CCC-C	Bonds are extremely speculative. The danger of a default is high.
	—	D	In default

WHEN TO BUY

Initial-issue bonds are marketed continuously, so quality is more important than timing. If you want to get into the corporate and muni bond market, keep your eye peeled for offerings by the most creditworthy institutions and agencies. Just because a big city or populous state is offering bonds, it doesn't mean that that bond is necessarily a good investment. Poorly managed municipalities in depressed areas can be just as risky as poorly managed companies in depressed industries. In general, though, corporate bonds issued by any blue chip company are worth considering.

One word of caution: Bond ratings can change over time. Just because you've owned AAA bonds from one issuer doesn't mean that the next initial offering will be similarly rated, or that its existing debt won't be downgraded. This latter problem becomes significant only if you attempt to sell your bond before maturity. If downgrading occurs early in your holding period, it won't affect the interest you receive—although it may suggest your company or agency may have trouble making all future payments.

For example, the notorious 1984 failure of the Washington Public Power Supply System (aptly nicknamed "Woops") to service or repay its $2.25 billion worth of debt was the biggest muni default in history. Although many munis now carry private insurance for principal and interest, the best way to avoid this calamity is to keep it simple: choose your agencies carefully and hold only shorter and intermediate maturities in your corporate and muni bond portfolio.

HOW TO BUY

Since new issues are available only through brokerage firms, you'll have to establish a brokerage account if you don't already have one. I'll give you complete instructions on opening such accounts in Chap. 8. For now, just be sure to state that the purpose of the account is to purchase a given amount of a specific new issue and that you want the bond certificate to be sent to you, and not be held by the broker. This ensures that you won't be tapped for any hidden administrative costs or pestered excessively by a broker for new business.

Minimum investment for munis often begins at $5,000. Corporate bonds often have a face value of $1,000 but are invariably sold in five-lot minimums, so the initial investment is the same. Since these riskier alternatives to Treasuries and high quality CDs are best used to add a little kick to your fixed-income portfolio's earning power, it may be wiser for smaller investors to bite the bullet and pay the nominal fees a mutual fund manager will charge for buying these investments with a smaller initial stake. Chapter 9 and Appendix C give you criteria for selecting a fixed-income mutual fund.

How You'll Be Paid

Corporate and muni bonds pay coupon interest semiannually (like Treasuries). If the payment period is of concern to you, ladder your bond portfolio for issues with different dates. Although some corporate and muni bonds allow direct deposit of interest in the manner of Treasuries, most simply send you a check for your interest, with the principal refunded in one lump sum at maturity.

If you sell your bond through a broker in the aftermarket, you'll receive your funds (actually, a credit to your brokerage account) within two to five days, depending on the NASD regulation pertaining to that type of bond. If you want the cash, you'll typically have to wait another week or so for your broker to provide a check. The problem here, of course, is that you'll be clipped for the sell transaction (commission and mailing fee, etc.) so Frugal Investors should normally reinvest in another bond rather than sell, when the new issue replacing the old one can be had without additional cost.

Callability is more common among corporate and muni bonds than with Treasuries simply because companies, states, and cities have less flexibility than the federal government in handling long-term, excessively high interest rates. This shouldn't be a problem for Frugal Investors, since your five-year maturity horizon for these issues generally falls within the call-exemption period.

What Direct-Source, Fixed-Income Securities Not to Buy

As I said at the beginning of this chapter, the American economy depends more on debt than equity to keep the wheels of progress turning. Securities dealers know this and have come up with an almost endless array of debt-based securities to satisfy borrowers and lenders in any economic niche. Few of them, however, are really suitable for smaller investors and *none* meet my criteria for direct-acquisition frugal investing. Here is why.

Taxable Munis

Taxable municipal bonds are the fixed-income world's new kid on the block. Although it seems like a contradiction in terms (munis, almost by definition, are tax-exempt) these securities have some advocates because of their unusually high returns: they pay a coupon similar to corporate bonds despite ratings that would normally suggest a lower yield.

My problem with taxable munis is twofold. First, there is no free lunch—what one level of government gives in higher yield, another takes away in taxes, so what is the point? Second, taxable munis, with their higher return and therefore subtle suggestion of slightly higher risk for a given safety rating, are too new (currently only 2 percent of the entire muni market) to have a reliable track record. Until their economic niche becomes clearer, stick with better established muni options.

Secondary Market Corporate Bonds and Munis and "Junk" and Convertible Bonds

Although Moody's Baa and S&P's BBB and above muni and corporate bonds are acceptable, the so-called high yield debentures or "junk" bonds aren't unless you thoroughly understand the risk. Although their high interest rates are seductive, they're almost always part of some complex financial strategy hatched by the management of troubled companies, turnaround specialists, takeover sharks, or insolvent municipalities. (Even bonds in default have their customers: occasionally companies *do* turn around and bondholders have priority over stockholder when it comes to picking over liquidation assets.) Philosophically, though, investing in low-rated bonds is much closer to market timing than frugal investing so you'll want to avoid them.

Similarly, purchasing discounted corporate and muni bonds in the secondary market is really an exercise in interest rate arbitrage, not serious long-term investing. It also requires the use of a broker, which makes an iffy proposition even less desirable, and any profit, less profitable. Use the secondary market to sell your bonds, if necessary, but use the proceeds (or newly allocated fixed-income cash) to buy new issues only.

Another bond to avoid is the so-called convertible, a debenture that may be converted to a fixed amount of common stock. This hybrid investment had its genesis when "diversification" meant only stocks and bonds and there were few, if any, mutual funds. At the time, this seemed like a "dream" security to many but the reality was and is far different. Convertibles pay lower interest to compensate the issuer for the stock liability and virtually all of them are callable. Even worse, overall asset growth can never be comparable to an equivalent investment that began as stock since the drag of the low-return bond hampers those first few critical years. In short, if you want the benefit of a fixed-income asset, *buy* a quality bond. If you want the growing power of equity, *buy* a quality stock, it's just that simple.

Zero-Coupon STRIP Securities

These are Treasury securities whose semiannual interest payments have been "stripped" away, leaving only the principal, which is sold to you at a deeply discounted price. When the T-note or T-bond matures, you receive the full face value in a lump sum and therein your profit. The gimmicky nature of this product is reflected in the various names (sounding more like sports cars than securities) cooked up by the brokerage firms that first touted them: TIGRs, CATs, and LIONs. Even the normally staid Treasury Department bureaucrats joined the circus, offering its own version called—with a certain charming lack of imagination—STRIPS. Their big appeal was the guarantee of a fixed amount (euphemistically sold as "growth") that could be used for a specific future expense, such as college tuition. It was a financial planner's dream and a godsend to brokers who had trouble luring investors back after the Reagan-Volker recession.

The big problem with STRIPS, besides the outrageous fees that brokers charge, is that they achieve neither growth nor income while promising the benefits of both. True growth is open-ended, as experienced with stocks. STRIP "growth" is hocus-pocus based on a predetermined payback amount: bond investing by any other name. Similarly, true income dampens asset volatility by paying a little back as you go along. STRIP "income" is bogus because the discounted amount is buried for ten, twenty, even as long as thirty years, during which the STRIP's value can fluctuate wildly. Even worse, Uncle Sam taxes you each year on the interest you defer!

In sum, if you want growth, buy stocks. If you want income, buy bonds. If you want cats, tigers, and lions, go to the zoo.

Non-Treasury Government Bonds

Non-Treasury or "agency" government bonds marketed direct to private investors by the fed include Fannie Maes (Federal National Mortgage Association) and Ginnie Maes (Government National Mortgage Association), as well as their packaged offspring (Collateralized Mortgage Obligations, or CMOs) plus their lesser known cousins ranging from World Bank securities to packaged student loans. What these various and disparate agencies all have in common is hazy product (they tout "best yield possible" rather than specific rates or discounts) and great sensitivity to interest rate fluctuations. This means their volatility is generally outside the scope of what I look for in fixed-income assets, making them the province of speculators rather than serious long-term investors.

While all of these exotic fixed-income securities can make great cocktail party chatter, the investors who actually buy them may wind up caging drinks in exchange for their colorful tales while *you're* buying rounds for the house with your far more certain earnings. If you want higher returns than Treasuries, bypass the Agencies and go directly to high-grade corporate and muni bonds.

In my next and last chapter on direct-buy investing, I'll show you how to tame the most exotic beast of all: international securities—without having to tip the guides.

To Remember Before Going On

- In fixed-income investing, time and return are inextricably connected; and yield equals return *only* when a bond is held to maturity. Keep these in mind when evaluating any fixed-income security.
- T-notes and T-bonds are to your fixed-income allocation what T-bills are to your cash equivalents allocation: its core—safe, competitive, and liquid, but even more affordable.
- The maturity dates of all fixed-income securities in your portfolio should be intelligently laddered to help you take advantage of higher interest rates and not be unduly penalized when rates are low. Laddering helps you avoid secondary market risk.
- Intermediate-term CDs bought directly from a solvent bank can be suitable for Frugal Investors provided the return is two to three percent over T-notes of comparable maturity. Avoid gimmicky CDs that play with variable rates and maturities or are tied to other asset categories.
- Investment-grade corporate and municipal bonds can be suitable for Frugal Investors only when bought as an initial issue, avoiding any commission.
- Avoid "taxable" munis, convertibles, zero-coupon STRIPs, Fannie Maes and Ginnie Maes, and any bond offered in the secondary market, since these are either gimmicks or depend on interest rate arbitrage to make money.

6

The No-Toll Road to International Securities

The information highway is often paved with bad data. When it comes to foreign ventures, that's sometimes the only way you get there.

Take Columbus. When the plucky Italian set sail for the New World, he was so worried that his crew would mutiny because of the immense distance of their journey that he kept a false logbook showing they had come only half the actual distance. Significantly, the fudged numbers turned out to be more accurate than Columbus's original, secret record.

In the adventure of foreign investing, yesterday's received wisdom, too, often becomes tomorrow's obsolete fact.

Old Worlds and New

Who would have thought even a few years ago that by the mid-1990s the "evil empire" of world communism would have vanished like a bad dream, Europe would become one giant marketplace for jobs, goods, and services, and the biggest threat to American security would come from our own poorly educated kids and "huddled masses" yearning for affordable health care and a piece of the middle class pie. Indeed, the new global community—financially and politically—looks a lot more like the world of the nineteenth century than our previous shimmering visions of the twenty-first.

For Frugal Investors, such "merchantilistic" ideas as interconnected currencies, interdependent economies, and international cartels and consortiums dominating world trade offer plenty of opportunities for wealth—provided your explorer spirit is strong and you're willing to trust your intuition as well as numbers on a page. And when it comes to foreign securities, some of those numbers are impressive.

For example, foreign markets returned an average of 19.2 percent per year (in U.S. dollars) to American investors over the last ten years. Indeed, one mutual fund investing in international securities ranked among the top ten in this country. It will also surprise some died-in-the-wool, buy-American investors to know that the largest equity market in the world is no longer found on Wall Street, but in Tokyo.

With a financial logbook like this, even the least adventurous economic explorers can ill afford to keep their investable dollars tied up to the American dock.

Direct-Buy International Securities

Because foreign investment opportunities, by definition, cross political as well as economic boundaries, a lot of red tape must be stepped over, pulled away, or cut. This provides a lucrative field for financial intermediaries—territory on which neither cautious investors nor domestic regulators seem too anxious to tread. Charles Schwab, in fact, despite being the largest discount broker in the country, refuses to buy or sell *any* foreign stock that doesn't trade over the counter in the United States.

As a result, good individual foreign securities are often hard to find and the only direct-buy (no commission) individual foreign securities currently available in the U.S. are initial (and some secondary) issues of foreign stock and debt, including foreign securities "bundled" by banks and offered to outside investors as American Depositary Receipts, or ADRs. Although these are unsuitable vehicles for most smaller investors, frugal or not, they have a role to play in some portfolios and certainly foreshadow an era—probably not too far in the future—when a wider variety of lower risk international securities will be available directly to U.S. investors.

WHERE TO GO

Unless you're exceptionally wealthy and knowledgeable, the best place to go for your international asset allocation is to Chap. 10 of this book. At present, the high minimum investment, transaction complexity (which often translates into cost), and unusual risks involved in direct-buy foreign securities (ranging from generally *un*accepted accounting practices to the risk of armed revolution) can easily override the initial advantages of no-commission investing. For most of us, the modest management fees charged by the better international funds more than pay their way.

One often overlooked alternative to direct foreign investment is to buy shares in, or the bonds of, U.S.-based, multinational companies that do a substantial amount of their business in foreign countries. Although you may have to buy your initial shares through a discount broker as I describe in Chap. 8, you can buy *new* shares through these firms' DRP and OCP programs without a commission and so build one segment of your "international" portfolio avoiding the drag of commissions and mutual fund management fees. Such investments can also minimize your exposure to currency exchange risk, although you'll never escape this entirely in any foreign-dependent investment.

Notice that I put "international" in quotations because, strictly speaking, these stocks will exhibit characteristics of both foreign *and* domestic equities. Since the purpose of an international allocation is to reduce the volatility of your U.S. stocks by the dampening action of an out-of-phase foreign economy, the following multinational stocks I recommend should be viewed as a complement to, but not substitute for, genuine foreign issues.

For example, equity markets throughout the 1980s showed a fairly low (40 percent) correlation between stock price changes in the United States and similar changes on the German (West German), United Kingdom, Hong Kong, Japanese, and Indonesian stock exchanges— although this correlation has increased somewhat in recent years. Foreign versus domestic bonds also show a similar weak relationship. This means, paradoxically, that slightly higher risk foreign securities *can* actually lower the overall risk of your multiasset portfolio simply by dampening its price volatility.

My final caveat about American multinationals involves what ought to be the simplest part of any investment: cashing your dividend check. Although your investment and distributions will always be denominated in U.S. dollars, you won't escape foreign exchange risk entirely. Even if necessary currency conversions are accounted for internally by the firm, a U.S. company selling products or buying labor, capital, and raw materials abroad must still deal in foreign currencies at some point, then convert that money back to U.S. dollars to pay investors like you. If value is lost due to unfavorable exchange rates anywhere during that process, it isn't going to magically reappear simply because your check is denominated in U.S. currency.

Having said all that, I'll now provide a ranking (according to *Forbes* magazine, July 20, 1992) of those U.S. firms whose foreign revenues and assets comprise a substantial portion of that firm's total revenues and assets—in two cases over half!—and contribute to *more than half* of that firm's total profit. Some names on this list of "all American" companies may surprise you. Others have been big players in the international arena for generations. The company's phone number (and, if available, their toll-free investor line) is provided if you want to inquire about their DRP–OCP plans:

Exxon
(214) 444-1000

IBM
(212) 735-7000

Texaco
(914) 253-6084

Chevron
(415) 894-7700

DuPont
(302) 774-9656 or (800) 526-0801

Coca-Cola
(404) 676-2777 or (800) 446-2617

J.P. Morgan
(212) 791-3909

Allied Signal
(201) 455-2127

Of course, this doesn't exhaust the list of major American players in the global economy. U.S. firms whose foreign revenues, foreign profit, or foreign assets comprise at least *one-third* of their total revenue, assets, or profit are:

General Motors
(313) 556-2044 or (212) 791-3909

Procter & Gamble
(800) 742-6253

Eastman Kodak
(716) 258-5853 or (716) 232-5000

3M
(612) 450-4064 or (612) 733-1110

Goodyear
(216) 796-3751 or (216) 796-2121

Woolworth
(212) 553-2000

Merck
(908) 594-6627

McDonald's
(212) 791-6422 or (800) 621-7825

Caterpillar
(309) 675-4619

If you acquire shares in these multinationals, you can be sure that their performance will offset, to some degree, both bad and good trends in your purely domestic stocks. As your portfolio appreciates along with the general market, its overall price volatility should be at least a little bit lower because you own these stocks.

However, all these firms still bear the "Made in the U.S.A." label. If you're intent on acquiring foreign securities directly, it *is* possible to buy international IPOs, including debt, commission-free through domestic brokerage firms.

As is the case in the United States when companies want to raise money, they hire an investment banking firm (which specializes in launching new securities) who then provides, or "underwrites," the issue to one or a few retail brokerage firms who then dispense it to their customers, institutional and private. In some cases, the investment bank also acts as the retailer, keeping a bigger share of those initial profits in house. The most active foreign IPO banker/brokers at this writing are Merrill Lynch, Dean Witter, Morgan Stanley, Solomon Bros., Kidder-Peabody, Smith-Barney Shearson, and Prudential Bache, so these are the firms you'll want to watch for new opportunities.

Unfortunately, because information about upcoming foreign IPOs is also a commodity, it's usually "rationed" first to the broker's best customers: very wealthy individuals (who run up big brokerage commissions) and institutional fund managers. To learn about new foreign offerings being underwritten by U.S. securities firms in time to participate, read *The Wall Street Journal*'s Money & Finance section every Monday. Although this notice won't give you offering dates or other practical information, it will tell you what issues are pending. It will then be up to you to contact the underwriter or broker and ascertain the project's status. (Some may be very close to the public offering date, others may still be developing a prospectus, so the timing of your call can mean everything.)

Also, according to securities law, foreign debt and ADR offerings must be "advertised." This doesn't mean billboards in Boca Raton, but usually a small display ad or legal notice (called a tombstone in journalese) placed among the classified ads in any daily issue of *The Wall Street Journal*. You can also take a look at the securities firm's investor newsletter and stories about developments in international business and finance in the *Journal*, and also in *Barron's, Forbes*, and other high-end financial magazines and newspapers.

Yet even the most conscientious and persistent arm's-length "data search" can still leave you out of the loop in this most clubby and cliquish process. If you're serious about foreign IPOs and don't have personal contacts in the brokerage community, prepare a letter of introduction for yourself explaining your intent and send it, along with a statement of your financial condition from your CPA or banker, to the branch manager of the brokerage firms with whom you'll most likely be doing business. This will establish you as a serious and qualified investor and, best of all, awaken the sales instincts of the broker, who will begin to sniff a hot prospect. You'll undoubtedly then receive not one, but a series of calls from a junior broker to whom your request has been given. This time, *don't* hang up. The name of the game here is to establish enough of a rapport to gain timely information about the foreign IPOs that interest you. With luck, a good one will come along before your rejection of the other "great opportunities" the broker had offered instead tags you as a hobbyist or a crank.

In any event, finding out *when* the "gravy train" leaves the station and how much the fare (minimum purchase) will be is only half the battle. You must still evaluate the various risks associated with the stock or debt issuer—all the risks that apply to domestic securities, plus those unique to a foreign investment, including political and currency exchange risk. (Don't be lulled by the demise of the Soviet Bloc and the capitalistic reforms of remaining communist nations. Nationalization can occur even in nonsocialistic countries and privatization of formerly state-run enterprises often change the ground rules for firms already competing in foreign markets.) Appendix C of this book will give you some suggestions for evaluating these opportunities.

Investments in Britain, Germany, and Japan are just about as liquid as their counterparts in the United States, but even in such advanced countries as France invested money can be hard to pry loose. Remember, even if many of our ancestors came from Europe and the Far East, modern investment markets are relatively new in both places—despite the flashy performance of their economies since World War II. The United States is still the standard-bearer in investment sophistication and regulation; and in the wide range and safety of financial products. Don't apply the same hunches, value judgments, and assumptions to foreign issues that you would for comparable domestic securities—our ground rules and historical experiences just don't match.

What You'll Save

As with the other direct-buy securities, you'll save a minimum of 3 to 5 percent in foregone broker's commissions, and even more (up to 10 percent or more, depending on how much of the security you buy) if you avoid the miscellaneous account-related charges the broker will steer you toward or let you fall into in the absence of information about your options.

On the downside, there is always a charge for currency exchange, even when the exchange rate is in your favor. Currency dealers, including banks, make money on the spread between "biding" price and "asking" price: what they will pay for a currency you have and what they'll charge for the currency you want. This spread is never less than one percent and can be as much as five percent or more, depending on economic conditions and the dealer you use. Governments are the most expensive money changers; banks are a little better; and the spread decreases quickly thereafter in proportion to the size of the dealer. That's why foreign cab drivers and mustachioed people on street corners wearing dark glasses and a fez tend to give the best exchange rates of all!

Tax Implications

With a few exceptions, which will be touted loud and clear in the offering circular and its collateral sales material, dividends and capital gains from foreign securities are taxed in the United States and possibly even by the government of the nation issuing the security—although the United States has treaties with many nations seeking to avoid or minimize such double taxation. To benefit from these treaties, though, you'll have to submit certain forms, which the IRS must certify, verifying your tax status—a tedious process at best. Be advised, too, that some countries automatically withhold substantial taxes (up to a third) on interest paid to noncitizen investors—enough to make some otherwise attractive investments questionable. In all these cases, let a knowledgeable CPA or tax attorney be your guide.

What to Buy

The lowest risk among these higher risk IPOs are foreign bonds, so I recommend starting with them. Remember, even though you'll be purchasing a debt investment, it will be part of your *international*, not your fixed-income allocation. The same is true for an IPO of foreign stock, or a new bundle of ADRs offered by a bank. Like the relative size of U.S. equities to debt, the foreign fixed-income market is larger than the foreign market for stocks, although the two markets are closer in size than their American counterparts.

Fortunately, foreign fixed-income opportunities closely resemble similar products offered in the United States. To maximize safety, start with the treasury debt of foreign governments, then add foreign corporate bonds—many of which will be denominated in U.S. dollars. Such instruments are called *Eurobonds* even if an Asian nation offers them—"Euro-" being the generic prefix for any investment based on U.S. dollars circulating outside American sovereignty (and therefore beyond the reach of the fed and IRS).

No matter what they're called, though, a foreign security at some point will be affected by the U.S. dollar–foreign currency exchange rate. This can be as infrequent as when the security matures (if debt) or is sold in the secondary market; or as often as the monthly, quarterly, or semiannual dividend or interest payments you'll receive. If you ask for such payments in U.S. dollars rather than reinvesting them immediately in securities denominated in that nation's currency, you'll be short-changed if the exchange rate is against you.

WHEN TO BUY

New foreign debt and equity investments are offered fairly frequently, although foreign treasury debt of different maturities may be offered on specified calendar dates. Naturally, when economic times are good, there are more new equity offerings than when the foreign economy shrinks. Unfortunately, many of the companies making these offerings won't be around at the end of the next business cycle. Thus debt and equity opportunities may be slightly safer if they come during a slower period in a nation's economy, since only the hardier, long-term players will likely be participating. This is doubly true for debt offerings, since a high level of economic activity often brings increased inflation, and you don't want to "go long" in fixed-income investments in a highly inflationary economy, even if it's somebody else's.

HOW TO BUY

As I mentioned, brokerage firms don't like to deal with smaller investors or infrequent traders anyway, and they especially don't want them involved in IPOs. Consequently new foreign stock or ADR offerings simply won't be sold in odd lots, so if you can't afford the 100-share round lot minimum (and even then, many brokers won't take orders for less than several round-lot multiples) you just won't be allowed in the pool.

For debt, minimum orders usually start at $25,000. Since these riskier fixed-income vehicles should never form more than 10 to 20 percent of your international allocation anyway, you can see why I call such acquisitions a "rich person's game."

If you're used to buying stocks on the margin, or with a portion of borrowed principal, you may be disappointed in foreign stocks. Although leveraged purchases are possible on both foreign issues and ADRs, the fed decides which stocks qualify for margin trading, and since its job is primarily to help promote the growth of business in the United States, you can draw your own conclusions.

When you're ready to order, you'll have to open a brokerage account; see Chap. 8 for full instructions. Tell the broker that you want stock and/or bond certificates registered to you (yes, you're willing to pay the extra fee for this service—in the long run, it's worth it) and sent to your address. You don't want the brokerage firm to hold the shares for you in "street name" since there is always an extra charge for that and, even worse, you'll be forever locked out of the company's DRP–OCP program. While you're at it, make sure you're not inadvertantly (or intentionally) put into a fee-charging account which assumes you'll want access to other services, such as a wrap account.

Once you take custody of the stock or bond certificates, put them in a bank safe deposit box or other secure place, since they're your only evidence of ownership.

How You'll Be Paid

Unless you own a Euro-security, all distributions on foreign securities are made in the issuing country's currency. If you're registered for a stock's DRP or a bond's automatic rollover plan, your reinvestment will be made in the foreign currency and you'll run no exchange risk at all—at least until you want to get your money out. If you liquidate your asset or take dividends or capital gains distributions, you'll have to convert the currency to U.S. dollars. The statement you receive from the security's transfer agent will show the custodial bank (almost always a foreign bank) that made the conversion and the exchange rate used.

Unfortunately, you have no control over this process or opportunity to play "amateur arbitrageur" by specifying forward exchange dates or otherwise locking in a particular exchange rate. If you're curious about whether you've been stung, you can always calculate the effective (after exchange) return you earned and compare it to the one promised or declared on the distribution statement (this rate will match the payment originally received in foreign currency). If the preexchange return is lower, it means you made money because of a favorable currency exchange rate: U.S. dollars happened to buy more units of the foreign currency on that particular day. If the pre-exchange return is higher than the one you calculate, it means you lost money because the currency exchange rate was unfavorable: U.S. dollars were worth less that day with respect to the foreign currency, and that difference ate into your profit.

Bear in mind, though, that governments of all nations with convertible currency work hard to keep exchange rates stable, since it promotes international trade. From a practical standpoint, unless there have been unusual developments on the world political or financial stage, differences due to exchange rate fluctuations won't be great enough to make a good investment bad; and both gains and losses due to exchange rate changes tend to cancel each other out over many years. However, such differences (plus the exchange fees) *can* modify your return in U.S. dollars by a few to several percentage points on each transaction. And, since Frugal Investors know all profit resides in the margin, these gains or losses *will* affect the rate of compounding you enjoy. A string of negative exchanges and consistently high fees can sometimes make a good investment mediocre and a bad investment terrible.

Generally, though, U.S. investors in foreign bonds or income stocks pray for a weaker dollar, since that means foreign currencies can buy more of them, and a given dividend or interest payment will be increased in terms of U.S. dollars.

Direct-Buy International Securities You Don't Want

Throughout this chapter, I've referred to foreign exchange risk—the dicey game of converting one currency to another in an open market. Since this inevitably involves a spread (yen, U.S. dollars, and British pounds, for example, don't instantaneously adjust to a three-way equivalence when demand for one changes), it creates an opportunity for speculation. Indeed, when an American investor sells a Japanese stock for a 10 percent capital gain, then notices he or she has made *another* 10 percent just because of that day's unusually lopsided exchange rate, it's hard to keep them from becoming instant currency speculators. However, although options and futures in foreign exchange are sold on both U.S. and international exchanges, I don't recommend them. They carry all the risks of stock and commodity options and futures and then some—including the chance you'll lose a lot more frequently than you win. But don't be discouraged. If many or all of these direct-buy opportunities are too rich or risky for your blood, I'll show you in Part III how to find the deepest discounts for all of these securities and more, and with minimum investments that anyone can afford.

To Remember Before Going On

- International securities are a basic asset class. For Frugal Investors, it's not a matter of *will* I invest internationally, but when, how much, and in what securities.
- Direct-buy foreign securities available in the United States are limited to foreign IPOs (and some secondary issues), including American Depositary Receipts, or ADRs, which are sold like stocks on major exchanges. However, the high minimum investment, complexity, and unusual business and market risks involved in direct-buy foreign issues can easily outweigh any advantage in saved commissions.
- A portion of your international allocation can be in the form of the stock or debt of American multinational firms deriving the majority (or a substantial portion) of their income from foreign economies. These securities are suitable for all Frugal Investors, provided their international portfolio is rounded out by genuine foreign securities, such as those available through a good, no-load international mutual fund (see Chap. 10).
- Although currency exchange risk is part of any international investment, exchange rate arbitrage is a rich person's game and should be avoided by Frugal Investors.

Part III

Demand and Get the Deepest Discounts

Making the Most of Money Market Mutual Funds and Investment Deposit Accounts

Bing Crosby—the affable crooner and film star as widely known for his relaxed demeanor as his success—was once asked how he stayed so calm. Der Bingle pulled a huge wad of cash from his pocket and said, "Well, this helps."

In the high-stakes entertainment industry, fools and their money are soon parted; but Crosby wasn't one of them. In addition to his considerable talents, he knew the value of cash. Like that other famous singer–investor, Gene Autry, Crosby was said to have been a clever businessman who never invested a dollar unless he was sure to make two or three. To stay active in the game of gain, both these Hollywood giants stayed liquid—good advice for Frugal Investors.

Nowhere is the competition to separate you from your cash reserves more intense than the battle waged between America's banks and their sworn enemies: the money market mutual funds. Unless you've got the bankroll of a Crosby or Autry, though, you'll probably have to do business with one or both of these fee-charging intermediaries to fully invest your cash-equivalent allocation.

In this chapter, I'll show you how to cut through all the propaganda to find the one cash-equivalent bank investment that still makes sense. I'll also take you on a guided tour of non-bank money market mutual funds—still the best place for most first-time or smaller investors to park their ready cash.

To Bank or Not to Bank

Throughout this book, I've both praised and damned (and sometimes damned with faint praise) the blurring of old lines between banking and investing. On the positive side, consumers have never had more choices about what to do with their money—and despite the S&L crisis (which was bad news mostly for taxpayers), our investment supermarket continues to be the safest in the world. On the downside, most of these investments do little more than break even once you subtract the commissions, fees, charges, taxation, inflation, and other financial wear and tear caused by the various marketing gimmicks designed to reinforce the middleman's profits—always at your expense.

Why Don't Banks Offer Better Cash-Equivalents?

Decades ago, Congress threw a bone to the securities industry in the form of the Glass Stiegel Act. This was supposed to keep banks out of the investment business, but all it really did was make them more clever about how they tapped that lucrative market—a process only accelerated by financial deregulation in the 1980s.

The banks' most recent strategy has been to subcontract their highly advertised investment operations to independent broker-dealers, most of whom were drop-outs (or flunk-outs) from the major brokerage houses and possessed only Class 6 NASD licenses—not to mention second- or third-class money minds. These marginal or unqualified salespeople then hung up their "investment counselor" shingles in the lobbies of host banks. This gave those banks the appearance of following the regulation while giving their affiliate "counselors" the gloss of bank respectability.

These bank "lobbyists" sell a variety of investments, including insurance-related products like annuities, to a gullible public. I say gullible, because many of these customers assume that because the products are bought through a bank, their principal must be insured, which it isn't. Although banks don't overtly misrepresent this aspect, they don't exactly go out of their way to correct this impression, either. In a 1994 investigative report, undercover financial writers from the *San Francisco Chronicle* approached both mutual fund salespeople and bank lobby brokers with the same investment query. They said they had between $7,500 and $10,000 to invest for two to five years to pay for a home-improvement project. The mutual fund representatives all gave an immediate and fair appraisal of investment risks, but only *one* bank salesperson mentioned risk (namely, that the principal would be uninsured) without prompting.

Even worse, two 1994 studies of the nation's fifty largest banks conducted by Prophet Market Research of San Francisco showed that women get even worse treatment than men in this regard. According to Prophet's cofounder, Scott Galloway, "Women had more difficulty reaching a bank investment representative, had a tougher time scheduling meetings, and were less likely than men to have important disclosures about securities products explained to them." Although the banks' low numerical scores improved slightly between the spring and summer surveys, Galloway characterizes this improvement as a move from "very bad" to "just bad."

Another misconception bank customers have about bank-affiliated investments is that they're somehow commission-free, or at least cheaper than nonbank investments because of competition among the banks. In truth, not only do bank-lobby brokers charge commissions as high as the wire houses, but they split them with the bank. In medicine, this practice is called a kick-back and is universally condemned. In broadcasting, it's called payola and disk jockeys can lose their jobs over it. In banking, it's called *revenue sharing* and customers aren't supposed to care—assuming they ever find out about it. In fact, some banks charge *an additional* "annual maintenance fee" on the investments they sell, usually less than 1 percent, just for giving your account number the privilege of sitting around in their computer.

All this would seem to be yet another case of *caveat emptor*, or buyer beware, requiring only consumer education and new regulations (even as I write this, Congress is debating a new law to force banks into more complete disclosure about their products), but I think the problem goes deeper. Since banks are the place most novice investors go when they think about money, and since banks now offer more and more investment-oriented (as opposed to traditional banking) products, their power to do harm is just tremendous and a lot of damage—to public confidence, personal finances, and even the economy—has already been done.

When Can You Trust a Bank?

Frugal Investors should look to banks only for the things banks traditionally do best: checking accounts, ATM service, short-term CDs, loans (if you need one and the rate is competitive), and for certain cash-equivalent investments offered by the bank, and *not* their branch-lobby broker.

For these last investments, the bank will allow you to establish, and make periodic contributions to, a federally insured account paying close to money market rates *without* exacting a fee in proportion to the size of the assets you deposit. They can do this because (strictly speaking) they don't manage a portfolio of cash-equivalent investments like a mutual fund, but use your deposit as the basis for banking operations, such as loans. Thus, such products stay solidly on the "banking," and not the investing, side of the banker–broker battle lines. If the money market rates these banks use to determine their interest are high enough, and if their other terms are reasonable, some of these accounts, often called "investment savings" or "money market deposit" accounts (or some other impressive name), can be suitable for those very conservative Frugal Investors who put a premium on insured accounts.

WHERE TO GO

A large number of banks and thrifts now offer money market deposit accounts or investment savings accounts. Shop for these exactly as I described for bank CDs in Chap. 3—although you'll sacrifice CD-type interest in order to get the liquidity of a money market-style account.

WHAT YOU'LL SAVE

The bank will charge you nothing to open an investment savings or money market deposit account and you'll save the annual management fee charged by a true, outside money market fund, although your return will be lower than that offered by such independent funds. The real perk is that your principal is insured by the FDIC.

TAX IMPLICATIONS

Interest on an investment savings or money market deposit account is taxed as ordinary income by federal, state, and (if applicable), local authorities. If you're in a high tax bracket with few deductions, a nonbank tax-free money market fund may be a better choice. Although these tax-exempt investments pay less than their taxable cousins, (and are *not* federally insured, although their risk is usually low) their after-tax return may be superior.

WHAT TO BUY

Be sure you ask your bank for a *money market deposit account* or *investment savings account*. Although these products are advertised under various names by different banks, you'll get what you want if you make it clear that you're after a deposit and not an investment, and insist that your principal be insured by the FDIC.

As with many nonbank mutual funds, your money market deposit account may allow check-writing privileges, although these are usually limited to a few each month and for amounts above a specified minimum.

WHEN TO BUY

Bank money market deposit accounts may be opened at any time. Although short-term interest rates can change quickly, the money market rates on which your interest is based are almost always less than short-term CD rates (and in those rare instances when they're not, banks make quick adjustments). If you have your heart set on this product and don't have your cash-equivalent allocation fully invested, there is no point in waiting to open an account.

HOW TO BUY

A bank money market deposit account is opened like any other bank account. If you're already a depositor with the bank (have a fee-based checking or, preferably, a NOW account) the initial deposit can be made as a transfer without having to write a check.

HOW YOU'LL BE PAID

Money market deposit accounts pay monthly interest that can be issued as a check or deposited to another account at the bank, such as a checking or savings account. If you own CDs with the same bank, you can usually have the interest from those CDs deposited automatically in your money market deposit account, thus earning "interest on your interest" that's superior to that paid on most NOW or passbook savings accounts. If the bank's CD interest *and* its money market deposit interest are good and are compounded frequently, this can increase your overall cash equivalent return to a level that may be competitive with nonbank money market mutual funds—particularly if those fund shares were bought with a load or have unusually high management fees.

Remember, though, banks that try too hard to be both investment companies and banks usually wind up being poor at both—all caused by a kind of professional schizophrenia that permeates from top management down to the lowest levels of teller and lobby services. This little speech by an eighteenth century investor in Patrick O'Brian's *The Thirteen Gun Salute* holds just as true today:

> Nothing could be simpler than carrying on a banking-house. You receive money, you write it down; you pay money out, you write it down; and the difference between the two sums is the customer's balance. But can I induce my bank to tell me my bal-

ance, answer my letters, attend to my instructions promptly? I can't. When I go to expostulate, I swim in chaos. ...I don't say they're dishonest (though there is a fourpence for unexpected sundries that I don't much care for) but I do say they're incompetent, vainly struggling in an amorphous fog. Tell me sir, do you know of any banker that really understands his business?

Taxable and Tax-Free Money Market Mutual Funds

If you've come this far in my book, you're undoubtedly one of the vast majority of private investors who recognize the value of group investments. These pool the financial resources of many smaller investors to gain economies of scale (such as very large round-lot share purchases) and professional management that, even if it doesn't add tremendously to your return, at least saves you from a lot of tedious paperwork. Mutual funds have become so popular, in fact, that as of December, 1993, investors had pumped more than $2.14 *trillion* into such vehicles. While Frugal Investors are always sensitive to costs, they should never let fees alone outweigh the potential benefits of any investment. As I say, all profit resides in the margin. If the extra costs you'll pay for a group investment, like a mutual fund, pays returns in excess of what you can achieve on your own (due to an unaffordably high minimum investment, for example, as well as a more diversified securities selection), I say: Go for it. The problem then becomes one of finding a superior investment at the lowest possible cost—what Frugal Investing is all about!

Understanding Mutual Fund Fees

Most investors these days know that mutual funds come in two basic flavors: load and no-load. Unfortunately, these categories, like so many other things in investing, have become blurred in recent years. Still, distinctions do remain, and it pays to know about them for money market as well as equity funds.

In mutual fund parlance, a *load* is an up-front sales fee, or commission, the broker or financial salesperson charges when he or she sells you your mutual fund shares. Naturally, all mutual funds bought through a broker, including a bank-lobby broker, carry a load, usually from 3 to 8.5 percent of the amount you invest. Although some load funds have performed well over the years, they almost never return as much to investors as funds that lack this up-front tariff—and even the high-performing loads can take years to payback the commission. As a result, I consider all load funds off-limits for Frugal Investing.

When consumers arrived at a similar conclusion many years ago, *no-load* funds were developed. Shares in these funds are purchased directly from the investment company or from a deep-discount brokerage firm, so theoretically, the sales commission is zip. I say theoretically, because some equity no-load funds have a *12b-1 fee* after the SEC regulation that allows such funds to recoup some of their marketing costs by taxing the assets under management on a daily basis. Still, at 0.25 to 1 percent of assets, these 12b-1 fees are far less onerous than loads—and, again, they do *not* apply to money market funds.

Another nuisance fee charged by some load and no-load funds is the so-called liquidation cost, or *redemption fee* (sometimes as high as one percent) deducted if you sell your shares within the first six to twelve months of ownership. Again, this is less than a brokerage or full load commission, but it can still reduce your short-term return significantly just when you need it most.

One fee common to *all* mutual funds is the *annual fund operating expense*—the annual percentage of assets the investment company deducts as its compensation for running the fund. Fortunately, funds—especially no-load funds—compete significantly in this area, so bargains among even high-return funds are possible. The annual fund operating expense consists of the investment company's management fee plus miscellaneous other expenses, such as the 12b-1 fee (if applicable) in an equity fund. When this amount is divided by the value of assets under management, the *expense ratio* is determined. This is the best common denominator available for comparing the cost of similar funds. Each percentage point of the expense ratio reduces investor return by an equal amount.

How well do mutual fund companies acknowledge these costs in their literature? Thanks to SEC regulations, quite well—and certainly better than banks. All fund expenses must be stated in the prospectus and fund performance is often quoted *after* expenses have been deducted. However, some funds don't follow this convention, so be sure you compare apples to apples.

Unfortunately, the expense ratio, as useful as it is, doesn't cover all costs that might be relevant to a particular account. Not only are brokerage commissions excluded, but certain optional or even required costs are often listed separately, such as wire-transfer fees for investors with direct deposit accounts for their distributions, one-time fees for establishing or closing an account, and the fees some funds charge for switching money out of one fund and into another operated by the same company.

Still, these extra, marginal fees seldom make or break an investment, even for Frugal Investors, so you can't go wrong letting the expense ratio be your primary guide.

WHERE TO GO

Currently, over 800 money market mutual funds offer shares to the general public. Since all of these are no-load funds (I don't consider an in-house brokerage fund's account fee a true load, although I would never advise you pay it), you'd have a big job screening the prospectuses of every one.

I therefore recommend you scan *IBC Donoghue's Money Fund Directory*, available at larger libraries, first. (If your local public library doesn't have a copy, try the library at the nearest college or university that offers business courses.) If you live in the boondocks or otherwise prefer to do all your investing by mail or modem, you can obtain your own copy for $27.95 by contacting:

IBC Directory
290 Eliot Street
Ashland, MA 01721
(800) 343-5413

Another good source of information about any mutual fund is *Morningstar Mutual Funds*, a Value Line-style data bank offering both objective statistics and qualitative evaluations. An annotated sample data page from this useful publication can be found in Appendix C.

A list of higher performing money market funds can also be found in *The Wall Street Journal* every Monday, which also gives you a standard for comparing current, competitive yields. Unfortunately, these listings say nothing about operational costs or management fees, but if you contact the companies mentioned using the entries in *Donoghue's* or *Morningstar*, you'll receive complete investor information, including a prospectus and order forms. I'll tell you how to interpret and evaluate information for all types of mutual funds in Appendix C.

WHAT YOU'LL SAVE

A front-end load can range as high as 8.5 percent of your investment—money you'll never have to earn back if you stick with no-load funds. Management fees, fortunately, seldom add up to more than 2 percent, although this can significantly reduce return in a money market fund, where average returns are typically low to begin with. Thus it pays to shop for higher yielding, lower cost funds, especially in this asset class, where the portfolios all contain pretty much the same underlying assets, although in different mixes.

TAX IMPLICATIONS

Money market funds give you great flexibility in managing your tax liability. Distributions received from taxable money market funds are taxed as ordinary income by federal, state, and if applicable, local authorities. Distributions received solely from U.S. Treasuries are exempt from state and local taxes, but are taxable by the IRS. Distributions received from funds specializing in municipal bonds issued in your state are generally tax exempt at *all* levels, but there are exceptions, so read the prospectus carefully. Because all money earned is paid out to shareholders (after covering fund expenses), there is no capital gain potential with a money market investment.

Also, mutual funds of any kind are favorites for tax-deferred 401K retirement plans. Check with your employer to see if your plan excludes specific types of investments.

WHAT TO BUY

Some experts say that high expense ratios are worth it if the fund's long-term performance is superior, but I think that's generally poor advice. After all, what such advisors are *really* saying is that the fund managed to earn back its fees, and then some, for *previous* investors—no guarantee that it can or will do the same for you. Even worse, such advice carries the hidden message that you're somehow safer by investing in a "demonstrated winner," that the odds will somehow be in your favor if you invest in the highest return fund currently available. In reality, higher than usual returns almost *always* means higher than usual price volatility—what goes up usually comes down, and the faster it goes one way, the faster it's liable to go in the other.

Fortunately, these aspects apply more to equity than to money-market funds, but the principle is the same. For cash equivalents, you'll probably do best by choosing a no-load fund with at least average returns and a significantly *below average* expense ratio. Why? Because while those better-than-average returns can and do fluctuate, a low fixed cost never does. As John Markese, president of the American Association of Individual Investors said in a 1994 interview:

> If you look back, you can say "I would pay two percent in fees
> to get that thirty percent rate of return." But going forward, the
> only thing you know for sure is the fee.

Thus you have a much better chance of enjoying long-term good returns—a consistent margin of profit—with a fund that doesn't risk a lot of money trying to make a fair return get even bigger.

For money market funds, I like managers who emphasize T-bills, since these returns are safe, predictable, and always competitive. If you're in a high tax bracket, I would consider a tax-exempt government fund, or a standard money market fund which is usually a mix of both taxable (CDs and banker's acceptances, etc.) and tax-free bonds. I also like managers who buy assets with maturities of six months or less.

For smaller investors who can't afford the minimum ante for a Treasury Direct account, or for wealthier investors who simply like the idea of frequently laddered T-bills and excellent liquidity, a low-cost Treasuries-oriented money market fund is without question the next best thing to do-it-yourself.

Other features you might want include *switching privileges*, which is a no or low cost way to transfer money from your money market fund to an equity, fixed-income, or even international fund operated by the same investment company. (I'll give you instructions on how to use these services to full advantage in Part IV of this book.) However, funds in different asset classes must stand on their own, and saving a few dollars to switch a portion of your money-market allocation to an unsuitable equity investment simply because it happens to be in the same "mutual fund family" is absolute folly. It's the kind of false economy—penny wisdom and pound foolishness—that separates true Frugal Investors from people who are merely cheap or suckers for a well-targeted sales gimmick.

One feature that makes more sense is a wire-transfer provision. If you plan on withdrawing your distributions in cash, you might appreciate the convenience of a direct deposit service in which current income is wired to a specified bank or brokerage account.

In any event, I've selected the following money market funds as good bets for Frugal Investing:

Fidelity Spartan Money Market Fund
(800) 544-8888

Olde Premium Money Market Fund
(Offered through a discount brokerage without account fee.)
(800) 872-6533

Vanguard Money Market Fund
(800) 622-7447

WHEN TO BUY

Initial shares of money market mutual funds may be purchased directly from the company at any time, and many mutual fund companies offer automatic reinvestment of distributions—a good way to increase the value of your cash equivalent allocation if you don't need the current income. Additional cash purchases can also be made easily using the simplified order form (often called a deposit form) that accompanies each monthly statement. Some money market funds also offer the convenience of regular payroll deposits—a time saver that, over the years, can add measurably to your return.

HOW TO BUY

Contact the companies that interest you using their toll free number or write to request investment information. You'll receive in return an investment brochure plus a prospectus that contains the share order form. See Appendix C for instructions on how to interpret and evaluate the most important parts of a typical mutual fund application and prospectus.

After you've made your choice, complete the form and send it in with your check. Don't worry about current share prices, the cost of odd versus round lots, or the need for an ongoing cash balance that some brokerage accounts demand. If your initial check doesn't purchase an even number of shares, the company will keep adding fractional shares until the entire amount is invested. This is true, too, for the distribution reinvestment plans most mutual funds offer.

HOW YOU'LL BE PAID

Distributions from money market funds are made monthly. You can receive a check for this amount, if you require current income, but I suggest you enroll right away in the fund's DRP—the distribution reinvestment plan. This costs nothing and, since you'll always have a cash-equivalent component to your multiasset portfolio, it's a painless way to increase the earning power of a good fund. If you want to take money out of your account, you can simply write a check for the amount you desire (most money market funds have check-writing privileges) and the fund will liquidate, or redeem (in essence, buy-back) the number of even and fractional shares corresponding to the amount of the check.

Cash Equivalents You Don't Want to Buy

Cash equivalents I don't recommend on a direct-buy basis, such as Banker's Acceptances and Commercial Paper, become feasible when purchased through a money market mutual fund. However, some of the more exotic cash equivalents are still a bad idea, even in group investments.

Gambling on Government Paper

You already know that municipal bonds are fixed-income investments used by states and cities to fund capital improvement projects (infrastructure like bridges and airports) or to raise money for general operations without troubling the local taxpayers. What you may not know is that these municipal authorities have their own cash-equivalent "equivalent": the muni analog to short-term Treasuries, namely *tax anticipation notes (TANs)* and *bond anticipation notes (BANs)*. These short-term vehicles do just what they say: raise money for ongoing government operations whose real source of funding—a tax increase or new bond issue—is expected to be available in the near future. In this respect they're like a "bridge" loan from a bank that sustains you, say, while you're waiting to receive funds from an escrow account, or, if you're in business, a loan made on the strength of your accounts receivable—money owed to you by good customers that you expect to receive shortly, but need right now.

The big problem with TANs and BANs is that they're no safer than the revenue source they anticipate, and are always a good deal riskier, since the underlying cash infusion they depend on may not materialize, or may be delayed by litigation or political wrangling. Unless you like subsidizing profligate politicians, stay away from them.

Passing Bad CDs Along to the Customer

In Part II, I said bank CDs longer than six months—no matter how high paying—were a bad idea, and such CDs get no better when your fund's manager picks them for your money market portfolio. Unless interest rates are very high and the bank is an immaculate credit risk, these intermediate term investments just tie up money and add nothing to a portfolio that a good selection of laddered Treasuries (with a 10 to 15 percent allocation, perhaps, to commercial paper) can't provide. Seek funds whose policy limits commercial bank CDs to one-hundred-eighty days or less.

In the next chapter, I'll take the idea of group investing one step further and show you how to put it to work in the core of your multiasset portfolio: your equity investments. If individual stocks are still your bag, I'll also show you how to locate and use the best of the deep discounters or, if worse comes to worse, how to get more mileage from the full-service brokerage account you may already have.

To Remember Before Going On

- Use banks for checking account, ATM, loan services, and some deposits—not for investments. Bank lobby brokers are a particularly bad source of financial advice for any purpose.
- If you want a federally insured cash-equivalent "managed" by a bank, ask for an *investment savings* or *money market deposit* account but never invest in a bank's money market fund.
- Nonbank money market mutual funds are among the best cash-equivalent investments around since they offer low costs, competitive returns, and great flexibility on controlling your tax liability.
- The expense ratio is the best common denominator for comparing the cost of similar mutual funds in any asset class. A fund with a low expense ratio and average returns is usually a better long-term bet than an expensive fund with superior returns.
- Stay away from funds holding so-called government paper and CDs with maturities greater than six months.

8

Taking Stock of Deep-Discount Brokers and Equity Funds

I'll say one thing about the advice of most stockbrokers: what it lacks in quality, it makes up for in consistency. As one battle-worn investor put it: "I can't ask my broker for new tips; I'm still paying for the old ones!"

Because you'll probably have to pay a stockbroker or mutual fund manager at least *something* to establish your portfolio—such as buying an initial share of stock you simply can't get elsewhere, or for managing a fund that's perfect for your objectives—it's nice to remember that a multiasset, buy-and-hold philosophy means, among other things, you don't have to use all the expensive advice you've paid for.

In this chapter, I'll show you how to evaluate and do business with both traditional brokerage firms and the growing number of *alternative* securities dealers: those offering lower commissions and a fairer shake than the big Wall Street wire houses. And for those Frugal Investors who don't mind putting the middleman on the payroll, I'll show you how to screen and select a cost-effective equity mutual fund; one that not only earns more than it spends, but also gives you the best chance of meeting your long-term investment goals.

Holding Your Own with Full-Service Brokers

Investment lore is full of horror stories about people who spent years working with the "wrong" broker and never knew it. They include income-oriented investors teamed with options specialists; first-timers matched with "financial consultants" who actually knew less than they did about money; people who expected 30 percent returns in a relentlessly 6 to 8 percent world and got ripped off by every sharper in town because of it. For these reasons and all the others you've learned elsewhere in this book, it pays to find the right broker.

Why Use a Full-Service Broker?

There is really no practical reason for anyone to do business with a full-service brokerage firm. However, some people have obligations that transcend their better judgment. Perhaps you have an old friend or family member in the business or your spouse will never speak to you again unless your brother-in-law handles your transactions. Perhaps you already have a brokerage account and have luckily stumbled onto that rarest of rare birds: the honest, knowledgeable, experienced, and customer-oriented broker. Or perhaps you have an account with a firm you like, are used to reading their statements, but don't particularly like your broker and would like to find another. Maybe you have fun trading a portion of your portfolio in small-cap or OTC stocks and like being able to kick around ideas with a broker who has made money for you in that field. Maybe you've set your sights on no-commission IPOs, including foreign IPOs, which are simply not available through discount brokers.

No matter what the reason, though, anyone sticking with a full-service house can make their dealings a lot easier, more productive, and a *lot* less expensive by heeding a little hard-won advice.

Tip #1: Know Who You're Dealing With

Just because your current (or candidate) full-service house has slick TV commercials and full-page ads in financial journals, it doesn't mean they're a good choice to do business with. If you're already working with a specific broker but suspect you may not be hearing the truth, the whole truth, and nothing but the truth in all your dealings, contact your state's securities regulatory agency and ask for a copy of the broker's *Central Registration Depository*, or CRD file. This will list the broker's employment history and show if any disciplinary actions have ever been taken against the broker by the SEC, the state's securities regulatory commission, or by the brokerage industry itself. The record will also show instances, and the results, of any arbitration or lawsuits.

Another source of similar information is the NASD, which you can call directly at (800) 289-9999. If you don't like what you see or hear, don't hesitate to switch to someone else—and you don't even have to give a reason.

Don't forget to screen the broker's firm as well. Although no full-service brokerage firm is ever totally immune from sharp practitioners, those holding seats on the major stock exchanges (not all brokerage firms do) receive a little extra scrutiny, and are just that much more anxious to avoid excessive customer complaints. The average quality of brokers you find here will be a notch above the average broker elsewhere, but this doesn't mean that *any* broker you draw will be the best for you. Therefore...

Tip #2: Don't Deal with the First Person You Meet

If you drop in cold to open an account, you'll be assigned to the *broker of the day*—that is, the rooky whose turn it is to process walk-in customers.

Chances are, this junior broker will be polite and attentive until he or she learns that you're not the "coconut" they had hoped for: an off-the-street Donald or Marla Trump who just happened to drop in to make them rich. At this point the rookie may suddenly get very busy, remember some phone calls he or she forgot to make, and otherwise show clearly that your new account isn't a very high priority.

That's why I recommend bypassing this useless and embarassing ritual from the beginning and ask as soon as you come in to see the branch manager, sometimes called the managing director or resident vice president (RVP). In a businesslike way, explain the purpose of your visit, your investing objectives (as you've determined them personally and as I've outlined in this book), and ask to be introduced to two or three candidate brokers. Don't pretend to be an expert if you're not, and don't suggest that you're richer than you are in hopes of getting better service. If the brokers are any good, you'll very likely have to make appointments to see them, but it's worth the extra trouble—a little effort now can save you hours of grief and many dollars down the line. Above all, ask what investment products "make up the broker's book" (that is, the securities the broker trades regularly) and be sure these coincide with your area of interest: not just buying an initial share of a dozen or so specific blue chips, which any broker can do, but (if they're part of your allocation plan) ADRs, IPOs, small-cap stocks, or other special products. If you don't ask this question early, you'll be shunted to a salesperson for the firm's proprietary mutual funds—a waste of everybody's time.

Your initial interview shouldn't take more than ten minutes. Time is money for any professional, and since you'll never be the broker's biggest customer, don't waste it asking for advice you'll never take. Don't ask a lot of standard questions about the firm when basic information is available in the brochures you obtained before the meeting. The purpose of the interview now is to give each of you a thumbnail sketch of the other from an investing perspective. The broker you choose should be customer-oriented, knowledgeable about multiasset allocation and long-term investing, experienced in the securities you want, and willing to do business on the frugal terms I've outlined in this book. Don't worry about checking references. Brokers usually plead "client confidence" to this question anyway, and since you'll seldom ask your broker for advice, the broker's track record at anything other than taking orders efficiently is really beside the point.

Tip #3: Remember Why You're There

Don't be surprised if the broker tries to sell you some or all of the firm's fee-based and commissionable services—that's why he or she is there. Remember, though, the main reason *you* are there is to purchase that *first* share (not a round lot) of a handful of specific stocks you've already selected so that you can begin participating in those companies' DRP and OCP programs; and, perhaps, to get on the broker's list for early information about IPOs or other commission-free products.

Of course, the broker will raise all kinds of objections to this plan, mostly because it will prevent him from purchasing those additional shares for you at a commission. These arguments will range from why the few stocks you've chosen don't represent adequate diversification or that better capital growth (or income, or whatever) prospects are available elsewhere—usually in the firm's proprietary load funds. Some brokers are masters of the "silent sell," and simply smile condescendingly until you're so embarassed you actually *ask* for advice just to keep from feeling stupid!

If you stick to your guns, though, a halfway decent broker will soon realize that, whether he or she agrees or not, you're determined to have your way and will spare you further aggravation—at least for the moment. After that, your job is to make sure you're getting all the information and services they're going to ask you to pay for—and not one bit, or penny, more.

Tip #4: Insist on Full Disclosure

As a Frugal Investor, your first, and perhaps only, buy order will be short and sweet. Since you won't be buying any of their proprietary products or establishing a complex account (such as a Wrap account) and you'll only be buying a single share of probably no more than ten or twelve different stocks, the fees and commissions you'll face will be minimal—but you can still pay more than you have to if you're not prepared.

First, ask the broker to list on paper absolutely *all* the fees and commissions that might possibly apply to your transactions. Then ask which of those can be avoided or minimized (this means negotiated) depending on the level of service you desire. Don't be misled if the broker dismisses certain fees as "negligible" or "minor" or "next to nothing." If they're so unimportant, ask the broker not to charge them.

Another favorite nonexplanation is that a fee is "standard" or "standard for the industry." To this you may respectfully ask, "So what?" The firm's standard gouge or fees the industry has conspired to fix to deny consumers any real choice isn't necessarily what *you* should have to pay! In this case, the broker will usually respond like a bad postal clerk or car dealer.

The bureaucrat's defense goes like this: "Hey, I just work here—I don't make the rules!" The best offense for this defense is to say, "Show me." Chances are, the broker will prefer to make some concessions than leaf through a half-forgotten policy binder, or admit that a company policy is *not* an SEC regulation.

If the broker elects to wear you down, like some auto salespeople do, the broker will say, "I understand your concern, but my boss has to approve any discounts or deviations. Wait here and I'll see what I can do." To counter this approach, insist on tagging along on that trip to the manager's office. If the broker doesn't relent and give you some concessions right then, the manager probably will. If both still treat you like a leper, thank them kindly and head for the door. You're dealing with the wrong company.

In sum, your objective here isn't to argue every single cost, but to *insist on the value you deserve.* If your demands are reasonable and still offer the broker fair compensation, the firm will likely go along.

Second, once you've agreed on the package of costs and commissions that will apply to you, get it in writing. Even if the broker insists all the information you ask for will be "furnished later" or is in the boilerplate of your agreement, have the broker sign a brief memo to that effect. It should cover the quotation for basic commission rates, nonrecurring fees to open a no-frills, no-annual-fee securities trading account, processing fees for handling every trade, and any costs for preparing and mailing your statements and stock certificates. In my experience, *all* brokers will insist on their usual commission, a postage and handling fee, and often a "miscellaneous" fee of two to three dollars per transaction for back office support. The yearly "account maintenance" fee of forty to sixty dollars most brokers try to charge is pure profit—you get absolutely nothing for your money—and no investor should pay it. If the broker balks at this simple concession or refuses the courtesy of putting his or her promises in writing: take a walk.

Above all, come prepared with specific *written* instructions, or a signed *letter of authorization*, or LOA, which you'll leave behind. (To have effect, an original LOA must be in the broker's file—a fax or photocopy isn't acceptable.) Although there's no standard format for the LOA, it should clearly state the transactions you have in mind, including the particular guidelines I've given in this book for establishing the account, registering the security in your name, and ensuring good delivery of your stock certificates. If all this is in your file from the beginning, nobody can claim later that you authorized something else.

And by all means, keep a record of all your communications, including a phone log covering conversations during which fees, commissions, and your objectives and instructions are discussed. Such "real time" document made during or just after a disputed event are much more persuasive to those who can help you than a hazy, self-serving recollection made many months after the fact.

Finding the Discount Broker Who's Right for You

I'll say one thing for capitalism: when a crying need develops in one area, free enterprise usually comes to the rescue—and the securities business is no exception.

From its humble beginings in 1975, when the SEC eliminated its fixed-commission structure and Charles Schwab and Company first opened its doors—to many hoots and catcalls from the industry—(not to mention sly jokes on the *Tonight* show) the discount brokerage business has grown to include more than 100 practitioners. Most of these firms buy and sell the same secondary securities as the big wire-houses, using exactly the same system (the NYSE DOT system, which allows real-time telephone confirmations) with exactly the same efficiency—but for well-below the rates of traditional brokers. In a recent study by Mercer, Inc., a New York research firm that publishes a discount brokerage directory, the average cost of twenty-two identical transactions involving a variety of securities and prices was 57 percent cheaper at a discount brokerage (as opposed to a full-service house), and 77 percent cheaper at one of the even newer "deep discount" firms—and all this at a time when full-service commissions and fees just keep on rising! True, discounters tend to cater to middle-class value hunters rather than the old-money hoi polloi, and you probably won't meet the Donald, Leona, or Robin Leach sipping espresso from

Wedgwood china at your local discounter's office. But you *may* see Bill and Hillary Clinton come through the door: our forty-second President's and First Lady's IRS Form 1040 lists a Schwab account among their assets! The growth of this new market has been so fast and furious, in fact, that it has now blossomed into three clearly defined segments: the original "big three" discounters; the newer, deeper discounters; and less visible bank affiliates who try to trade on this phenomenon but offer anything but value.

Doing Business with the Big Three

In most new industries, those who get there first do best and grow the fastest—until they, too, begin to show signs of complacency, greed, or just plain bureaucratic inefficiency. So far, the discount brokerage business has largely escaped this "mature industry" sickness, although some customers think the leaders have begun to sputter and wheeze a little.

Far and away, the biggest of the big three discounters is Charles Schwab, whose two-hundred offices in forty-six states cover all U.S. metropolitan areas and then some. Like the branches of your local bank or drug store, Schwab offices are now sprouting up even in suburban shopping malls so that harried homemakers and retired people can stop in, check on their portfolios, and make a few trades on the way to pick up the kids or play a few rounds of golf. Even on vacation, Schwab customers are seldom far from a branch—good news for heavy traders, retired or not.

Right behind Schwab is Fidelity Brokerage Services, a subsidiary of the mutual fund giant, with eighty offices; then Quick & Riley, an aggressive marketer who offers slightly fewer outlets. Although these three leaders pioneered the field of no-frills, low-cost service for investors who already know what they want, they have also heard the siren's call of proprietary brokerage products. Over the last few years all have begun to sell more and more securities "alternatives" similar to those products offered by brokerage firms charging higher fees.

For example, every Big Three firm (and many deep discounters) now offers cash management accounts, custodial accounts, IRAs, and have developed close ties with dozens of no-load mutual fund families which offer access to over three-hundred "no transaction fee" funds, which include switching services. Like similar products offered by full-service houses, restrictions usually apply to these securities, from a limit on the number of buy-sell transactions you can make in a given period of time, to surprisingly high liquidation fees. Some consumers ask: "Are all these really demand-driven, value-oriented customer services or simply another 'big company' way of roping clients into buying proprietary products they wouldn't otherwise choose—then using arbitrary restrictions to keep them 'in the family'"? You be the judge.

You can get Big Three account and branch office information from:

Charles Schwab & Co.
The Schwab Building
101 Montgomery Street
San Francisco, CA 94104
(800) 648-5300

Fidelity Brokerage Services, Inc.
164 Northern Avenue
Boston, MA 02210
(800) 544-7272

Quick & Riley, Inc.
120 Wall Street
New York, NY 10005
(800) 221-5220

Whether these trends can continue without these bigger players becoming top-heavy and noncompetitive remains to be seen. What *is* clear is how quickly the market has reorganized itself to offer value-oriented investors even better and lower-cost options.

Enter the Deep Discounters

Today, about 20 percent of the discount brokerage market is held by what have become known—for lack of a better term—as *deep discounters*. These more recent entries in a very competitive field have calculated that a substantial number of existing discount customers are disenchanted with the Big Three's infatuation with "bigness" and believe even more potential investors can be attracted if the discount industry returns to its roots, which means taking, not making, investment orders. Their chief means of operating cheaply, in addition to fewer "partial service" services and proprietary investment products, is to offer fewer branch offices. This doesn't mean people outside their local area can't use their services, just that it's less convenient. By traditional marketing standards, this doesn't facilitate new customers—particularly when a shiny new Schwab, Q&R, or Fidelity office has just opened around the corner. More significantly, perhaps, it means customers may have more difficulty straightening out problems over the phone or through the mail that could otherwise have been solved by a brief, personal visit.

One value of a local branch became clear during the infamous Stock Market Crash of 1987. Once discount customers got wind of the growing calamity on the radio or during their lunch hour, they began calling their brokers in droves, overloading the companies' telephone systems. Many investors could not get through for hours—bad enough if they just wanted information; deadly if they had to make an important trade. Customers with local branches who could not get through on the phone simply went down to the branch in person, where most of their questions were answered and orders were promptly filled.

Another potential shortcoming of the deeper, smaller discounters is that most don't offer as large a selection of no- or low-load mutual funds. Although most of these funds can be purchased directly from the investment company anyway, discount customers with individual as well as group investments sometimes appreciate the ability to conduct all of their business at one place.

You can find a listing of smaller, deep discount brokers in your area in the Yellow Pages of your local phone book. Not all handle foreign stocks, ADRs, OTC issues, or certain securities that aren't listed on the major stock exchanges, so be sure you find one that can accommodate your particular needs. Those deep discounters that I've found to be particularly supportive of the frugal investing philosophy include:

Barry W. Murphy & Co.
270 Congress Street
Boston, MA 02210
(800) 221-2111

Jack White and Co.
9191 Town Center Drive, Ste 22
San Diego, CA 92122
(800) 233-3411

Kennedy, Cabot & Co.
9465 Wilshire Blvd
Beverly Hills, CA 90212
(800) 252-0090

Which to Choose: Big Three or Deep Disounter?

Any discounter will save you money over a full-service broker, but not all will save you the same amount, and not all offer the kinds of services you may need. Here are some criteria that might help you choose the one that's right for you.

Use a Big Three discounter if you:

- Plan on using your home computer or touch-tone phone to make your trades. All offer free software and twenty-four-hour service— as well as an additional 10 percent discount—for computer traders.
- Buy unusual securities (such as ADRs) and want a consolidated statement for all your investments.
- Value a local branch office. Americans are mobile people. Even if a deep discounter happens to be located near you now, if you move, you may lose that convenience.

Use a Deep Discounter if you:

- Plan to do your own research. The Big Three often charge for specialized information—although these charges are nominal and only on request. Nothing they provide, however, can't be found in reference material in your local library for a much better price: free.
- Trade infrequently. Unless you're a computer techie, you simply won't be buying or selling securities often enough to justify a computer hook-up. On the contrary, the ease of such trading may seduce you into making more transactions than you really need, and even discounted commissions take a bite out of your portfolio's long-term performance.

If you want a directory of *all* discount brokers, including those outside your local area, write to:

New York Stock Exchange
Directory Service
P.O. Box 1971
Radio City Station
New York, NY 10019

When Is a Bank Not a Bank?

When it acts like a brokerage firm! The third and currently smallest (but who knows what the future holds) segment of the alternative securities brokerage market, about ten percent, are brokerage operations acquired or established by commercial banks following deregulation in the 1980s. Although they lack the high visibility of the Big Three and committed followers of the deep discounters, bank-related brokers have two very powerful forces on their side.

First, they have access to vast numbers of potential clients through their retail banking operations. Banks and their lobby brokers aren't sup-

posed to "trade lists" of prospects, but it's a short walk from the teller's
window to a resident broker's desk when the term on a banking customer's CD is about to expire.

Second, banks have potential access to "instant" institutional millions
in funds held by the bank and its bigger clients and venture partners. In
addition to brokering transactions for the bank's own portfolio, the affili-
ated houses may be used increasingly as brokers for "business partnerships" (securities and lending operations linking banks, or a consortium of
banks, with businesses, developers, U.S. and foreign government agencies,
community groups, and others) in packaged deals that provide the broker
with hefty current transactions and a source of future customers.

Although banks are prohibited by law from buying stocks directly for
customers, nothing prohibits them from giving investment advice, and
investment advisory services for big depositors has long been a staple of
high-end banking operations. More recently, big institutions like Bank of
America and CitiCorp have used their brokerage affiliates to start their
own mutual funds, which can be purchased just like any other equity
fund directly from the company.

One way even small banks have gotten onto the mutual fund band-
wagon is through the "hub and spoke" concept. Under this scheme, a
smaller bank starts an equity mutual fund but hires an outside investment
company to be the fund's manager and advisor. Thus one investment
company can act as a "hub" with many different banks (which provide
only SEC registration, marketing, and audit functions) acting as its
"spokes." There is nothing illegal about such operations, but the resulting
funds offer no more than true, independent mutual funds can offer and
frequently cost a lot more to run.

Naturally, I recommend that *all* Frugal Investors give such bank-
related investment schemes a wide berth.

Getting the Most from Your Discount Broker

A true discounter has little time to discuss investment products, and
certainly won't call you out of the blue—as most full-service and bank-
related brokers will do—to ask why you've been able to live so long without the firm's latest securitized goodie. Consequently, since the discounter doesn't prospect for new sales, her firm has no need for a
"research department" (really a PR factory that manufactures rationales
for the broker's sales pitch)—and that saves you money, too.

Thus the first test I make of any discount broker is his disinterest in
talking to me about anything other than the order I've called to place. I
may ask such brokers to clarify some point (such as making sure if the

buy or sell order means "at market price" or "at the last quoted price"—the two may not be the same) or explain what is going to happen next in the transaction. But I'll never ask them for an opinion or recommendation on the transaction itself. If I hear one, or worse, if one is volunteered, I smell commission: nature's way of telling you to find another broker.

Here is a list of minimum services you should get from *any* discounter—deep or not—depending on your specific needs. Insist on an account that has:

• *Twenty-four-hour service.* Many discounters save money by investing in high-tech automation rather than relying on layers of clerks and administrators. Most have toll-free 800 numbers and will take your orders twenty-four hours a day, seven days a week—although orders taken when the market is closed won't be executed until the next business morning.

• *A discount structure appropriate to your most frequent type of trade.* Each discounter tries to attract a particular type of customer—the niche in which it feels it can compete most effectively against other discounters. For example, Boston's Brown and Co. offers rebates to customers whose commissions exceed $350 per month. This should appeal to high-volume traders, right? But Stock Brokers of Detroit likes high-volume so much they charge *no* commission for amounts over $500,000. Another discounter, Acu-Trade of Omaha, thinks price-based commissions (even low ones or those with sliding scales) are bogus and it hopes you think so, too. It charges a flat rate of three cents per share, but only after a $48 minimum. The point is, *self-knowledge*—about your portfolio's needs and your expected trading pattern—is the key to finding the right discount broker, then getting the most out of the one you choose.

• *No minimum balance or minimum number of annual transactions to keep your account current.* One way some discounters try to pad those discounts is by holding some of your money hostage, requiring a certain dollar-value in assets (cash or securities) or occasional trades just to keep your account open. Needless to say, these kind of takebacks are entirely for the firm's benefit, not yours. As long as alternatives are available, do business somewhere else.

• *Insurance coverage.* The Securities Investor Protection Corporation, or SIPC, won't insure you against market losses, but it will protect your brokerage account against fraud up to $500,000 ($100,000 in cash and $400,000 in other securities). Many brokerage firms advertise additional insurance coverage adding up to many millions. This is useful *only* if your account is that big—it offers no additional benefits beyond the SIPC maximums for smaller accounts.

How to Open a Discount Brokerage Account

Obtain an account request application from the firm of your choice in person or by mail. Fill it out as you would any other credit application form, which is basically what it is (although the industry refers to them as "cash accounts"). Be sure to indicate any other people who will have access to your account, such as a spouse, your attorney, or your accountant. To activate your account, you'll have to put something in it: cash, if you want to buy new securities; or old securities, if you plan on using them to finance your purchase, or contemplate selling them soon. If you currently hold stock certificates, you'll have to surrender them, with proper endorsement on the back, if you want them sold. Securities held by your previous broker in "street name," can be transfered to your new broker in the same manner.

How to Use Your New Brokerage Account

To buy a stock, phone your broker with the name and trading symbol of the stock and say you want a market order of so many shares. (If you're following my Frugal Investing procedures, you'll buy only one share of each stock, since that's all you need to get started in the issuing firm's DRP and OCP programs.) This means that your broker will buy the stock at its current market price. Similarly, a market order to sell means you want to dispose of the stock at the current bid price.

Experienced investors sometimes use other kinds of orders to buy and sell securities only when they reach a certain price, but that doesn't apply in Frugal Investing. I'll tell you more about the mechanics of, and strategies for, selling your shares in Part IV of this book. A market order will be completed within a few minutes of its receipt by your broker.

If you want to see how much a stock will cost, you can check the previous day's quotation in the newspaper (Appendix C shows you how to interpret the listing), but even a one-day delay can be many dollars out of date. A better way is to simply phone your broker and ask "Where's the market?" for the desired stock. The broker will reply with the stock's *trading range*, or high and low prices for the day. Don't worry if this range is considerably different from the one you saw for the stock in Value Line or another reference book. Your strategy isn't to low-ball a first-time purchase (least of all a one-share purchase!) but to simply get into the DRP–OCP game. Be sure to tell the broker at the time you place your order that you want "good delivery" of the share certificate.

The date on which your broker purchased your stock is the *trade date*. The date on which you must pay for them is the *settlement date*, by regulations five working days later. This means that if you have insufficient funds to pay for the shares, plus commission, on trade date, you have a week to increase the balance.

After you've made your transactions, check your monthly statement closely—this is no less important a document than your usual bank statement, and it should be just as accurate.

What Happens If You Have Problems with Your Broker?

To be fair, most broker-related problems (even with full-service houses) are caused by miscommunication rather than fraud or deceit. Even when everyone is on the same wavelength and nobody is trying to take advantage of anyone else, securities trading can be a fast-paced, nerve-wracking business. It's easy for an important bit of information to get garbled or for some detail to fall through the crack—and not always on the broker's side of the table. Since no one, not even your mother, will care about your portfolio as much as you do, it's up to you to make sure you know what you want and how and when you want it, and to make sure those instructions are transmitted clearly. (Remember, Mom was right when she said an ounce of prevention is worth a pound of cure.)

Here are a few suggestions for keeping the most typical stockbroker problems from happening:

1. *Put your instructions in writing.* Even if you're going to give your instructions by phone, write down what you want to say first, then use it as a script or "talking points" when you speak. This will save valuable phone time, increase accuracy, and give you a record of what was said. If the situation permits and the writing is legible, fax the sheet to the broker as a backup. Whenever you buy or sell a stock, be sure you know it's trading symbol.

2. *Look before you "lip."* If you detect a discrepency, ask your broker or the appropriate person in the accounting department for an explanation before you write an indignant letter; it may not be necessary to put your complaint in writing. Always keep a phone log of your brokerage firm contacts and requests. This allows you to follow up—you know who you talked to and when, and what you were promised. It also creates a quality control history for your account. Too many discrepencies, even if they're resolved, may indicate the need to shop for a more reliable broker.

3. *Let an expert solve a really bad problem.* There are lots of things you can do for yourself to troubleshoot a brokerage problem, but there are some things best left to specialists like CPAs and attorneys. If the problem is too technical, or if you're being asked to make choices you don't understand (but may have important tax or financial consequences), or if you sense that the brokerage firm is no longer working *with* you but against you, it's probably time to call for reinforcements who can speak the technician's language. Sometimes this can keep a merely annoying problem from becoming needlessly adversarial.

As a matter of course, I *always* set and communicate to the other person a deadline for solving the problem or, if that isn't possible, make a telephone appointment for a certain date and time just to check back and make sure the problem isn't forgotten. Since most customers don't insist on this, the mere fact you even mentioned it will often give your problem or request a higher priority.

What to Do About Administrative Problems

After inaccurate or undesired trade executions, most brokerage complaints have to do with mixups in client accounts. These can range from late or bounced checks and simple clerical errors (like transposed numbers) to really annoying problems like recurring charges for fees and commissions that don't apply to you. As a precaution, I check every transaction statement against my log, and spot-check other account information randomly every few months.

All I can say when such problems occur is: Don't cut down the cherry tree when the trouble is sour apples. In most firms, sales and administration are two different functions. If you have to kick a minor account problem upstairs to get it resolved, take it to the office manager first, not your broker. If your problem isn't resolved expeditiously (another reason to insist on deadlines) or involves a transaction (be sure your position is corroborated by your phone log) complain in writing to the branch manager or RVP. If you don't get satisfaction there, write to the company's Chief Executive Officer at the firm's headquarters, even if you've been given the name of another intermediate or regional manager to contact first. Your letter may wind up on the same desk, but it makes a big difference if the hand that delivers it comes from the mail room or the corner office.

What to Do About Securities Problems

The worst problem of all, of course, is when you suspect (or know!) something is wrong with an asset you bought. Neither your broker nor a company issuing a security is responsible for market action, such as capital loss on a stock, but it certainly is responsible for fraud, misrepresentation, or failure to honor a contractual commitment, such as payment of scheduled interest. If you think you may be a victim of this sort of thing, I recommend the following steps:

1. *Take the problem to your broker.* Even if the trouble isn't with the brokerage firm's own product, your broker should be able to help you. Often, what appears to be malfeasance or even shady dealing can be explained by a loophole in the law, the sales contract, or the prospectus. If so, demand proof, not just an oral explanation. If the broker can't show you "chapter and verse"—that is, where a specific and relevant explanation can be found—escalate to the next level.

2. *Ask to see the brokerage firm's compliance officer.* Every licensed securities dealer has a specially trained employee called the *compliance officer.* The officer's job is to make sure that SEC rules are followed by the firm's employees and by companies that provide the securities they handle. If the mistake has been an honest one, the compliance officer will usually find out about it quickly and offer a timely solution. However, if the problem seems to involve fraud or some other illegality, and the brokerage firm seems to be distancing itself from the matter rather than helping you resolve it, or if you encounter active opposition or unreasonable delays, you'll have to escalate.

3. *Write a certified letter to the appropriate securities exchange.* Both major exchanges and NASDAQ (the OTC market maker) have a *Broker/Dealer Compliance Department* which governs the activities of brokerage firms who hold seats on those exchanges. As a condition of the rights granted to them by these exchanges, the brokerage firm has already agreed to submit to binding arbitration in case of disputes with its clients. More than likely, your own account contract will also commit you to arbitration in case of such disputes. Although problems with a third-party security aren't strictly the brokerage firm's responsibility, they *are* required to support you in your attempts to solve any problems with securities bought through their firm. If they're reluctant to do so, the Broker/Dealer Compliance unit can help get them moving. If necessary, send a certified letter, return receipt requested, detailing your problem, along with photocopies of any relevant exhibits, to:

Broker Compliance
American Stock Exchange
86 Trinity Place
New York, NY 10006

or

Broker Compliance
New York Stock Exchange
11 Wall Street
New York, NY 10005

or

Broker Compliance
National Association of Securities Dealers
1735 K Street, N.W.
Washington, DC 20006

If the appropriate compliance department fails to achieve a satisfactory resolution, or if they determine that the problem exceeds the exchange's power to arbitrate, it's time for the ultimate escalation.

4. *Complain to the Securities and Exchange Commission.* The four-hundred-pound gorilla in the investment world is the SEC (and, for broker-dealers, the NASD—an agency of the SEC). Its administrative law powers are vast and although it moves with all deliberate speed (and is sometimes criticized for being a bit too glacial when it comes to errant insiders), its justice is usually much swifter than that delivered by state or federal courts. It has an active Consumer Services Department which handles complaints about individual securities and group investments, such as mutual funds.

For stock problems, write:

Enforcement Division
Securities and Exchange Commission
450 Fifth Street, N.W.
Washington, DC 20549

For mutual fund problems, write:

Division of Investment Companies
Securities and Exchange Commission
450 Fifth Street, N.W.
Washington, DC 20549

Naturally, these letters, too, should be sent by certified mail, return receipt requested.

How to Handle Arbitration

Unless you're extremely wealthy, are backed by some consumer interest group, or are a total masochist, you probably won't sue your brokerage firm, no matter how badly they have treated you. Fortunately, arbitration in recent years has taken the place of litigation in many broker–client disputes—making true justice that much more attainable and affordable for smaller investors. To use it effectively, though, you must know something about it:

• *Aribitration isn't small claims court.* Attorneys are allowed to represent you and rest assured, if you get that far, your brokerage firm will have one.

• *Arbitration panels aren't toothless.* Binding judgments may be entered in any court having jurisdiction over the matter and can be used to enforce your claim.

• *Your brokerage account contract will probably state the procedure for evoking arbitration.* Find that clause, read it, and understand it (this usually means consulting your attorney) before you take any action. Be sure to note if the location of arbitration is specified. It *may* be where your branch is located, but some contracts require arbitration to take place in the state where the company is incorporated or has its headquarters.

Aside from attorney fees (which may be based on contingency, if your claim is sizable) arbitration costs are fairly economical—especially when you consider the alternative: a lengthy and protracted lawsuit. A claim of $2,500 or below can cost less than $100 to arbitrate, while claims of $100,000 or more can run several times that much. Still, it's a bargain at twice the price.

How to Transfer a Brokerage Account

If you want to switch from a full-service to a discount firm, or if you simply want to shift your account from one wire-house to another, the procedure is the same.

First, open the new account before you inform your current broker. This will give you a place for your assets to be transferred and speed up the entire process.

Second, as it is when you close a bank account, your old broker may want to retain some assets (especially cash) to make sure any final liabilities are covered. This is especially true if your old account had check-writing privileges. This is a reasonable request, but it shouldn't be used to prevent you from transferring sizable assets (assuming your account balance exceeds any fees or expenses you still owe).

Finally, make sure any third parties are informed of the switch. This includes CPAs, attorneys, and the Treasury Department if your T-bill or T-note direct-deposit account is held by your brokerage firm.

Above all, don't let the old brokerage firm act like it's the utility company, post office, or IRS and bully you because you're a lame-duck client they will no longer be able to pluck. You're still a customer until your last paperwork clears their office. Know your rights and demand the timely, accurate service you're entitled to.

Equity Mutual Funds

For most of the 1980s, pension funds and big corporations jockeying assets for (and to prevent) buyouts and takeovers were the stock market's biggest players. Now, half-way through the 1990s, mutual funds have become the tail that wags the Wall Street dog.

Equity mutual funds are not only more numerous than individual listed stocks, they outnumber them two to one! Although their $140 *billion* in new investment money since 1990 (most of it drained from low-interest paying banks) accounts for only 10 percent of all stock ownership, funds now account for between 30 and 40 percent of all trades—and nearly a billion dollars in new investment money pours into fund coffers every day. Overall, stock and bond mutual fund assets totaled $1.4 trillion by the end of 1993. If you multiply this number by the average fund expense ratio, you can see that the mutual fund industry took in *at least* $15.5 billion that same year.

All this has double significance for smaller investors.

First, it means that because of low interest rates at banks, a lot of people are putting what used to be considered their life savings into the stock market, principally into mutual funds that, when marketed through banks, can give the illusion of being insured. The key word here, of course, is *illusion*.

Second, it means that the value of many mutual fund shares are now not only as volatile as the shares of their underlying stocks, they're actually *more volatile* as an exploding population of funds battles for a steadily shrinking percentage of investable assets.

Fortunately, as a Frugal Investor, you'll never be dangerously overconcentrated either in stocks or mutual funds, but if you anticipate making all or a lion's share of your equities allocation through such vehicles, you'll have to keep these new facts of life in mind as you make your choices.

Everything I said in Chap. 7 about money market mutual funds generally applies to domestic equity funds as well. One big difference, though, is that with an equity fund, you *can* literally "buy the market" with a variety of index funds that replicate the Dow or the S&P 500 (and many other indexes) with astonishing accuracy. If you're thinking about bypassing index funds because they seem stodgy or unproductive, remember that the S&P 500 has shown a long-term growth of 14.87 percent per year, and that over the ten years ending December 31, 1993, fully 60 percent of the *non*indexed funds performed *worse* than the indexes.

WHERE TO GO

One thing is certain in mutual fund investing: the investment companies sponsoring them aren't shy when it comes to touting their wares. According to Competitrack, a securities industry watchdog, general mutual fund advertising rose from $34.8 million to over $51 million in 1993; and equity fund advertising (a separate category) rose to $73 million from just under $60 million during the same period.

This is significant to investors because along with increased ad volume comes increased margins for misinformation, disinformation, and outright lies. One recent complaint involved a fund's apparent attempt to intentionally confuse "no load" with "no fees"—the two aren't the same. Another dealt with a fund's blanket assurances of safety that didn't quite match investment history. With pressure now on the SEC to allow funds to sell shares directly from newspaper coupons, this emphasis on sizzle instead of steak will only increase—and increase your need for vigilance.

With this caveat, I recommend that your first step be to scour the mutual fund ads in *The Wall Street Journal, Forbes*, and *Investor's Business Daily* (including Doug Rogers' daily column, which often features good information on mutual fund portfolios, rankings, and research) before you tackle any of the big and more complicated analytical guides. Why?

First, ad information isn't only free, it educates you in a decidedly "user friendly" way that lets you compare how different investment companies approach the same investment problems: growth, income, growth *and* income, aggressive growth, or matching a desired index. Say what you will about advertising, a lot of smart people go to a lot of trouble figuring out what ought to go into it—and for securities, SEC watchdogs also play a role. In 1994, for example, new rules went into effect requiring fund companies to disclose the source of their rankings (if used in their ads) and track record since inception or over the last ten years, whichever is shorter. Even more important, funds can no longer rank themselves simply by size, or use bogus self-ranking criteria (such as "highest-ranked fund in the ABC fund family"); and *all* performance rankings must take loads and fees into account.

With such controls, most ads will distill not only what the fund's manager thinks are the most important aspects of the product, but how that product generally compares with its competition. I'm not saying you should take an ad as the last word on a particular fund, but it often makes a much better place to start than a page full of diagrams and statistics.

After you've clipped enough ads to give you a sense of what is currently being offered in the types of funds that interest you, go to the library and look up those funds in *Morningstar Mutual Funds* (a guide to reading a typical fund data page is provided in Appendix C) or *Forbes'* annual mutual fund survey for the most recent year. (Remember, you're screening only for equity funds, not funds "balanced" between stocks and bonds or funds with an international component.) Jot down the data most relevant to both frugal investing and your own investment goals: expense ratio, historical return, and so on. Be sure to notice the letter rating Forbes experts assign the funds that interest you—they grade each fund's performance in both bull and bear markets. If your library is well equipped, you'll also find the current edition of the *No-Load Mutual Fund Association*'s guide (or you can obtain it by writing 475 Park Avenue South, New York, NY 10016) that provides similar data and evaluations. Use the information given about the funds you know from ads to begin exploring similar funds whose ads you *didn't* see.

One alternative to direct mutual-fund buying for people planning on investing in several different equity funds (including funds in other asset categories) is to open a single mutual fund account with a discount broker who offers mutual fund services. This can allow you to purchase some load funds without the usual commission (converting them instantly to no-load funds), but you'll have to ask if a specific broker offers this option on a specific fund. For example, a mutual fund account at Fidelity brokers will allow you to purchase shares in many of Fidelity's proprietary load funds without a commission, especially if you've earmarked them for an IRA account.

Still, over 95 percent of all load funds carry 12b-1 fees (see Chap. 7)—a tariff even these otherwise good buys can't avoid.

The biggest advantage of these consolidated mutual fund accounts, though, is to allow you to buy several funds at direct-from-the-company prices but receive your accounting all on one statement, in one easy-to-read format. You can even buy shares in a fund outside the discounter's "family" of funds through such accounts, although you'll have to pay an additional one-time load of around $6 per thousand dollars invested.

All Big Three discounters offer this service, as do deep-discounters Muriel Siebert and Waterhouse. This option may make particular sense if you're interested in Janus, Benham, Twentieth Century, Dreyfus, Invesco, Montgomery, Neuberger & Berman, SteinRoe, and Strong.

WHAT YOU'LL SAVE

Loads on individual funds sold through brokers can run from as little as 1 percent (which is still 1 percent too high, as far as I am concerned) to as much as 8.5 percent—and load funds *still* charge an annual operating fee. When you buy no-load funds direct from the company, you can have the satisfaction of adding the load percentage you *didn't* pay directly to your return. Over many securities and many trades in this largest of all asset categories, the money you *didn't* have to pay in fees and commissions (and therefore don't have to earn back) can sometimes be enough to send a kid to college!

TAX IMPLICATIONS

Equity funds can yield both current income and capital gains, both fully taxable at all levels. Capital losses up to $3,000 in any one year can offset other capital gains and can be carried forward from one tax year to another. Depending on the fund, capital gains are paid to shareholders once or twice each year. These are real, not paper, distributions, so the money you earn can be received in a check or, even better, put back to work through the fund's DRP. Be aware, though, that long-term capital gains are taxed as ordinary income and if they're significant enough, can push some investors into the next higher tax bracket.

Some advisors suggest buying individual stocks after the "ex-dividend" date, or the first trading day after a dividend is declared, to avoid the tax liability and to take advantage of the slight drop in price such stocks usually experience. Since mutual funds go "ex-div" quarterly and other factors influence NAV (and its resulting share price) more significantly, this has always seemed to me like a useless precaution but committed bargain hunters might want to keep it in mind.

WHAT TO BUY

If you've been conscientious in your "Where to Go" data search, you'll now have anywhere from a half-dozen to ten or twenty candidates. All probably seem like great funds, so which ones should you choose?

I recommend eliminating any fund whose assets are less than $50 million because such funds are probably too small and unseasoned to give you the economies of scale and safety implicit in any fund investment. You also want to be leery of any fund with exceptionally high performance, since this also implies exceptional volatility, either in the fund's own shares or in the value of the underlying stock.

Of course, you don't want to go to the other extreme, either, and pick funds so lifeless that even the buzzards won't touch them. In general, you want a fund whose average annual return is sufficient to reach your investment goals—*not* one that has set a recent return-on-assets record and may be riding for a fall. For most Frugal Investors, that means a fund that consistently performs at least with the market averages. A good income fund can perform slightly worse as long as distributions are predictable; an aggressive growth fund should score slightly better most of the time—but be prepared to see some down years along the way.

The best choice, though, for most Frugal Investors who don't want to try to beat the market averages will be an index fund—preferably the ASM Fund, which gives the closest replication of the DJIA; or one of a number of funds that try to match the much larger, but not quite as productive, S&P 500. I recommend the Vanguard 500 Index Trust, which earned 14.56 percent for the ten years ending December 31, 1993 (and is also one of the least expensive, with an expense ratio of .27 percent). This is especially admirable when you consider that the average general equity fund earned only 12.11 percent during this same period. As Nobel Laureate economist Paul Samuelson put it succinctly, "Hardly one of ten thousand [money managers] perform in a way that convinces a jury of experts that a long-term edge over indexing is likely"—a view endorsed not only by me, but by John C. Bogle, one of America's premier mutual fund moguls, and Peter Lynch, mastermind of Fidelity's highly successful Magellan Fund, who says in his popular book, *Beating the Street* (Simon & Schuster, 1993):

> All the time and effort that people devote to picking the right fund, the hot hand, the great manager, have in most cases led to no advantage. Unless you were fortunate enough to pick one of the few funds that consistently beat the averages, your research came to naught.

As you'll see when you compare equity funds, operational expenses run anywhere from a small fraction of a percent to over two. If you're buying an index fund, I can't imagine how a firm could justify anything over half a percent. According to *Morningstar Mutual Funds*, though, the average expense ratio on stock and bond funds in 1993 was 1.11 percent, but this includes active management—a dubious service you don't want to pay for, and certainly don't need with an index fund.

If you've earmarked a portion of your domestic equities allocation for small-cap stocks, a number of funds specialize in these riskier but higher potential issues. One of the least expensive is Schwab's Small Cap fund, which mirrors the performance of a thousand companies too small to be included in their massive Schwab 1,000 which tracks the market's biggest players.

Although a fund or funds in the seven basic market categories for equity funds (capital appreciation, growth, mid-cap, small company, growth and income, index, and income) I described in Chap. 4 should be adequate for the vast majority of Frugal Investors, you may want to assign a portion of your equity allocation to funds operating in an area, or economic sector, in which you have special interest or knowledge. If so, keep any allotment to these so-called sector funds to 10 to 15 percent (or less) of your total domestic equity allocation and avoid the impulse to try and capitalize on short-term price fluctuation through market timing; or switch between sector funds frequently to try to catch any updrafts in the changing economic climate. Price volatility means just that—frequently changing prices—and the whole purpose of a mutual fund is to hang onto it long enough to let whatever growth rate that's inherent in the sector to do its thing.

However, if you're bound and determined to do a little sector speculation, here are the current sector fund categories, based on Lipper Analytical Service's *Mutual Fund Performance Analysis*, along with my comments, recommendations, and caveats for each (*Note:* Unless stated otherwise, funds in these categories have at least 65 percent of their assets invested in that sector):

- *Health/biotechnology funds*: These funds consist of health care, medicine, and biotech stocks. These could take a shellacking if and when the U.S. government enacts its plans for "socialized" medicine. Invest with caution or wait until the political crystal ball clears up.

- *Natural resources funds*: These funds consist mainly of stocks in the basic materials and energy sectors. Traditionally, these have been extremely volatile stocks, so wear an asbestos suit and handle with care.

- *Environmental funds*: These consist of stocks and stock convertibles of companies judged to be contributing to a cleaner environment, usually drawn from the industrial sector. These usually make more sense for socially conscious investors than those just out to make a buck. Which are you?

• *Science and technology funds*: These funds own stocks drawn from the technology sector. If you know something about these industries, you may be able to make some wise choices.

• *Specialty and miscellaneous funds*: These are catchall funds holding stocks from companies not conveniently grouped with other fund types. Examples include funds specializing in transportation, retailing, etc. My advice is the same as above.

• *Utility funds*: Utility funds hold stocks from the ultilities sector. These usually pay the highest income of all stocks, even better than the best dividend-paying blue chips, although their growth potential is low. Income-oriented investors may skew their holdings in this direction, but not so much that their stock portfolio begins to look like bonds. The main culprit here is inflation.

• *Financial services funds*: These contain stocks from the financial sector. This sector often seems to have a few winners and lots of losers, or the floor drops out for everyone. If you know enough about the industry to make an intelligent choice, I suggest buying the individual stock and avoid the funds.

• *Real estate fund*: Real estate funds hold stocks of companies engaged in real estate investing and operations. This sizeable, specialized market is viewed by some analysts as a separate asset class worthy of continuous allocation. They reason that, because real estate has tended to follow its own market cycles regardless of changes to stocks and bonds (although it is dependent on local levels of business activity and is certainly sensitive to interest rates), it has a dampening effect on a multiasset portfolio's overall volatility. I don't deny the logic of this reasoning, but the linkage among assets is too close for my liking. However, if you have other reasons to like real estate, you may want to keep a more or less continuous proportion of your equity allocation in real estate funds—but I recommend never more than 10 to 20 percent. For most Frugal Investors, the four basic asset categories are more than enough to provide the safety and returns multiasset allocation is intended to give.

• *Gold oriented funds*: These funds hold shares from the basic materials and financial sectors of any stock dealing with gold mining, mine financing, bullion, coins, etc. Some analysts view previous metals the way other analysts view real estate, as a separate asset category. I say: Keep away from both. The strongest argument for precious metals is their reputed value as "chaos hedges"—a store of tangible value when more civilized markets crash, as tends to happen during catastrophes such as total war. If that's the case, your shares in gold funds won't be worth much anyway, so unless you horde bullion under your bed, it's hard to see how these funds help anyone but their sponsors.

After you've settled on a handful of finalists, call the firm's toll-free number (or invest in a stamp and write to the company) requesting the "investor's kit." Be sure to ask for the fund's *Statement of Additional Information*, too, which contains a more comprehensive list of portfolio holdings, subadvisors and agents, outside directors, and other evaluation material not normally included with the kit.

The firm will reply promptly with a prospectus and order form, and most likely with some slick literature summarizing the fund's best points. While many inexperienced investors rely solely on the glossy "brochure" to make their comparisons and their choices, Frugal Investors don't. In Appendix C, I'll give you some ways to make plowing through the prospectus's often dense and impenetrable language fast and informative. This isn't to say that the brochure that accompanies the prospectus is all propaganda—far from it. Most investors (even some very experienced ones) don't realize that SEC approval is required, too, for this potentially useful document. The main criteria the SEC uses for the brochure is that it can't misrepresent anything in the prospectus, or offer new information that the prospectus doesn't contain. In fact, if the brochure reveals something unflattering about the fund—a deal-breaker from your perspective, such as a very recent reshuffling of the fund's management—it can save you a lot of eyestrain with the prospectus. So, read the brochure first, and if nothing has turned you off, go on to the prospectus.

After you've extracted the necessary information from the prospectus, group your finalists according to their *Forbes* annual survey letter grade. From now on, you're only interested in the top-ranked prospects, although if one becomes disqualified for some reason, the runner up will take its place. Here is the criteria I use to select the "best of the best" in a given area:

- The average annual total return for the fund must be at least as good as the average for that market category of stocks over the last business cycle. That is, the candidate should score no worse than the average annual total return for other capital appreciation, growth, mid-cap, small company, growth and income, index, or income funds for the last three to six years. (If necessary, go back to Chap. 4 to refresh your memory on the significance of these market categories.) If the fund has not been around that long, forget it.

• The fund's current management team must have been in place during the last two years, and hopefully for the whole last business cycle. If management has changed recently, it will likely take the new players a year or two to adapt and you don't want to pay for their learning curve in foregone returns.

• For a capital appreciation, growth, income, small company, or mid-cap fund (in short, for any nonindexed U.S. equity fund), the expense ratio should never be more than 1 percent, no matter how actively managed or aggressive the fund's policy may be. The only possible exception to this—and it would be rare—is if the fund's long history of clearly superior returns would, if continued, pay back that extra fee in one to two years and give you a growing margin of compounded profit over the nearest rival. For an index fund, the ratio shouldn't exceed 0.5 percent.

• The fund's assets should not have increased astronomically in a single year. Some "free lunchers" are astonished by this advice; they can't imagine how a fund that increased its assets by three or four times, say, in a single year could possibly be a bad bet. Unfortunately, history gives plenty of examples of talented fund managers who got in over their heads when new money poured in too fast. I have no problems with little acorns sprouting into mighty oaks; I just don't like it when they try to compress that 5- or 10-year cycle into one year, or two.

• The fund must have a dividend or distributions reinvestment program. This is basic Frugal Investing and by now should need no special explanation.

As I've said, I don't put much value on "switching privileges," or special low- or no-cost deals for transferring money among different funds within the investment company's mutual fund "family." This idea was cooked up primarily to keep money from leaving a particular investment company when economic conditions changed, and to attract market timers—neither of which appeals to Frugal Investors.

When to Buy

No-load equity mutual funds are sold continuously by the investment companies operating them. Although some advisors suggest waiting to buy your shares after quarterly dividends have been declared, I think this is false economy. Because of the power of compounding, you're usually much better off putting your investable funds to work as soon as possible, especially in equity markets.

How to Buy

The sales contract accompanying the prospectus specifies the fund you're buying, the amount you're investing (there is usually a minimum, but it's invariably low, often $1,000 or $250 if the shares are for your IRA), how share ownership is to be registered, how you want future transactions conducted, and tax status information. Be sure to indicate that you want to participate in the dividend reinvestment program—a core Frugal Investing technique for this core asset category!

You may pay for your shares with a personal check. The number of whole and fractional shares you buy will depend on the net asset value, or NAV, of the shares computed at the end of the business day *prior* to the company's receipt of your order. The NAV is calculated by subtracting the fund's liabilities from its assets (which includes both cash and securities). The share price is then computed by dividing this amount by the current number of shareholders. Obviously, this method of share valuation is different from listed stocks, since individual stocks derive their price from direct market action, which is only one factor contributing to NAV. Still, if the stocks purchased by the fund appreciate, so will NAV.

How You'll Be Paid

After your order has been filled, you'll receive a statement that will tell you the number of shares you've purchased and the NAV that was used. This is the cost basis of your investment, and future changes in share prices will constitute a capital gain or loss. Appendix C will show you how to read a typical mutual listing in the financial pages of your local newspaper.

As a Frugal Investor, you'll want to double check the statement and make sure you haven't been charged for any special services, such as direct deposit, you haven't ordered. Since your account is a bookkeeping entry, you'll receive no engraved certificates as evidence of ownership, and there is no "good delivery" of shares. Each statement will reflect the growing number of whole and fractional shares you've purchased through the fund's DRP.

You can liquidate any or all shares using the method you've agreed to in the purchase contract, which can include a telephone order to sell. Unlike a broker selling a client's stocks, though, the fund *redeems* your shares—essentially buying them back at the previous day's NAV—out of the fund's cash reserves. This allows open-end funds to stabilize prices and redeem shares without cannibalizing their portfolios. Of course, a panic can put lots of pressure on a fund's cash reserves, and

NAV can plummet if the underlying assets have to be sold in a down market to pay shareholders.

By law, the company will cut your check (or you'll receive direct deposit credit) within seven days of the company's receipt of your sell order.

Equity Mutual Funds You Don't Want to Own

All the funds I've discussed in this and the preceding chapter are *open-end* funds. That means they're open at any time to anyone who wants to invest. Shares are issued based on the NAV calculation and redeemed by the fund, so they're highly liquid. Not all mutual funds possess these desirable qualities.

Closing the Door on Closed-End Funds

One category of fund that features both slightly less liquidity and slightly more price volatility than open-end funds are the so-called *closed-end funds*. These funds feature a fixed number of shares that are traded like the stocks comprising their portfolios: according to supply and demand. This may sound great, except when you want to sell and buyers will only pay *less* than the fund's NAV. Thus, closed-end shares almost always trade at a discount. Why should a new buyer pay more? This doesn't mean you can't make money on closed-end funds when the underlying stocks appreciate, only that you'll seldom make as much as you would have on a comparable portfolio held by an open-end fund. Understandably, there are relatively few closed-end funds (less than a hundred—their glory days were the late 1980s when the sponsoring brokerage firms were hard-pressed to keep funds flowing into their houses) and most of those are highly specialized, compared to the thousands of open-end funds.

Trimming Your Interest in Hedge Funds and Derivatives

You already know that derivative investments like options and futures are off limits to Frugal Investors; so are the *hedge funds* that trade in puts, calls, naked and covered options, short selling, and other market timing techniques—and for the same reasons. These investment "casino games" may be great fun, but they make cash consistently only for the fund's management and brokers. Unless you're willing to follow the gambler's dictum and never invest more than you're prepared to lose, you've got no business in these "investments."

Tipping the Scale on Balanced Funds

Investment companies have gotten very creative in their packaging of mutual funds. It's now possible to buy shares in funds that not only acquire equities, but mix them with securities from other asset categories as well. This may sound great—like diversification or even asset allocation—but Frugal Investors have a couple of serious problems with these funds.

First, someone else has made the allocation decision for you. You're always at the mercy of somebody else's idea of the asset mix and have no ability to change it. Second, most balanced funds are far from balanced, but contain only stocks and bonds—giving you the illusion of multiasset allocation safety but not the essence.

Finally, allocation funds can have some of the highest expense ratios around. They're very complex and costly to administer—and these operational costs are invariably passed on to investors. Why pay a fund manager to do the things you can do better, more cheaply, and less frequently yourself?

In the next chapter, and again in Chap. 10, I'll show you how to cut through all these hybrids (with their smoke, mirrors, and big fees) to find the group and brokered investments in our two remaining asset classes—fixed-income and international securities—that *make sense* for Frugal Investing.

To Remember Before Going On

- If you must use a full-service brokerage firm, pick a broker who's customer-oriented and is knowledgeable about multiasset allocation, long-term investing, and has made money in the specific securities you want. Insist on full-disclosure of all commissions and fees and document your investment policy in a written letter of authorization.
- Deep discounters may not necessarily be cheaper (or have access to the same inventory) than the Big Three discounters for the specific securities you want, so it pays to shop around before opening a discount trading account. Under no circumstances should you deal with a bank "lobby broker" for any investment.
- To avoid problems with a broker: put your instructions in writing; follow-up with the appropriate person; and call in an expert if needed. If problems arise anyway, try to resolve it first with the broker, then the firm's compliance officer, then the appropriate exchange, then (if all else fails) with the SEC.

- Equity mutual funds now vastly outnumber the listed stocks that comprise them, giving any investor a large number of choices. Unless you have very aggressive goals, extra cash, and special knowledge of a particular industry, though, a good index fund is preferred for frugal investing.
- To pick the fund that's right for you: Study the ads, look up the firms you like in one of several widely available mutual fund guides, send for the "investor's kit" of the better prospects, then make your selection based on your goals, the guidelines in this chapter, and my criteria in Appendix C.
- Avoid closed-end funds, hedge funds based on derivative stock market products, and the so-called balanced or allocation funds where the all-important allocation decisions are made by somebody else.

9

Fixing the Cost of Fixed-Income Investments

Diamonds are forever; so are bonds and CDs (at least they seem that way!) if you're stuck with low yields in a rising market. Because one good bond decision is worth a dozen second thoughts (requiring chancy trades in the secondary bond market, for example), I've counseled you to buy and hold-to-maturity quality fixed-income securities—and that's still good advice.

What happens, though, if you can't get the bond laddering you want as a hedge against volatile interest rates, particularly in the longer term? What happens in a crisis when you need more cash than you can conveniently draw down from cash equivalents or stocks without gutting your portfolio?

From this perspective, the "cost" of fixed-income safety may be the nominal expense of a well-managed mutual fund that deals in bonds and other debt-based issues—particularly those that may have been too expensive or complex for you to procure on your own. Unlike all but the biggest private bond portfolios, which require a principal of several hundred thousand dollars for minimum liquidity, almost any bond fund can yield spendable cash within a week while the remainder continues to crank out dependable interest. And, best of all, you can do it for cut-rate prices.

Which Bond Funds Are Worth the Money?

In Chap. 5, you explored the range of cost-effective fixed-income investments you could buy direct from the issuer. If you're a typical smaller investor, some of these sounded great, but required an initial investment beyond your means or meant you'd be holding a significant chunk of change to maturity, risking a loss of purchasing power if interest rates went up or, if you had a cash-consuming emergency, illiquidity or even loss of principal. What was left was an array of bank-sponsored CDs that may or may not have filled your bill; but even those with longer terms paid lower interest than the buy-direct debt securities that the bigger players get to choose from.

Once again, the name of the fixed-income investing game is summed up by two words: yield and time. The fixed-income funds that provide both increased yield and increased liquidity (over the buy-direct options) all have these things in common:

- *They do not emphasize government bonds.* Remember, we are talking about long-term, fixed-income investments, not cash equivalents where T-bills are king. Once you're beyond the range of T-bill maturities and their high initial ante, you're *into* the most affordable types of Treasuries: T-notes and T-bonds. Since you can buy these yourself and ladder them intelligently, you won't need a fund manager to do this for you. As Peter Lynch (one of the nation's best known and most successful mutual fund managers) says, "I simply can't understand why anyone puts money in a government bond fund." I can't either, and as a Frugal Investor, you shouldn't.

- *They do emphasize the bonds you can't or shouldn't buy on your own.* These can include mid-rated (B-level—slightly better than junk) corporates and munis, as well as certain callables and mortgage-backed securities, where much higher yields can be obtained with good levels of safety *if* you know what to look for. That's the kind of expertise that justifies a bond fund's management fee and it's a skill that doesn't depend on trading. Also, most tax-exempt municipal bonds, including those with the highest ratings, are sold in $5,000 minimums. A good bond fund pools the resources of thousands of investors and opens a whole new range of good paying, dependable munis for a fraction of this price. In fact, mutual funds are now the biggest buyers of munis on the planet and play an increasingly important role in providing debt capital for mature and expanding corporations, not to mention for home mortgages.

- *They act like stewards, not gamblers, with your fixed-income allocation.* I am always amazed at how many people put good money into speculative debt investments when lower risk, but equally high yielding alternatives are available in other asset classes, such as equities. Apparently, the perceived but illusory safety of any interest-bearing vehicle—from high-yield bonds to second mortgages and private debt placements—overrides their better judgment and sharpens that "free lunch" appetite. Whatever the reason, your fund should stay away from such securities.

• *They charge less than a percent—and not an arm and a leg—for their expertise and service.* The average taxable bond fund charges 0.89 percent of assets for its services; the average tax-exempt fund: 0.76 percent. You can pay more for a fund, but why would you? To justify these higher ratios, the funds usually invest in riskier or more complex issues that require more analysis. If you wouldn't want these kinds of investments individually at any price, would you like them better in a group?

• *They manage volatility through laddered bond portfolios, not by playing the aftermarket.* Bond prices in the secondary market fluctuate daily— whenever interest rates wiggle. This isn't due to uncertainty, but from the *dead* certainty that comes from mathematical relationships between time and yield: old bonds get cheaper or dearer depending on the spread between their nominal rate and the prevailing interest rate for similar securities of the same maturity. Except for thinly traded, high-risk/high-yield and very low rated bonds, there is very little "horse trading" with bonds, because everybody knows instantly how much quality bonds are worth. "Active" bond fund managers who try to achieve higher total returns by frequent trading usually have to pay the piper at some point since in bond investing, at least, a "greater fool" seldom comes along to save you from your mistakes. All this is avoided when yield and return are the same, and that's *only* when bonds are held to maturity, with safety and liquidity ensured by an emphasis on shorter term issues and intelligent laddering. In other words, while you usually can't swap your way to success in bonds, you certainly should be able buy it.

WHERE TO GO

The most extensive quotations of bond mutual fund prices are published in *The Wall Street Journal, Investor's Business Daily,* and *Morningstar.* These publications also offer annual reports on bond advisory newsletters, and the better of these newsletters (those that emphasize intelligent portfolio design over clever aftermarket trades) can help you in your choice.

Beyond these, the same publications mentioned in Chap. 8 as sources for advertisements and features for equity funds also feature similar information about bond funds. Since these are all major, nationally distributed periodicals, you can use them for free in most libraries.

What You'll Save

Fixed-income load funds typically charge a 1 to 6 percent sales commission—a cost your no-load fund simply won't have to earn back. This is an even more significant savings in fixed-income securities, which lack equities' upside potential. Beware of the 12b-1 fee, though, and shop for the lowest rate consistent with your other objectives.

One advantage of fixed-income funds over buy-direct bonds is the ability they give you to invest odd amounts. By this I mean sums that aren't just *different* from the minimum and incremental amounts required for direct-buy Treasuries and munis, but uneven cash amounts. For example, suppose you wanted to invest in quality municipal bond with a $5,000 minimum purchase with $5,000 increments beyond that. If your allocated amount was $8,500, you'd be stuck for a place to put that remaining $2,500. With a bond fund that invests in that type of muni, though, you can invest 100 percent of either the odd or original amount.

Tax Implications

Distributions paid by funds investing in corporate bonds are taxed as ordinary income. Capital gains and losses are possible if and when the bond is traded in the secondary market. Capital losses may be carried forward from one tax year to the next. Income from most municipal bonds is exempt from federal taxes, as Treasuries are from state and local taxes.

As tax rates rise in the 1990s, more investment companies are developing tax-exempt funds. Two of the biggest, Vanguard and Fidelity, both offer funds featuring intermediate-term California bonds offering tax-free, better-than-money-market yields to residents of that state. (Such funds are formed only for affluent, high-tax states, so one may not be available where you live.) Unfortunately, the minimum for Fidelity's Spartan California Municipal Portfolio is $10,000, and Vanguard's Insured Intermediate-Term Fund is $3,000. The Vanguard offering is the first bond fund to insure its investors against loss in case any of the portfolio's bonds default. Such insurance has been offered to direct-buy bond holders, but never before to mutual fund investors.

More affordable is Value Line's Tax-exempt Fund—High Yield, specializing in a wide variety of munis. Although this fund trades often and so is a bit more volatile and costly than some others, it makes a good point of comparison for shopping around if you're a tax-sensitive investor.

Fixed-income funds have all the bells and whistles of equity funds, plus a few extra. In addition to the DRP provisions that are mandatory for any frugal investment, some offer check-writing privileges like money market funds, and even tax-free income.

After the expense ratio, a key qualifier for Frugal Investors to check is the fund's average maturity, which should be no longer than ten years. As long as this seems, this is still only an "intermediate maturity" portfolio.

If you can't find the one ideal fund that fits this profile, split your allocation between an investment grade (high rated) corporate and muni bond fund and a high-yield fund, letting your direct-buy T-notes and T-bonds anchor your fixed-income portfolio. The mix I recommend here would be 15 to 25 percent of assets in the investment-grade fund; 5 to 10 percent in the high-yield fund; and 70 to 75 percent in your Treasury Direct account. Risk tolerant investors may use the higher percentages for the high-yield and investment-grade funds, but the Treasury portion should remain the same for almost all Frugal Investors.

Individual muni bonds or funds specializing in such bonds make sense only for investors in the highest tax bracket. In either case, I suggest buying your funds or bonds from a good deep-discount broker rather than trying to master the direct-buy process yourself—even to the extent necessary to evaluate a competent all-muni fund. And don't be misled by bond funds that advertise their investment as "government insured" or "government guaranteed." What is "guaranteed" are the underlying securities, or a portion thereof, and not the fund shares you'll be buying.

If you have a taste for high-yield junk (low- or no-rated) bonds, a high-yield bond fund is vastly preferred over individual issues, even if you can afford them. In addition to beating the high initial investment hurdle, your fund's portfolio will be big enough to increase the percentage of winners and keep you from bearing the burden of any big losers, or defaulters, all by yourself. (In truth, most high-yield bonds are a lot safer than the popular press lets on, but what risk there is is only magnified when your sampling of such bonds gets smaller.)

In no case should you choose a fund with an expense ratio greater than one percent (some run as high as 1.25 percent). A tax exempt fund should have a ratio of about half of that, but may go higher if you like the fund's objectives, management policy, and other features of direct importance to you.

I recommend the following fixed-income funds as especially suitable for Frugal Investing because of their portfolio laddering, quality asset acquisition policy, and rock-bottom management fees (see Figure 9-1):

Fidelity Short-Term Bond Fund
(800) 544-8888

Neuberger & Berman Ultra Short Bond Fund
(800) 877-9700

Janus Short-Term Bond Fund
(800) 525-8983

Vanguard Fixed-Income Short-Term Corporate Fund
(800) 662-7447

For tax sensitive investors who want low-cost funds yielding average income with lower-than-usual price volatility (due to a policy of investing in shorter term bonds), I recommend:

Vanguard Municipal Short-Term Fund
(800) 662-7447

Fidelity Municipal Bond Fund
(800) 544-8888

For investors wanting low-cost funds investing in lower rated, more speculative bonds, including "junk" bonds, I suggest (see Figure 9-2 for ten-year returns):

Federated High-Yield Trust
(800) 245-5040

PIMCo High-Yield Fund
(800) 800-0952

Fidelity Capital & Income Fund
(800) 544-8888

Vanguard Fixed-Income High-Yield Corporate Fund
(800) 662-7447

WHEN TO BUY

As with any open-end mutual fund, fixed-income funds may be purchased at any time directly from the investment company.

Figure 9-1. Ten-Year Cumulative Returns.

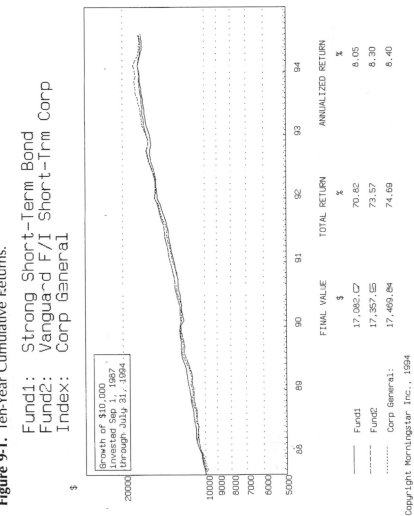

Fund1: Strong Short-Term Bond
Fund2: Vanguard F/I Short-Trm Corp
Index: Corp General

Growth of $10,000
invested Sep 1, 1987
through July 31, 1994

	FINAL VALUE	TOTAL RETURN	ANNUALIZED RETURN
	$	%	%
Fund1	17,082.07	70.82	8.05
Fund2	17,357.56	73.57	8.30
Corp General:	17,469.84	74.69	8.40

Copyright Morningstar Inc., 1994

Figure 9-2. Ten-Year Cumulative Returns.

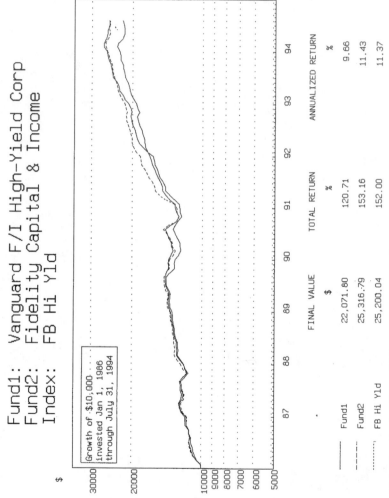

Fund1: Vanguard F/I High-Yield Corp
Fund2: Fidelity Capital & Income
Index: FB Hi Yld

Growth of $10,000
invested Jan 1, 1986
through July 31, 1994

	FINAL VALUE	TOTAL RETURN	ANNUALIZED RETURN
	$	%	%
Fund1	22,071.80	120.71	9.66
Fund2	25,316.79	153.16	11.43
FB Hi Yld	25,200.04	152.00	11.37

Copyright Morningstar Inc., 1994

Curiously, the price of bond fund shares tends to run opposite to interest rate changes, so rising rates can signal bond fund bargains. That is, when interest rates rise and old bonds drop in value, investors tend to move their money out of bond funds and into direct-buy fixed-income securities like CDs and Treasuries. Since the fund must redeem shares on demand, a heavy "run" on the fund can quickly deplete cash reserves and force the fund manager to sell old bonds on the already devalued market. When this happens, the fund's NAV (not to mention prices on the overall secondary bond market) drops even faster. This can open a window of opportunity for bond fund buyers seeking a fundamentally good investment that's temporarily undervalued. Just make sure the fund you're buying is only on its knees and has not fallen through the floor!

How to Buy

Shares in fixed-income funds are purchased just like shares in equity and money-market funds. The sales contract accompanies the prospectus and allows you to specify form of ownership, amount to be invested (often as little as $1,000), and enrollment in special programs, like DRP, direct deposit of distributions or proceeds from liquidated shares, and fund switching privileges—although I discourage the use of the latter.

Like all mutual funds, the precise number of shares your initial check buys will depend on the NAV calculated the day prior to the receipt of your order. For bond funds, the NAV is the sum of the market value of all bonds or other securities held by the fund, including its cash reserves, less liabilities. The share price is computed by dividing that number by the number of shares outstanding.

How You'll Be Paid

The best way to manage your fixed-income distributions is to recycle them immediately in the fund's DRP program. You may also have the interest from your direct-buy Treasuries wired to your fixed-income fund account. That way, you have the next best thing to a "Treasury DRP" account and can keep your fixed-income proceeds employed at higher than money-market rates.

Fixed-Income Funds You *Don't* Want to Buy

Although some investors are happy with bond funds that other investors wouldn't touch, some funds shouldn't be touched by *anyone.*

Don't Put Your Trust In Unit Trusts

Unit trusts sound like the perfect fixed-income vehicle for Frugal Investing: they buy portfolios of corporate and muni bonds you usually can't get on your own and hold those securities to maturity, paying out the interest to investors. As a result, their management fees are among the lowest around. Unfortunately, they have two fatal flaws.

First, they're "self-liquidating," which means you can't hold them in perpetuity, but must reinvest in a new unit trust when the last underlying asset matures. This leads to the second major fault: They're brokerage firm products that can only be purchased (or sold before maturity) through the brokerage firm that organized them, making liquidity poor and transaction cost high. As long as comparable, more liquid, no-load and open-end mutual funds are available, why would you be interested in these?

Opting Out for Interest Rate Options

Some people will bet on anything, and investors who want the thrill of interest-rate risk without laboring through all that tedious business about "yield" and "maturity" cut right to the chase when buying *interest rate options*.

Like any option contract, this one promises to buy or sell an asset (in this case, an interest-bearing security) at a particular price in the future. If the investors guess right, they make money on the option because the underlying security is more valuable. Not only is this example of extreme short-term market timing unsuitable for Frugal Investing, it's unsuitable even for most short-term market timers because even if you guess correctly, the required interest change might not occur within the time period of your option contract! This is a sucker bet that only the idle rich (and their wealthy brokers) are qualified to take.

In the next and last chapter in this Part, I'll show you how to round out your multiasset portfolio with group or brokered investments in the flashiest and perhaps highest potential asset class of all: international securities.

To Remember Before Going On

- Frugal Investors want fixed-income funds that do *not* emphasize securities they could buy themselves, like Treasuries, or securities they would never want to own, like mid-rated corporates and munis. They *do* want funds that avoid secondary market trading, ladder intelligently, and have lower than average expense ratios.

- Tax-exempt fixed-income funds are suitable only for Frugal Investors in the highest tax bracket.
- All Frugal Investors avoid unit trusts, and funds emphasizing interest rate options and other fixed-income derivatives.

10

International Funds That Pay the Freight

Things can get lost in foreign translation.

Norwegian adventurer Thor Heyerdahl arrived in London for an appearance on the BBC. His hosts assured him that a driver was on the way to take him from his hotel to the studio. But after a long wait in the lobby, he stepped onto the sidewalk and approached a cockney gentleman in a flat cap leaning against a car.

"Excuse me," the Noregian said in a thick accent, "I'm Thor Heyerdahl. Are you looking for me?"

"No, mate," the man replied, "I've been sent 'ere to pickup four airedales for the BBC."

I love this story because it shows how little miscommunication it really takes to totally confuse a situation. This happens too often when investments cross international boundaries and financial journalists, tip-sheet jockeys, brokers, academes, and others try to cash-in on the confusion by peddling their own interpretations, if not outright disinformation.

Fortunately, investors don't have to rely on these self-serving intermediaries to get the straight facts on the international securities they need to complete their multiasset portfolios. All of the low-cost brokered or cost-efficient international mutual funds I'll recommend in this chapter can be procured right here in the United States, denominated in American dollars, with everything you need to know spelled out in English. Why, it's so simple, even an airedale could do it.

Group Investing in the Global Environment

We truly live in a global community. About forty percent of the total revenue earned by the "Dow 30" industrials comes from international business and the volume keeps growing year by year. Although you hear a lot about NAFTA costing American jobs in favor of low-wage countries like Mexico, labor in the United States costs about *half* what it does in Europe, keeping our goods and our workers (believe it or not) in demand among the major industrialized countries. Although almost 60 percent of the world market is capitalized overseas, only 25 percent of American investors hold portfolios containing foreign assets. With American multi-nationals and our powerful, innovative, and well-regulated securities industry at the hub of this accelerating international "wheel of fortune," Frugal Investors have no excuse for not allocating at least a portion of their multiasset portfolios to this high-potential asset category.

WHERE TO GO

All the information sources I cited in Chap. 8 apply to international funds as well. I especially like the international coverage of *MorningStar Mutual Funds*, which is carried by most public or college libraries; the *Charles Schwab Mutual Funds Performance Guide*, which is available free at any Schwab office; and Doug Roger's column in *Investor's Business Daily* which sometimes features an international focus.

If you want to track share values, price quotations for larger funds are published in *The Wall Street Journal* and *Investor's Business Daily*, as well as many major metropolitan newspapers.

WHAT YOU'LL SAVE

Buying your international fund direct from the investment company will save you the usual two to eight percent broker's load on mutual funds, but that's not the end of your savings. If you select a foreign index fund, you'll also benefit from the more "passive" portfolio management approach through a lower annual operating expense. At the present time, one of the leading foreign indexing firms, Vanguard's European fund, boasts an expense ratio of only 0.32 percent to an average 1.8 percent charged for actively managed foreign stock funds—and index results were *superior* to even the best actively managed funds; another case of Frugal Investors getting more *because* they insist on paying less!

Now, some sharp-eyed, load-hungry stockbrokers will point to this same example and say, "Look, Vanguard charges a 1 percent transaction fee when you sell your shares, why don't you tell your readers about that!" I certainly will, mainly to point out that this fee does *not* go to the fund's manager, the way loads go to stockbrokers, but is plowed back directly into the portfolio to prevent such fees from becoming a drain on performance. Thus, fund manager compensation (by way of the annual management fee) is still based solidly on the value of the asset pie which benefits, and doesn't penalize, investors—vastly different from the commissions and other broker-related costs that detract from, and never contribute to, returns.

TAX IMPLICATIONS

Capital gains and income received from funds investing in foreign stocks are treated as ordinary income. Capital losses can offset capital gains in other areas, of course, and can be carried forward to the next tax year.

Any tax complications involving foreign governments with respect to stocks within the fund are handled by the fund's management. You don't need to file certifications, etc., with the IRS to avoid double taxation or contend with a foreign government's dividend withholding as you might if you owned the underlying stocks directly. If you're owed any credits because of all this bureaucratic paper shuffling, it will be declared on your fund's year-end statement.

WHAT TO BUY

Currently, the SEC receives new filings from mutual funds with at least a portion of their portfolio in international securities at the rate of one or two *per day*. This could lead naive investors to think there is a lot of choice out there, which is true—but not all choices are equal.

Lipper Analytical Services uses the following categories to identify international mutual funds; to these I've added my own observations and advice:

• *Global funds:* These funds invest at least 75 percent of their portfolios in securities traded outside the United States, 25 percent of which can't be in more than one country. They also include the stock of high-cap multinationals receiving a large portion of their revenue from beyond our borders. Despite these features, I don't recommend global funds for Frugal Investors because the domestic stocks they own are redundant to your equity portfolio and cause your international portfolio to be continually underallocated. This is another case where other people's allocation decisions simply don't pay off for you.

• *Global small company funds:* At least 65 percent of the securities these funds hold are in small-cap companies, and at least 25 percent of them must trade with other nations. Since these are really companies doing international business, not foreign-based firms, and are subject to higher than usual foreign exchange risk, I don't view them as suitable for your international portfolio.

• *International funds:* Securities within these funds all come from companies whose primary trading markets are outside the United States. This doesn't preclude domestic corporations, but it at least confines them to those with a lion's share of business abroad. At best, I categorize these as conservative choices, which, like a portfolio of U.S. multinationals, should be augmented with true foreign-based securities to reap the full benefit of an international allocation.

• *European region funds:* These funds concentrate on equities that trade or operate in the European economic community, or even within a single country. In other words, these are true foreign, or international funds. If you like a European fund, though, you'll want to balance it with a fund (and preferably more than one) specializing in other parts of the world.

• *Pacific region fund:* These funds are similar to the previous ones, but with an Asian orientation. The same advice applies.

• *Emerging markets funds:* These funds are the foreign equivalent of capital appreciation or growth funds in the United States. They're even riskier than these funds, however, because they seek to "cherry pick" winners (at least 65 percent of their portfolios) in developing countries where everything from social upheaval, political instability, and natural disasters can turn a promising young economy to shambles in a virtual blink of an eye. One highly awaited entry to this field is Vanguard's Emerging Markets Index Fund, launched in April, 1994, which hopes to "buy the market" in potentially fast-growing economies of Southeast Asia (Malaysia, Indonesia, Thailand), Latin America (Mexico, Chile, Argentina, and Brazil) and even developing countries on the periphery of Europe, like Turkey. They even beat other emerging markets funds with a penny-pinching 0.6 percent expense ratio compared to the sector's 2 percent average. Admittedly, the prospectuses, brochures, and annual reports of such funds make exciting reading, but if you crave international adventure, stick with the novels of Fredrick Forsyth, Robert Ludlum, or Ken Follet and leave these funds alone.

• *Japanese funds:* These funds invest only in "Japan, Inc.," so if you think the next century belongs to Japan, put a big share of your international allocation here. Personally, although I think a bit of Japan belongs in every international portfolio, it's only as one component of the global economy. Balance these securities with a fund, or funds, from other regions and you'll probably do better.

• *Latin American funds:* These are like the other regional funds, but concentrated in the (quite considerable) area south of the Rio Grande. Some analysts think this is a region whose time has almost come—the fastest growing economy in terms of equity appreciation during the 1980s was Chile! However, I believe the region as a whole has a lot of house-keeping to do with respect to population stabilization, workforce education, political reform, and infrastructure development before it shines like a galaxy instead of a few exceptional stars. Place a bet if it makes you feel good, but hedge that bet with substantial investment in other regions.

• *Canadian funds:* These are the funds that invest exclusively in our often overlooked northern neighbor. For decades, friendly, hard-working Canadian companies cranked out respectable, stable returns, particularly in debt issues. Unfortunately, the twin jaws of socialism (and its crushing tax burden) and the Quebec separatist movement are now snapping at investors who dip their toes in this once placid investment pool. NAFTA will help Canadians, but I think it will help Americans more. In any event, I view Canada as so closely linked with the U.S. economy that it's virtually another American region. Place your international allocation elsewhere.

• *Global flexible portfolio funds:* "Flexible" is Wall Street code for allocation. Since you're doing it yourself, why pay for someone else to make such decisions? Besides, these funds can be as little as 25 percent invested abroad—you'd get more foreign exposure from the "Frugal 10" or multinationals I recommended in Chap. 6.

• *World income fund:* This sounds like a televangelist's crusade, but funds in this category can be good bets for Frugal Investors. First, they invest in both Euro- and nondollar fixed-income securities around the globe, offering both broad international diversification and the higher yields foreign bonds often pay. Second, they can and do invest in foreign equities, mainly for dividend yield—another Frugal Investing plus. If you can find one of these funds you like (and that meets my other criteria), I would recommend investing up to a third of your international allocation in this area.

• *World equity funds average:* These are allocators who invest in other funds, including equities, gold-oriented funds, small company funds, internationals (as previously defined), globals, global small-company funds, regional (both European, Pacific, and Latin American) as well as funds specializing in Canada and Japan. In my opinion, these funds get you nothing but two layers of management expenses and shares in companies and in countries you may eventually wish you never heard of. When you can get comparable return, safety, and volatility dampening in other, cheaper funds, that's where you should go.

After you've received the investors' kit (prospectus, brochure, and order form) from the international funds that interest you, here is what you should look for:

• *Time is of the essence.* How long has the fund been in business? For a domestic stock fund, index or not, the company (and even more important, it's current management team) should have weathered at least one market cycle: four to six years. For an international fund, I prefer *double* this experience—partly because foreign markets tend to run out of phase with American exchanges; partly because the added unknowns and risks of foreign economies put a greater premium on experience. I also like funds that show a foreign advisor for each market, as well as domestic managers—there is simply no substitute for the local perspective. This will limit your choices now, especially if you index, but when you're ready to reallocate (see Chap. 11) the list of candidates will probably be longer.

• *Go for consistently average, not spectacular returns.* This sounds like investment heresy, but, second to seasoning, it's probably the best qualification your fund manager can have. Why? Because superior returns implies marketing timing, or luck, and the increased risk that a dependence on either brings. At minimum, it guarantees above average share price volatility in an asset class that's already volatile enough. Besides, hot hands always cool and every old gunslinger eventually gets picked off by the next Billy-the-Kid. Unfortunately, the only way you know if your guru's time has passed is *after* the bubble bursts—and then you must add the back-end or 12b-1 fees to the losses you've already sustained when you switch to the next rising (you hope!) star. Forget all that. Buy quality then let good old-fashioned competence and time grind out the compound returns you need.

• *Consider funds that invest in foreign debt as well as equity.* All rules have exceptions, and so does the one I have proposed eliminating "balanced" funds from Frugal Investing. Because the international asset category depends upon *all* aspects of foreign economies to boost the performance and dampen the price volatility of your total portfolio, it really should include foreign fixed-income and money market securities as well as foreign stocks. If you can find an international mutual fund that meets all my other criteria *and* invests in bonds, you'll get more bang for your international buck.

• *Inches count in horseshoes, football, and investing, so buy the lowest cost fund that meets your other objectives.* This often repeated maxim doesn't need explaining here, other than to repeat that you shouldn't have to pay for analysis and fancy footwork you don't want. Inevitably, a foreign index fund will be the cheapest way to go, and probably the best. Remember, the primary purpose of an international allocation is to balance countercyclically the movement of your U.S. stocks: As domestic share prices fall, they rise in foreign economies, and vice versa. This has the net effect of lowering the overall price volatility of your portfolio, even if you happen to be invested in some very aggressive domestic growth stocks. The surest way to do this is to "buy the market" on one or a few of the bigger foreign exchanges. International index funds, now obtainable on the NYSE as easily as our own domestic issues, is the lowest cost way I know to accomplish this goal.

But indexing your international stocks makes sense from another perspective as well. For years, U.S. analysts avoided foreign indexing because they assumed the markets were too volatile, too new and inefficient, and the firms comprising them too unseasoned to offer the same kind of results indexing gives investors in the United States. Even worse, the post-World War II environment created a kind of "dictator-of-the-day" mentality that clouded many analyst's view of the political stability of even the most prosperous nations, including Japan (which has pioneered productive links between government and industry rather than undercut them) well into present times.

All these concerns, in my view, ultimately boil down to one thing: the American securities industry's preoccupation with short-term results. Volatility, track record, trading history, legal and regulatory stability *all* tend to fade as problems over time. Since Frugal Investors are long-term investors, the factors that scare market timers and speculators should mean very little to you.

To illustrate my point, the best actively managed international fund, the Templeton Foreign Fund, posted a spectacular 387 percent total cumulative return for the decade ending May 31, 1994, while the Morgan Stanley Capital International EAFE (Europe, Australia, and the Far East) index grew by an even more spectacular 428 percent! Since it's the nature of indexes to be even tougher to beat over longer periods than shorter, results like this have convinced me that indexing is now as good an idea abroad as it is at home.

If you like the idea of foreign indexing, the biggest funds currently offering this choice are (*Note:* All are based on the Morgan Stanley EAFE index):

Vanguard International Equity Index Fund—Pacific Portfolio
(800) 662-7447

Vanguard International Equity Index Fund—European Portfolio
(800) 662-7447

Schwab International Index
(800) 526-8600

The Schwab fund may be particularly attractive, despite its small load, since it invests in both Europe and Asia, as well as Latin America, and seeks to minimize capital gains distributions—a tax nuisance many high-bracket investors should avoid.

One word of caution, though. The EAFE-Pacific index is heavily weighted toward Japan, since that powerhouse currently dominates the region. Thus a bet on the Pacific region in such a fund is really a bet on Japan. (It's a little like a company starting a "NAFTA fund" hoping that the economies of Mexico and Canada will somehow counterbalance events in the United States—it just isn't going to happen!) Since the minimum purchase in these funds is low (only $250 for IRA and $500 for non-IRA investments, although a few go as high as $1,000), you should plan on buying both, weighting your Pacific/European allocation approximately fifty-fifty. (If you don't like Vanguard, you can also make similar splits in comparable index funds as they become available over the coming years.) This way, you'll be able to stabilize your international portfolio by anchoring them to economies literally at "both ends of the earth."

If indexing still bothers you and you prefer an actively managed but still well-diversified fund, I recommend:

Harbor International Fund
(800) 422-1050

T. Rowe Price International Fund
(800) 638-5660

Scudder International Stock Fund
(800) 225-2470

Vanguard International Equity Index Fund—Europe and Asia
(800) 662-7447

As you can see from Figure 10-1, these no-load funds all have an excellent ten year record and otherwise meet my Frugal Investing criteria.

WHEN TO BUY

As I've said, with a few exceptions under very specific circumstances, over the long haul stock prices overseas tend to run if not countercyclical, then at least out-of-phase with stock prices at home. This means that, all other things being equal, a time of inflated stock prices in New York is a good time to find bargains in Tokyo, Bonn, London, Singapore, and elsewhere—and most international fund managers know this.

Figure 10-1. Ten-Year Cumulative Returns.

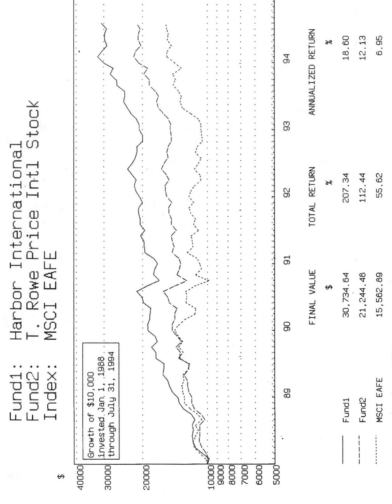

Fund1:   Harbor International
Fund2:   T. Rowe Price Intl Stock
Index: MSCI EAFE

	FINAL VALUE	TOTAL RETURN	ANNUALIZED RETURN
	$	%	%
Fund1	30,734.64	207.34	18.60
Fund2	21,244.48	112.44	12.13
MSCI EAFE	15,562.89	55.62	6.95

Copyright Morningstar Inc., 1994

Fortunately, we are still surfing happily on a long standing wave of higher prices in domestic stocks, making mutual funds dealing in foreign securities, which are climbing out of a global recession, a little (to a lot) undervalued. If the trend toward higher U.S. interest rates continues into the late 1990s, U.S. indexes will cool off and, since all indexes do well in rising markets, foreign funds investors can reap the benefits of their foresight sooner as well as later.

Some analysts advise timing your purchase of foreign-based securities to low points in the dollar exchange rate. That's fine in theory, but even the experts have trouble telling which way foreign exchange rates will go, let alone when the bottom of a short-term cycle has been reached. I say: Grit your teeth and get fully invested in the index fund(s) of your choice as soon as your international allocation is ready and leave arbitrage to the gamblers.

HOW TO BUY

International funds are purchased the same way as domestic mutual funds described in Chap. 8. Like other mutual funds, too, they compute a net asset value (NAV) at the end of each business day, which, when divided by the number of shares outstanding, becomes the price used to sell or redeem shares the following day.

HOW YOU'LL BE PAID

Dividends from international funds are distributed, and proceeds from share liquidation are made, exactly as described in Chapter 8 for domestic funds. Virtually all international funds also offer DRPs, so you'll be able to reinvest those distributions frequently.

Buying American Depositary Receipts (ADRs) from Your Broker

Earlier in this book, I mentioned American Depositary Receipts, or ADRs, as one way wealthier private investors could get into the international market. These negotiable securities are simply certificates issued to investors by a U.S.-owned bank for rights to income and capital gains from foreign stocks held by the bank's overseas branches. These branches receive these stocks from foreign companies who use the U.S. bank as an intermediary for selling their securities to Americans.

ADRs are sometimes viewed as alternatives to international mutual funds, which makes sense only if you don't need or want a fund's diversification or orientation toward a particular objective, such as tracking an index, beating an index, generating income, or reflecting the performance of a particular region or economic sector. In reality, ADRs more closely resemble a sophisticated investor's portfolio of well-chosen individual stocks, with all the same strengths and weaknesses that implies, and are less advisable for the average Frugal Investor.

WHERE TO GO

ADRs in the name of a particular foreign corporation trade on the major U.S. exchanges and also in the OTC market just like stocks. *Morningstar American Depositary Receipts* provides Value Line-type information about almost any ADR that interests you. Appendix C gives you a step by step method for quickly interpreting a typical *Morningstar* ARD listing.

WHAT YOU'LL SAVE

If you invest through a discount broker, you'll save between 50 and 75 percent of the cost of a full-service brokerage firm. Otherwise, costs for ADRs are exactly the same as for listed domestic stocks.

TAX IMPLICATIONS

Tax considerations for ADR investors are the same as for shareholders in domestic mutual funds investing in foreign stocks.

WHAT TO BUY

You can ask for a foreign company by name, such as Sony, British Airways, Honda, Telefonos de Mexico, plus hundreds of other major companies—all of which are sold in the United States as ADRs. Stick with the company names you know and recognize from your own experience, or from diligent research, before you experiment with lesser known firms. Ideally, you should gradually build an ADR portfolio that mirrors a good international index or well-diversified international mutual fund, much as my "Frugal Ten" mirrors the Dow. Pick a few good stocks from Japan and the Western Pacific and Europe as the core of your ADR holdings, then move on to other regions or specific countries if you want to spice up your returns or if you have special knowledge of the economies in those areas.

Income-oriented investors will want to skew their overall foreign holdings in favor of dividend-paying ADRs. Growth-oriented investors will favor equities with roughly the same characteristics as good growth stocks in the United States. If you're one of these investors, choose a few ADRs with stocks in emerging markets, but don't go overboard. Your main objective here is to keep your total multiasset portfolio growing and compounding at a good pace, minimizing the high volatility that usually comes with aggressive objectives, and not to make a killing or time your trades to the vagaries of foreign markets.

Finally, favor ADRs with a DRP option, since this is the essence of Frugal Investing. If you can't find any ADRs you like with this feature, consider a mutual fund emphasizing the same region rather than committing yourself to DCA purchases through a broker. Here are some ADRs that feature DRP, along with the telephone numbers of both the company's investor relations department (first) and securities transfer agent (second):

British Airways
(202) 331-9068
(800) 428-4237

British Petroleum Co.
(216) 586-4101
(800) 428-4237

Glaxo Holdings
(212) 308-5185
(800) 524-4458

Novo Nordisk of North America, Inc.
(212) 867-0131 (company only)

SmithKline Beecham
(215) 751-5012
(800) 428-4237

Volvo North America Corp.
(212) 754-3300
(800) 551-6161

WHEN TO BUY

ADRs may be purchased like domestic stocks anytime the market is open. Orders placed with your broker after the market has closed won't be executed, though, until the beginning of the next business day.

Again, the time to acquire initial securities in any asset class is as soon as you're ready (don't try to out-psyche international political or economic developments—put your allocation to work as soon as possible) then build your holdings steadily. The laws of compounding, like the laws of physics, work the same at any place on the planet.

How to Buy

Orders for ADRs may be placed with your broker exactly in the manner described for individual stocks in Chap. 8.

How You'll Be Paid

ADRs pass on the same income and capital gain rights you would have if you owned the underlying foreign stocks directly. Dividends or capital gains received from ADRs are paid in U.S. dollars, so there is no significant foreign exchange risk associated with receiving your return, although any investment doing business outside the U.S. economy will encounter foreign exchange risk of some kind, and that can affect return. Best of all, all stock-related transactions are handled for you by the bank sponsoring the ADR. Therefore, no matter how many ADRs you own, your investment information will all be reported on a single statement, provided the same bank handles those ADRs.

International Group or Brokered Investments You Don't Want to Buy

Offshore International Funds

All mutual funds based in the United States must meet stringent SEC financial and disclosure requirements. As soon as you step outside the statutory limit, though, all these bets are off.

In the early days of mutual funds, some international funds were organized in the Antilles, Bahamas, and Cayman Islands—the proverbial "offshore" locations favored by money launderers, tax evaders, and other shady dealers. Many of these funds neither registered with the SEC nor followed its disclosure requirements and financial guidelines. When troubles arose, scandals followed. Although some offshore funds are perfectly legitimate, others aren't. With all the choices available through registered securities, it's pointless to consider the rest.

Individual Foreign Stocks, Including Those Traded OTC

Stay away from stocks listed only on foreign exchanges (including foreign OTC exchanges) and not listed on a major U.S. exchange. Such stocks not only carry with them all the usual and unusual risks of an international investment, but what information you do receive about them doesn't have to conform to SEC requirements. This doesn't mean the information you receive will necessarily be wrong, fraudulent, or incomplete, but that nobody (except you!) pays a penalty if it is. If you feel good doing business that way, be my guest. Otherwise, stick with one of the many better ways available for breaking into foreign markets.

Eurobonds

Eurobonds are bonds offered by foreign institutions anywhere in the world but denominated in U.S. dollars. Many sophisticated investors believe they can make a good contribution to an international allocation, complementing the return from equities with the superior yield often available through fixed-income securities issued in other countries.

The problem with Eurobonds is twofold. First, as vehicles based on U.S. dollars circulating abroad, they fall outside the purview of the Fed, the U.S. Treasury, or even the interest rate policies of our domestic banks—yet they still depend on the factors controlled by those agencies, in part, for their value. Second, the agencies that issue them aren't supervised by the SEC. Thus they tend to carry lots of risks we don't commonly associate with dollar-denominated securities. When you add to these imponderables the complexities of foreign tax laws (which aren't intermediated for you by a professional manager when you buy Eurobonds direct, say, through a U.S. branch office of a foreign bank), their advisability becomes questionable for anyone but the most sophisticated and well-heeled investor.

In short, if you like Eurobond yields, look for them in the portfolio of a good international mutual fund and leave the direct-buying to the experts.

Nondollar Foreign Bonds

Foreign governments and companies all issue debt securities denominated in their own currencies. These are as safe or risky (in terms of business, inflation, interest rate, and political risks) as any other fixed-income investment in that environment. But one risk they all have that U.S. fixed-income securities don't is foreign exchange risk: the chance that U.S. dollars will be worth more in terms of the foreign currency on the day you want to convert that currency, and so will make your investment less profitable. On occasion, for a particular transaction, this exchange loss can virtually wipe out the return of a very conservative foreign investment, although exchange rate fluctuations tend to dampen out over time. Consequently, I say leave these nondollar investments to the locals who understand them better and don't share this excessive risk.

Swiss Portfolio Accounts

Americans have known for decades about "Swiss bank accounts," where high rollers and international wheeler dealers—from Oliver North's motley Iran-Contra crew to the biggest global financiers and soon-to-be-ex-dictators from a variety of smaller nations—park their money, no questions asked. What many Americans *don't* know about are Swiss Portfolio Accounts where, for a minimum of $50,000, the Swiss bank's investment advisors will put you into a variety of foreign stocks.

Unfortunately, this James Bond-ish alternative to "good old Charlie Schwab" is one of the most expensive and, in my opinion, self-dealing of all money management schemes. First, the Swiss charge commissions on all buy and sell transactions, as do American brokers, plus a management fee (like a mutual fund or private fee-based advisor), *plus* a toll on any price fluctuations your shares may experience in the course of a trading day: minicommissions, in other words, on transactions they don't even make and you don't even profit from! The only reason clients put up with this "information highway" robbery (aside from the legendary Swiss discretion about giving up account numbers to foreign officials) is that much of the market for these stocks is made by the Swiss banks themselves. If you like the possibility of your foreign portfolio manager cooking up buy and sell prices with his opposite number over an expense-account lunch in Lucerne, go ahead and open an account. Otherwise, take your peanut butter sandwich to Schwab's or Quick & Reilly's or Fidelity's local office and watch the ticker tape for free.

If you've followed my advice in Parts II and III, you are, or shortly will be, fully invested in a multiasset portfolio. Normally, investment guidebooks stop there—but not this one.

In the next and final part, I'll show you how to make dollar-cost averaging contributions to your equity, fixed-income, and international portfolios, track the results of your investments, and reallocate intelligently from those classes that have hit home runs to those who are awaiting their turn at bat. In so doing, you'll discover how to cash-in on undervalued securities while keeping yourself from becoming overconcentrated in markets that may be riding for a fall.

To Remember Before Going On

- Although international funds specializing in a particular region are available, Frugal Investors prefer a good index fund balanced between the European and Asian economies.
- Unlike domestic mutual funds, international funds containing some fixed-income securities should be considered by Frugal Investors.
- ADRs are suitable for more experienced investors who have the same skills and resources needed to evaluate, buy, and hold a portfolio of well-chosen individual domestic stocks.
- Frugal Investors avoid offshore internationals, individual foreign stocks not traded on the major U.S. exchanges, Eurobonds, non-dollar foreign bonds, and Swiss portfolio accounts, even when they can afford the minimum investments.

Part IV
Grow and Rightsize Your Assets

11

How to Build and Reallocate Your Portfolio

Some people will believe anything.

In the Roaring Twenties, analysts noticed a connection between stock prices and hemlines: The shorter the skirts, the better the market. Other pundits observed that when the same horse won the Kentucky Derby, Preakness, and Belmont Stakes, stock prices took a dive. Later, more scientific soothsayers plotted a connection between eleven-year sunspot cycles and economic boom and bust—the market did better when solar radiation was low.

Similar correlations have been made between Super Bowl outcomes and market averages (sell your stock if the AFC team wins) and the ironic relationship between bulls or bears on the cover of *Time* and subsequent market developments (whichever it shows, the market will do just the opposite). Psychics and astrologers, too, have tried to predict the next uptick or downturn in investment markets, but with equally mixed results.

My point is: Where rationality ends, wishful thinking often begins. That's one reason why the very difficult question of what to do with an investment after you've made it is usually left unanswered in books like this. I'll try to correct that dismal record in this chapter, giving you some tangible advice on how to keep your multiasset portfolio healthy, happy, and growing—including occasional reallocations among asset classes when actual results threaten porfolio safety and the achievement of your goals.

Expanding Your Dividend Reinvestment Options

Earlier in this book, I mentioned how critical the availability of DRP services is to my frugal investing philosophy. Since the number of companies offering this service changes from time to time (the trend is up, with more adding the option every year), and since some mutual fund investors find themselves adding individual stocks to their equity portfolio as they gain experience, I'll remind you here of sources for both a further discussion of DRPs ...

Carlson's Newsletter
7412 Calumet Avenue
Hammond, IA 46324
(219) 931-6480

...and up-to-date directories of companies offering DRPs:

DRP Directory
P.O. Box 7631
Laurel, MD 20725-0763
(301) 549-3939

Standard & Poor's
Directory of Dividend Reinvestment Plans
25 Broadway
New York, NY 10004

Using Payroll Deductions to Dollar-Cost Average

You've already seen the incredible power of DCA to magnify the wealth-building power of dividend reinvestment and optional cash purchase plans. You also know, too, that successful Frugal Investors take full advantage of both.

One painless and cost-efficient way to implement an effective DCA progam is to establish an *automatic payroll deduction* plan at your company. Most employers and payroll services permit paycheck recipients to designate one or more institutions, such as a bank or investment company, to receive all or a portion of each check, or a portion of checks issued at certain intervals, such as once a month or at the beginning of each quarter. Some will also schedule regular deductions to these institutions, then stop them at a predetermined limit. Unlike tax and social security deductions, which work the same way, this system *pays you first*—to add value to the assets you've already selected—and saves you the time, trouble, expense (and let's face it: self discipline) of writing checks month after month, year after year. After all, money you never handle is less a temptation to spend.

Table 11-1 shows you how such automatic payroll deductions amplify the power of compounding to build your assets fast.

Frugal Investing for Financial Independence

Most people work to live. We become experts in earning and spending (the two usually increase together) and lifestyle often becomes our biggest dependent. Wouldn't it be great, though, to use your time anyway you wanted while still being assured of that comfortable standard of living?

That's what retirement at any age is supposed to be about, and except for lottery winners, it seldom happens by accident. At a time when more and more pension plans are underfunded and a cash-hungry Congress reneges regularly on IRA incentives and social security benefits, even younger workers are beginning to see that nobody is going to ensure their financial future but themselves. In fact, the ideal time to invest for eventual financial independence is in your twenties and early thirties; not to give you time to correct investment mistakes, but to give the awesome power of DRP, DCA, and compounding more time to work.

Table 11-1. Automatic Payroll Deductions Build Assets Quickly and Painlessly.

An Automatic Investment of	Each	for	Grows an Investment of	to
$100	Month	5 Years	$ 7,000	$ 8,887
$100	Month	10 Years	$13,000	$20,636
$100	Quarter	10 Years	$5,000	$8,399
$250	Month	5 Years	$16,000	$19,982
$250	Month	10 Years	$31,000	$48,261
$250	Quarter	10 Years	$11,000	$17,669
$500	Month	5 Years	$31,000	$38,473
$500	Month	10 Years	$61,000	$94,302
$500	Quarter	10 Years	$21,000	$33,118

This chart shows results of regular investments, each based on a $1,000 initial investment and an immediate monthly or quarterly dollar-cost averaging payment. Each investment assumes an 8% rate of return, compounded monthly. Yields and returns may fluctuate with market conditions. The examples do not take into effect any taxes that may be due on the income earned.

Frugal Investing Under Forty

People under age forty are usually more concerned about starting and raising families, establishing careers, and perhaps buying a house, than they are about securities investing. Fortunately, these goals are *not* mutually exclusive—provided you give increasing your net worth the high priority it deserves. This doesn't mean putting money ahead of people: actually, it's just the opposite. By assuring your financial independence at or before retirement age, you relieve your loved ones of the anxiety and responsibility for caring for you long after employers and bureaucrats have forgotten you exist.

Consequently, I urge every Frugal Investor to start building a multi-asset portfolio as soon as possible—and *not* just after they have bought a house. Why? Because, despite what realtors and relatives tell you, the purchase of a principal residence is mainly a lifestyle decision, not an investment choice. You can't "reallocate" your homeowner's equity in an overvalued market, and few people sell their home (or buy more homes) simply because local real estate prices have changed. Although home ownership often does have investment value (price appreciation and use of the home as collateral are just two of them), I suggest keeping the place you live solidly on the emotional, not the financial, side of the ledger.

That leaves the other four asset classes. Here is how I coach younger investors to begin building wealth in each:

CASH EQUIVALENTS

People in new careers relocate frequently, and young families often need lots of cash. Young adults now tend to use credit cards to maintain a desired lifestyle and meet unexpected expenses the way their parents used to tap cash reserves. Either way, liquidity is important, so I recommend putting around 10 percent of your total investable assets into a money market mutual fund, or even T-bills if you can afford them. A larger than usual allocation to domestic equities, as shown in the following, will provide additional liquidity if it's needed.

DOMESTIC EQUITIES

U.S. stocks are the main wealth-building engine of any portfolio and the sooner you get it in gear, the faster you'll reach your financial destination. If your objectives are very aggressive, I recommend allocating 20 percent of your investable funds to small- or mid-cap stocks, or funds dealing with these securities; 20 percent to a good index fund or individual blue chips like the "Frugal Ten" chosen to mirror an index; and 20 percent to "value" stocks, possibly in a good growth-oriented mutual fund. More conservative investors may distribute the 20 percent not allocated to small-caps to their blue chips, index fund, or growth stocks as they see fit.

FIXED INCOME

Younger investors need fixed-income securities to help dampen the volatility of their growth-oriented equities. I recommend putting 5 percent of your total assets into two-year T-notes or an investment-grade bond fund. If you're very aggressive and have lots of disposable income, you might put a portion of this into a well-managed high-yield fund—all within the limits I gave you earlier in this book.

International Securities

Younger investors should see the long-heralded promise of a true, global economy mature in their lifetimes. I suggest investing 25 percent of your total assets in an EAFE-type international index fund. If you're very aggressive, you might put all or a portion of this in a managed international fund. If all goes well, the increased volatility of such a fund, working out-of-phase with U.S. markets, will help dampen the increased volatility of your growth-oriented domestic securities, yielding some great compound returns along the way.

Frugal Investing in Midlife

The broad span of years from forty to sixty we call *middle age* breaks down into two distinct eras from a financial point of view. The first period, roughly forty to fifty, usually marks the culmination of a career. Those who are going to "make it" see their name on the office door or otherwise reap the rewards of hard work and good luck. Very likely, their income and wealth-building capacity will keep on growing from year to year. Those who have not been as fortunate usually realize, too, that they have arrived at a broad plateau—the high-water mark of their professional life. They'll make more money during the next ten or fifteen years, but those increases won't be as great and will come more slowly. The more ambitious among either group sometimes abandon old careers and look for new mountains to climb, frequently as entrepreneurs.

Both types of people, too, usually have grown families with children in or graduating from college. Other big expenses, such as a down payment for a home, are typically long behind them. Consumer credit balances, especially as a fraction of income, are traditionally low in this age bracket. People over fifty also begin thinking seriously about retirement, and make the maximum IRA contribution each year. Many discover they have unexpected wealth in the form of maturing investments, pension accounts, company stock options, and home equity. The more affluent among them may divert some of this wealth to luxuries like vacation homes, world travel, expensive toys like boats, planes, and collectables, or as gifts to loved ones and charities. However, many also find themselves burdened, if lovingly so, with elderly parents who for one reason or another depend on them for support. No matter what financial challenges or opportunities surround them, though, the typical attitude of people at midlife is, "How can I still do it all?" rather than "How long can I keep what I've got?"

Cash Equivalents

For many people, health problems begin to surface during this period—particularly after age fifty. I recommend keeping at least 10 percent total assets in T-bills to ensure adequate liquidity.

Domestic Equities

After you pass forty, I recommend reducing your small-cap allocation, if any, to 15 percent and confine your stocks (or mutual fund specializing in such stocks) to mid-cap issues. Keep the same 20 percent each in the index and value funds you started out with. After you pass fifty, reduce your mid-cap holdings to 10 percent and switch your 20 percent allocation in index funds to a fund specializing in growth and income, leaving you 20 percent alotted to value stocks alone.

Fixed Income

After forty, allocate an extra 5 percent to five-year T-notes, keeping your existing two-year T-note allocation. After fifty, keep this same 10 percent allocation (split the same way) in this asset class.

International Securities

Keep 25 percent allocated to the same index or managed international fund throughout this twenty-year period.

Preretirement Investing

After sixty, most people are preoccupied with making their dreams about "life after work" a reality. As the work force grows, more and more companies are offering older workers an early retirement option. However, many people, including those in the trades and professions and people who are self-employed, continue working well into their seventies. The big advantage of this stage of life is that if you've sown your investment seeds wisely, you'll reap a generous harvest and begin switching methodically from growth- to income-oriented securities in the equity and international asset classes. Many people at or near retirement often become real experts in money *managing*, as well as earning and spending, and that's all to the good. These skills will serve them well over the next twenty or thirty years.

And don't forget, after the legal retirement age, you'll be entitled to begin withdrawing benefits from your social security account. To get an estimate of what those benefits will be, contact the Social Security Administration at 1-800-772-1213 and ask for Form SSA-7004. Six weeks after you've completed and returned the form, you'll receive a personal earnings and benefits statement.

CASH EQUIVALENTS

Keep the same 10 percent minimum invested in T-bills, or increase this allocation to 20 percent if you have uninsured health expenses or other recurring needs for extra cash beyond your normal living expenses.

DOMESTIC EQUITIES

Keep your 10 percent mid-cap, 20 percent value stock, and 25 percent growth and income allocations as they are, but shift from growth to dividend-oriented companies within each allocation. This will probably mean switching from one fund to another or swapping some of your individual stocks, incurring a capital gain liability. Your tax advisor can help you with strategies for minimizing the cost of this necessary restructuring.

FIXED INCOME

Keep your 5 percent allocations to two-year and five-year T-notes respectively, and add to them new 5 percent allocations each for seven- and ten-year T-notes. You'll keep this laddering indefinitely for the remaining life of your portfolio.

INTERNATIONAL SECURITIES

Reduce your international allocation to 15 percent of total assets. You'll retain this allocation for the remaining life of your portfolio (although you may restructure, or change the specific securities that comprise them, as you get older).

Enjoying a Productive Retirement

Many newly retired people panic at the thought of no more paycheck and the loss of regular merit and cost-of-living raises. They stamp "capital preservation" on their forehead and refuse to think about anything other than hanging onto what they've got.

This defensive mindset may be understandable, even instinctive, but it's also a big mistake. If you look at actuarial tables like those insurance companies use, your life expecancy at retirement is *not* the same as it was when you were born: *it's usually much longer*. In other words, all other things being equal, a nonsmoking man born in 1930 who, at that time, was expected to live to be 71, doesn't have a six-year life expectancy at retirement in 1995, but may actually expect to live an additional 10 to 14 years. This extra longevity comes, in part, from the way mortality and probability statistics work: if you're healthy, the longer you live; and the longer you live, the better your chances get for living a little bit longer, at least until you hit the natural limit of human lifespans. This means that almost everyone who reaches retirement age will live longer than he or she thinks—one reason the guardians of social security and our health care systems are so worried!

In financial terms, this means that while retirement may be a time to rest on your laurels, your investments can't rest on their's. Your portfolio will still have to grow to some degree if the income you receive from it is to keep up with, or surpass, inflation—another of those immutable economic facts of life.

One unpleasant surprise some retirees get is the end of the favorable tax treatment given to their IRA contributions. After age 70½, withdrawals must begin to avoid tax penalties, forcing new decisions about spending, allocation, and investment.

Cash Equivalents

If the 10 percent in T-bills is no longer sufficient to meet your needs for ready cash, increase this allocation to 15 percent.

Domestic Equities

A lot of risk-averse investors get out the stock market altogether after retirement—a move virtually all of them live to regret. I recommend reducing your mid-cap holdings to 5 percent of total assets and adding the proceeds to your growth and income stocks (which should now be about 50 percent of total assets) keeping 20 percent in value stocks for the upside kick your future spending power depends on.

FIXED INCOME

Retain the 20 percent laddered mix of T-bills and T-notes you established during your last reallocation.

INTERNATIONAL SECURITIES

Retain the 15 percent allocation you currently have. If necessary, switch from index or growth-oriented internationals to income or balanced international funds.

Table 11-2 shows this dynamic relationship among time, risk tolerance, and appropriate securities selection at a glance.

Keeping Track of Your Total Return—Cheaply

One reasonable question Frugal Investors sometimes ask is: "Unless I get all my securities from one source, or through one brokerage firm, which can be expensive, how will I ever know the return of my *overall* portfolio?"

John Markese, president of the American Association of Individual Investors, has found a way. His simple formula provides a "quick and dirty," but surprisingly reliable, approximation of the total return calculations performed by complex computer programs used by high-priced investment advisors. To make it work, all you need is a simple hand calculator (or paper and pencil) and three basic facts from your investment account statements, no matter how many you have:

1. The account's annual or quarterly ending balance. (To compare apples to apples, make sure all your statements reflect the same period.)
2. The net contributions to the account. These are additions such as those made through a DRP or by DCA, less any withdrawals.
3. The account's balance at the beginning of the period.

Table 11-2. Recommended Allocations for a Lifetime of Frugal Investing.

CONSERVATIVE GOALS (Income Oriented)

AGGRESSIVE GOALS (Growth Oriented)

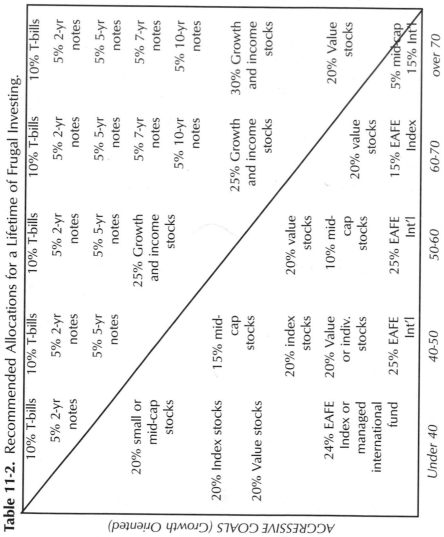

Under 40	40-50	50-60	60-70	over 70
10% T-bills	10% T-bills	10% T-bills	10% T-bills	10% T-bills
5% 2-yr notes	5% 2-yr notes	5% 2-yr notes	5% 2-yr notes	5% 2-yr notes
	5% 5-yr notes	5% 5-yr notes	5% 5-yr notes	5% 5-yr notes
			5% 7-yr notes	5% 7-yr notes
			5% 10-yr notes	5% 10-yr notes
20% small or mid-cap stocks	15% mid-cap stocks	25% Growth and income stocks	25% Growth and income stocks	30% Growth and income stocks
20% Index stocks	20% index stocks	20% value stocks	20% value stocks	20% Value stocks
20% Value stocks	20% Value or indiv. stocks	10% mid-cap stocks		5% mid-cap
24% EAFE Index or managed international fund	25% EAFE Int'l	25% EAFE Int'l	15% EAFE Index	15% Int'l

Here is the formula (in somewhat simplified form from the original version):

$$\frac{\text{Ending Balance} \ - .5 \ \times \ \text{Net Contributions}}{\text{Beginning Balance} + .5 \ \times \ \text{Net Contributions}} - 1.0 \ = \% \ \text{Return}$$

To keep things simple, suppose you had only one mutual fund in each asset category (the fund names below are fictitious) with the following annual statement information:

Name	Begin	Net Contributions	End
Cash-Money Liquidity Fund	3,000	0	3,120
U-Pickem Equity Winners	23,000	3,600	29,130
Boring Bonds Unlimited	8,000	0	8,680
Attila International Growth	6,500	1,200	8,025
Totals:	40,500	4,800	48,955

Plugging this into the formula, we get:

$$\frac{48,955 - .5 \times 4,800}{40,500 + .5 \times 4,800} - 1.0 = 8.5\% \ \text{total portfolio return}$$

Why is this number useful? First, it allows you to gage the overall growth of your assets. Are they keeping up with inflation? Is it sufficient to reach your long-term goals? Is it better than the lowest risk alternative to which your money might be put? All these are relevant investor questions and should be evaluated periodically. After several such measurements, you'll know, too, if your current asset mix is doing the job it's supposed to be doing, particularly in comparison to mixes advised by other allocation specialists.

Reallocating to Correct Imbalanced Performance

Reallocations due to changing financial circumstances or different stages of life make sense and are needed only rarely. What happens, though, when your portfolio "turns on you" and changes the allocations on its own? If you think this can't happen, take a look:

Thirtysomething Scott and Nancy were conscientious, Frugal Investors who were fully allocated early in their investment careers. They bought shares in a money market fund, an S&P 500 index fund, an EAFE international mutual fund, and a mid-term bank CD—all according to my allocation advice for their age bracket. At the end of their first complete, fully allocated year, their portfolio looked like this:

Total Assets Value, Initial: $30,000 (100%) Allocation to

Cash equivalents:	3,000 (10%)
Domestic equities:	18,000 (60%)
Fixed income:	1,500 (5%)
International securities:	7,500 (25%)

After four years, without drawing down any money, they had earned a return of 20 percent on their money market fund (averaging 5 percent per year); 28 percent on their bond fund (at about 7 percent per year); and a whopping 40 percent on their international fund. Their domestic stock portfolio, however, suffered a bear market and gained only 16 percent in value—a meager average of 4 percent per year. To keep things simple, let's assume the annual returns were *not* compounded and the couple made *no* DCA contributions during this period—all factors that would only increase the results you're about to see. Their "year four" portfolio looked like this (the decimal values are rounded off, and so do not add evenly to 100 percent):

Total Asset Value, End of Year Four: $36,900 (100%)

Cash equivalents:	3,600 (9.7%)
Domestic equities:	20,880 (56.5%)
Fixed income:	1,920 (5.2%)
International securities:	10,500 (28.5%)

Naturally, Scott and Nancy were surprised to see that, through no action of their own, their allocations had been skewed: slightly lower than they wanted in cash equivalents, moderately above what they wanted in internationals, and well below what they needed in domestic equities.

Thus, our couple's task at the beginning of year five, all other things being equal, is to reallocate about 4 percent of their total asset value *from* their international portfolio and put it *into* their domestic equities. From a practical standpoint, this meant redeeming about $1,400 from their international fund and reinvesting it as new capital in their index stock fund. (They decided that the minor differences in the other allocations are too small to worry about, so they left them alone.) Their new, reallocated portfolio now looked like this:

Total Asset Value, Beginning of Year Five: $36,900 (100%)

Cash equivalents:	3,600 (9.7%)
Domestic equities:	22,288 (60.3%)
Fixed income:	1,920 (5.2%)
International securities:	9,100 (24.6%)

This sort of portfolio fine tuning may seem like guilding the lily, but such discrepancies only get worse the longer they're left without attention. Eventually, Scott and Nancy's international allocation might have equalled their U.S. stock allocation—bad news, because what goes up must come down, and more volatile securities take bigger hits in down markets. Similarly, interest-bearing investments seldom keep up with inflation, so overallocations to them over a long period of time weakens your future purchasing power much more than you might think.

The message here is: Pay attention to your statements of account (and, if you own individual stocks purchased directly from the company, from the annual reports you receive). Periodically calculate your portfolio's total return and the *actual* allocations market action has left you with. When necessary, shift your assets from the overvalued markets to those whose time is about to come.

Another and even more frugal way to avoid or postpone a forced reallocation, which can cost you exit fees or broker commissions, is to vary your DCA contributions when you notice that price changes between securities in two asset classes have become pronounced. There is no hard and fast rule for this, and you certainly don't want to violate DCA's cardinal rules for regular and constant reinvestment just to tweak your allocations a percent or two. But cutting down new investment in an overvalued security and beefing up your acquisitions in one that's significantly undervalued can often keep your desired allocations on track—or at least within an acceptable range—while actually magnifying the chief benefit of DCA: namely, that you don't spend too much for inflated securities and buy more of a good thing when the price is down.

To illustrate, suppose now that part of Scott and Nancy's four-year return in both the U.S. and international funds were based on DCA contributions. For simplicity's sake, let us say *half* of the 40 percent return on the international fund, or $1,500, and *half* the 16 percent return on domestic equities, or $1,440, were due to such contributions.

Now suppose they observed the diverging price trends of these two asset classes in year two and cut their international DCA in half while doubling their contributions to domestic stocks: buying *less* of the high-priced shares and *more* of the undervalued shares. The resulting portfolios would look like this:

	Gain, Years 1 and 2 (Using old DCA)		Gain, Years 3 and 4 (Using New DCA)		Total
Domestic Equities:	1,440	+	2,880	=	4,320
International Securities:	1,500	+	750	=	2,250

This would give the following balances and allocation percentages by the end of year four in these two asset classes:

Domestic equities: $22,320 (60.5%)
International securities: $ 9,770 (26.4%)

As you can see, this rough and ready method isn't perfect, but it can help maintain a desired spread among allocation percentages *without* incurring fees, commissions, and other expenses associated with share liquidation. If you wait too long and the forced reallocation is sizeable, and your portfolio consists of individual stocks, the amount you must reallocate because of market action may actually exceed the upper limits allowed by the company's OCP program—so an ounce of prevention can literally be much cheaper than that proverbial pound of cure.

Of course, building and reallocating assets is only part of the portfolio management story. To be useful at any stage of life, money must be drawn down from your investments. Doing that cost-efficiently and in a way that doesn't throw a wrench in the rest of the wealth-producing machinery in your portfolio is the subject of the next and final chapter.

To Remember Before Going On

- Your employer's automatic payroll deduction system is one painless way to implement an effective dollar-cost averaging plan.
- Allocation percentages change as you pass from young wage earner to middle age to preretirement and into retirement years. All age brackets, even income-oriented retirees, need a growth component in their portfolio to offset inflation.

- Don't pay extra for a consolidated brokerage account or buy funds all from one fund family just to know your total return, which can be easily calculated yourself.
- Every few years you may have to reallocate among asset classes to compensate for market results and keep your portfolio balanced. If you see market-driven misallocations coming, reallocate using DCA to avoid paying extra costs and commissions.

12

How and When to Draw Down Your Investments

Many people spend their whole lives worrying about which securities to buy and how to buy them—to avoid paying extra fees, commissions, and taxes—but spend virtually *no* time at all thinking about when and how to sell them: for goal-related spending, income-generation, planned giving, estate transfer, or whatever.

And stockbrokers and other high-priced advisors aren't much help, even when you ask them. Experts who advised you to make an investment are notoriously reluctant to tell you when to get out. They often view a sell recommendation as an admission of failure, and I suppose that's human nature.

Some experts get around this by using such formulas as, "Sell when the P/E ratio equals the company's earnings growth," or "Sell half your holdings whenever the stock price doubles." Mechanical tricks like these may help brokers evade personal responsibility for their advice, but they also leave investor preferences, needs, and goals completely out of the equation. And newsletters aren't much better. Knowing their recommendations will hang around in print forever, few editors want to be reminded of the time in the 1950s when their publication told subscribers to dump Polaroid, Xerox, or IBM because their prices or earnings were "unreasonable."

There has to be a better way.

My solution is for investors to take the sell decision as seriously as any other; as one deserving of lots of forethought as well as hindsight, and with all the Frugal Investing techniques I've suggested brought into play.

The Liquidation and Restructuring Process

Frugal Investors believe that less is more when it comes to commissions, fees, unsolicited advice, unnecessary risk, and money they have but, for some reason, can't spend. As a result, virtually all of your portfolio management decisions should be made with an eye toward *maximizing* the discretionary dollars you'll have at the time you want that money—not necessarily managing for paper profits you can't touch.

The problem is: What time is the *right* time to sell a given security? How clear are those signals and are they different for different asset classes? For that matter, is it smarter to take and keep your principal and earnings in cash or reinvest them in another, more productive security right up until the time you need them?

These aren't idle questions. Every investor who's smart or lucky enough to ride a winner to the finish line will face them eventually. Here is my way of sorting them out.

Step 1: Decide How Much You'll Need Two Years Before You Need It

This rule applies mainly to sizeable lump-sum withdrawals. I say two years, because this is the longest interval I recommend before you begin to divest yourself of your most volatile investment in anticipation of major goal-related spending. For average Frugal Investors, the first source of funds they will tap will be their international securities. Very risk-tolerant, aggressive investors, would still begin with their international securities (particularly any value-oriented ADRs or managed emerging market funds) but they could also liquidate a portion of their small-cap stocks or funds, high yield bond funds, and similar risky domestic ventures.

The key idea (all other things being equal) is to draw down the needed funds *first* from your most volatile securities, then transfer the proceeds gradually into stabler vehicles until, by the time you need the cash, the full amount is in the appropriate check-writing account. This keeps your money working productively and *dependably* right up to the time you make the disbursement.

Just as important to the long-term health of your portfolio, never liquidate all your holdings in any asset class or specific security (after all, you'll still want no-commission access to the security to rebuild your asset through lump-sum OCP contributions, DRP, and DCA later), but after reducing it (at most) to 10 or 20 percent of its current value, go to the *next* most volatile and risky investment, even if it's in a different asset class. Continue drawing down the funds in this manner until you're within a few percent of the desired amount. If you've gone through all your securities this way and still have not got the needed amount, begin again. The key idea is to penalize the riskiest investments in the most volatile asset categories first, then nick the others with an eye toward preserving your original allocations as much as possible. This won't be perfect, but it will help preserve the benefits of multiasset allocation while making your remaining portfolio *safer* rather than more volatile when you can afford increased volatility the least.

Now, why did I say to draw down your investments to "within a few percent" of the needed amount and not the total amount itself? Because part of your liquidation strategy is to put the withdrawn amount into an interest-bearing, intermediate-term investment (a financial "holding pattern," so to speak) until it's needed—but more of that in its place. For now, just make sure you don't take a too-small fraction of the needed amount then try to speculate your way to greatness: gambling on options, futures, hedge funds, or the like to make up the difference.

This is also the time to begin factoring in, and planning to minimize, any liquidation costs associated with the withdrawal. These could include:

- Broker's fees and commissions
- Back-end or "stinger" fees charged by some mutual funds
- Wire transfer or other special cash-handling charges
- Taxes, including ordinary income and capital gain

Where taxes are concerned, be sure to add your DRP purchases back onto your original cost basis so that you don't pay taxes on them twice. Also, if you've previously sold shares using one of the four basic methods of calculating mutual fund costs, you'll probably have to stick with it. Check with your tax advisor to see which method applies to you.

Step 2: Put the Amount Drawn Down into the Best-Paying One-Year Fixed-Income Security Available

This will usually be a bank CD, but could also be a T-bill if the amount is sufficient. Rollover this interim investment until you're within six months of the need date, then deposit it all in your check-writing cash equivalent account.

To begin the liquidation and restructuring process, notify your broker or the fund company of your intention to sell. If your account has a telephone authorization provision, a phone call will trigger the sale immediately but will require a follow-up letter of authorization, or LRO. Some funds require a notary- or bank-certified signature on this letter, which can add a few dollars to the cost.

If the shares to be liquidated come from a mutual fund within a larger family of funds, you may be able to switch the desired amount into a domestic fixed-income fund without charge—but be sure there will be no additional fees or penalties levied when you liquidate this amount eighteen months later.

If the liquidated securities are individual stocks or ADRs, your *market price sell order* will be confirmed within twenty-four hours and settled within five days. Since you'll have received "good delivery" on your shares when you bought them, you'll have to surrender the stock certificates to your broker within this period, properly endorsed on the back, so make sure you know where they are. (Stock certificates are hard to replace; you should keep them with your other valuables in a safe deposit box.)

Once the shares are liquidated, don't delay in reinvesting them in the interim fixed-income investment of your choice. If you already have a good fixed-income mutual fund that you like better than CDs, go ahead and put the earmarked money there, provided you won't get nicked with a "premature exit" charge for the amount in question.

Step 3: Begin Reinvesting in the Depleted Asset Category (or Categories) at Once by Lump-Sum OCP Contributions and Restructured DCA Allocations

Some careful allocators panic when they see the gaping hole a sizeable withdrawal leaves in their portfolio. They're particularly concerned about the way their allocation mix may have been thrown off. Some of them even feel tempted to draw down the needed amount from *all* their holdings in proportion to their current allocations so that the mix isn't disturbed, but I think this is a mistake. From a financial planning perspective, a sizeable withdrawal that's not simply reinvested in another asset, like a house, decreases your net worth no matter how the withdrawal is structured. In my view, it's like running the video tape of your wealth-building adventure backward. Since you built your portfolio by going from stabler to more volatile investments, it only makes sense from a capital preservation standpoint to reverse this process when incremental amounts must be drawn down.

It also means that you should begin rebuilding your depleted securities by diverting any new lump sums (such as the next annual bonus check) and all your DCA contributions to them until the old asset mix is reestablished. This, too, is only common sense because continued DCA investment in the nondepleted securities will only increase or prolong any out-of-balance condition, not cure it.

But lump-sum, goal-related spending is only one reason you might liquidate and reallocate a portion of your holdings. What happens as you get older, and your investment objectives change?

Restructuring for Income

As you saw in Chap. 11, most investors eventually find their need for current income exceeds their need for asset growth. This may be temporary and can occur at any age—for example, by a need to generate income during a period of unemployment, extended illness, or low returns from a start-up business—but it's usually associated with retirement. Whatever the reason, there is *never* a reason to "gut" your portfolio and cut out its heart and muscle, its core wealth-building capacity to satisfy an increased demand for cash. With the intelligent reallocations you've already learned about and the thoughtful restructuring I'll teach you here, even a marginal multiasset portfolio can keep producing dependable, spendable cash, year after year. The key is to structure those withdrawals intelligently, meeting short-term needs without abandoning long-term goals.

Managing Systematic Withdrawals

Most mutual funds, and many stock DRP plans, have a *systematic withdrawal plan*, or method for paying out all or a portion of distributions that were previously reinvested, including the liquidation of whole or fractional shares. This feature was probably offered to you on the initial purchase contract (see the sample in Appendix B), although retired people investing for income are usually the only ones who check this option right away.

Typically, the systematic withdrawal plan requires a minimum balance of from $2,000 to $10,000 to begin. Most plans will also allow you to designate third-parties, such as mortgage companies, nursing homes, or other private individuals to receive the payments. This is handy for Frugal Investors who want their plan to work like a miniature trust, *without* paying those heavy legal and custodial fees!

Check the prospectus and account contract (or later company material if you've held the shares a long time—new programs or rules may apply) to see which options are available for you. Remember, you can modify a given withdrawal plan any time, and even cancel it and go back to the DRP option if your overall financial situation permits it. And nothing stops you, of course, from making new investments to the fund if you receive a windfall, but want to continue using the plan as a kind of personal "cash manager."

Remember, too, that proceeds from such plans always have tax consequences, including possible limitions on the maximum amount you can withdraw at a low- or no-tax rate if contributions were part of an IRA. Also, if the option you select involves share liquidation and frequent distributions, the cost-basis recordkeeping can quickly become very complex.

Finally, because of the extra paperwork involved in these plans and the fund manager's natural desire to keep people in the fund instead of letting them out painlessly, most systematic withdrawal plans carry extra costs. If you're at or near retirement age and such withdrawals (and their costs) are a real concern, you should know that Vanguard and Fidelity, as well as Charles Schwab funds, offer systematic withdrawal plans without additional fees.

You should also realize that not all funds offering systematic withdrawals are good candidates for this process. A very volatile, aggressive growth fund, for example, may pay well when times are good, but when the market is down, may pay insufficient distributions and force you to think about cannibalizing shares or switching funds to something more stable and thereby incur an exit fee or unplanned capital gains tax hit. In these cases, the sooner you begin an orderly transfer from growth- to income-growth securities, such as the reallocations I suggested in Chapter 11, the better off you'll be.

Here are the most common withdrawal options, listed in order of desirability for income-oriented investors:

• *Percentage of distributions plan:* This option, admittedly for more affluent investors, disburses only a portion of the distributions and allows the remainder to be reinvested. This provides for both continued DRP benefits and current income. Naturally, the account has to be pretty big to make this income meaningful, and a period of no (or low) dividends can wipe out any income at all. Its big advantage is that it never eats into your principal and allows continued capital appreciation, so if you can afford it, think about this option first.

• *Dividends and capital gains withdrawal plan:* This choice simply cancels your DRP option and instructs the fund manager to pay all distributions to you. This preserves your capital, allowing continued growth due to market appreciation—a partial hedge against inflation. The downside is that normal distributions will be irregular, making budget planning difficult; and if the principal isn't sizeable, neither are the distributions.

- *Fixed-dollar liquidation plan:* This retirement favorite allows you to withdraw a set amount of money monthly or quarterly to meet budgeted living expenses. If you're still working, even part-time, you can minimize this fixed amount by setting it to cover some major or troublesome expense, such as a mortgage payment, while your other earnings cover the remaining (and more discretionary) costs. The big problem with this is that if and when distributions sag, withrawals from your principal (that is, liquidation of shares) will be needed to make up the difference. If this happens too often, the capacity of your assets to either grow *or* pay income may be diminished considerably. I recommend this option only when the lowest expected distributions are sufficient to meet the budgeted amount, or you were planning to liquidate this investment anyway and have good growth sources in other areas.

- *The percentage of assets liquidation plan:* For people who are committed to getting out of an investment, but want to do so in an orderly, cost-effective way, this plan isn't bad. Under this option, a fixed fraction (often quite small) of your total asset value is disbursed each period. When the market goes up, most of the proceeds will come from distributions and few shares, if any, will have to be liquidated, keeping your assets working a little longer. When the market goes down, or if no distributions are available, all the money must come from the liquidated shares. If your goal is postponing the inevitable as long as possible and you can live with variable disbursements, this plan may be for you.

- *Fixed shares liquidation plan:* This plan, which sends you the proceeds from the sale of a set number of shares each period, is suitable only for people who want to liquidate their holdings fairly soon, but wish to do so in a way that minimizes tax exposure and prevents them from selling too many shares in a down market—as can happen with the fixed-dollar approach. The main problem with this, aside from being a one-way ticket out of the investment, is that the amounts will be irregular—high when share prices are high, and low when the market is bad.

The main thing to keep in mind with all these plans is that systematic withdrawal isn't an all or nothing proposition. A given plan can usually be changed or terminated as the situation warrants, and amounts can be minimized (minimizing the risk of undesired share liquidation) by restructuring your holdings within the asset category, or within other asset categories, to either augment the income you need or increase the growth rate of value-oriented investments.

It's an old dictum but true: winners plan to succeed and losers fail to plan. As long as you keep continuous allocations in the four basic asset classes and follow the frugal investing commandments (don't pay for things you can get for free; buy from the source or at the deepest discounts; use DRP and OCP-DCA to compound your assets quickly; and liquidate your holdings thoughtfully) few investment decisions will ever come back to haunt you.

A Last Word—and An Invitation

Throughout this book, I've tried to drive home my heart-felt belief that anyone *can* acquire and successfully manage an effective multiasset portfolio without paying a lot of commissions, fees, and other unnecessary costs. However, some people because of health, age, temperament, economic circumstances, or other reasons decide they wish to trust all or part of that job to an asset manager who shares their frugal philosophy. If you're considering such a decision and want to talk to me personally about your needs and objectives or the qualities I look for in value-oriented, fee-based money managers, call or write:

> Scott Spiering
> Spiering & Company, Inc.
> Four Embarcadero Center, Suite 730
> San Francisco, CA 94111
> (415) 398-4000

For those who enjoy Frugal Investing as a participation sport and want to keep up with the latest developments in buy-direct and no- or low-cost investment methods, products, and discount broker services, as well as cost-effective multiasset portfolio management techniques and do-it-yourself software, you may want to subscribe to my quarterly newsletter, *The Frugal Investor*, available at $195 per year.

No matter how you invest, though, I wish you the best of luck with your portfolio and hope you enjoy the "many happy returns" your diligence and forethought will have earned.

To Remember Before Going On

- Liquidation decisions are just as important as acquisition decisions.
- Draw down an amount to within a few percentage points of your desired sum two years before you'll need it. Start with your most volatile securities in your most volatile asset category first, then work your way down—like running a movie or video of your

wealth-building process in reverse. *Never* completely deplete any asset category or security, since you'll only incur unnecessary new costs when you replenish it.

- Invest the withdrawn amount in the highest paying fixed-income security available for the time period remaining (usually one-year minimum) then, six months prior to expenditure, deposit the amount in a cash-equivalent security with check-writing privileges.
- Begin replenishing the depleted assets at once by lump-sum OCP contributions, when possible, and temporarily modified DCA allocations.
- When restructuring from growth to income, begin by switching your current holdings from a DRP to a systematic withdrawal plan that meets your income objectives while preserving as much of your principal as possible. If that amount isn't sufficient, sell your more aggressive growth securities and reinvest the proceeds in more income-oriented securities, choosing the cash withdrawal option.
- With a little thought and planning, even modest portfolios can provide a reliable stream of income for a surprisingly long time.

Appendixes:
A Compendium
of Frugal
Investing Tips,
Tricks, and
Resources

Appendix A

Federal Reserve Banks and Treasury Servicing Offices

The following addresses and telephone numbers may be used to obtain additional information about, and tender forms for, all Treasury investments.

Addresses and Telephone Numbers of Federal Reserve Banks and Treasury Servicing Offices

For In-Person Visits	*For Written Correspondence*
Atlanta	
104 Mariette Street, N.W.	FRB Atlanta
Atlanta, GA	104 Marietta Street, N.W.
(404) 521-8653	Atlanta, GA 30303
(404) 521-8657 (recording)	
Baltimore	
502 South Sharp Street	Baltimore Branch
Baltimore, MD	FRB of Richmond
(301) 576-3553	P.O. Box 1378
(301) 576-3500 (recording)	Baltimore, MD 21203
Birmingham	
1801 Fifth Avenue, North	Birmingham Branch
Birmingham, AL	FRB Atlanta
(205)731-8702	P.O. Box 830447
	Birmingham, AL 35283-0447

For In-Person Visits	*For Written Correspondence*

Boston
600 Atlantic Avenue
Boston, MA
(617) 973-3810
(617) 973-3805 (recording)

FRB of Boston
P.O. Box 2076
Boston, MA 02106

Buffalo
160 Delaware Avenue
Buffalo, NY
(716) 849-5079
(716) 849-5030 (recording)

Buffalo Branch
FRB of New York
P.O. Box 961
Buffalo, NY 14240

Charlotte
530 East Trade Street
Charlotte, NC
(704) 358-2410 or 2411
(704) 358-2424 (recording)

Charlotte Branch
FRB of Richmond
P.O. Box 30248
Charlotte, NC 28230

Chicago
230 South LaSalle Street
Chicago, IL
(312) 322-5369
(312) 786-1110 (recording)

FRB of Chicago
P.O. Box 834
Chicago, IL 60690

Cincinnati
150 East Fourth Street
Cincinnati, OH
(513) 721-4787, ext. 333

Cincinnati Branch
FRB of Cleveland
P.O. Box 999
Cincinnati, OH 45201

Cleveland
1455 East Sixth Street
Cleveland, OH
(212) 579-2490

FRB of Cleveland
P.O. Box 6387
Cleveland, OH 44101

Dallas
400 South Akard Street
Dallas, TX
(214) 651-6362
(214) 651-6177 (recording)

FRB of Dallas
Securities Dept.
Station K
Dallas, TX 75222

For In-Person Visits	*For Written Correspondence*

Denver
1020 16th Street
Denver, CO
(303) 572-2477
(303) 572-2475 (recording)

Denver Branch
FRB of Kansas City
P.O. Box 5228
Terminal Annex
Denver, CO 80217

Detroit
160 West Fort Street
Detroit, MI
(313) 964-6157
(313) 963-4963 (recording)

Detroit Branch
FRB of Chicago
P.O. Box 1059
Detroit, MI 48231

El Paso
301 East Main Street
El Paso, TX
Call Dallas
(214) 651-6362
(214) 651-6177 (recording)

El Paso Branch
FRB of Dallas
P.O. Box 100
El Paso, TX 79999

Houston
1701 San Jacinto Street
Houston, TX
(713) 659-4433
(713) 652-1688 (recording)

Houston branch
FRB of Dallas
P.O. Box 2578
Houston, TX 77252

Jacksonville
800 West Water Street
Jacksonville, FL
(904) 632-1179

Jacksonville Branch
FRB of Atlanta
P.O. Box 2499
Jacksonville, FL 32231-2499

Kansas City
925 Grand Avenue
Kansas City, MO
(816) 881-2783 or 2409
(816) 881-2767 (recording)

FRB of Kansas City
Attn. Securities Dept.
P.O. Box 419440
Kansas City, MO 64141-6440

Little Rock
325 West Capitol Avenue
Little Rock, AR
(501) 372-5451, ext. 288

Little Rock Branch
FRB of St.Louis
P.O. Box 1261
Little Rock, AR 72203

For In-Person Visits	*For Written Correspondence*

Los Angeles
950 South Grand Avenue
Los Angeles, CA
(213) 624-7398
(213) 688-0068 (recording)

Los Angeles Branch
FRB of San Francisco
P.O. Box 2077
Terminal Annex
Los Angeles, CA 90051

Louisville
410 South Fifth Street
Louisville, KY
(502) 568-9236 or 9231

Louisville Branch
FRB of St.Louis
P.O. Box 32710
Louisville, KY 40232

Memphis
200 North Main Street
Memphis, TN
(901) 523-7171
Ext. 622 or 629
Ext. 641 (recording)

Memphis Branch
FRB of St.Louis
P.O. Box 407
Memphis, TN 38101

Miami
9100 N.W. 36th Street
Miami, FL
(305) 471-6497

Miami Branch
FRB of Atlanta
P.O. Box 520847
Miami, FL 33152-0847

Minneapolis
250 Marquette Avenue
Minneapolis, MN
(612) 340-2075

FRB of Minneapolis
P.O. Box 491
Minneapolis, MN 55480

Nashville
301 Eighth Avenue, North
Nashville, TN
(615) 251-7100

Nashville Branch
FRB of Atlanta
301 Eighth Avenue, North
Nashville, TN 37203

New Orleans
515 St. Charles Avenue
New Orleans, LA
(504) 586-1505
Ext. 293 or 294

New Orleans Branch
FRB of Atlanta
P.O. Box 61630
New Orleans, LA 70161

For In-Person Visits	*For Written Correspondence*

New York
33 Liberty Street
New York, NY
(212) 720-6619 (recording)
(212) 720-5823 (results)
(212) 720-7773 (new offerings)

FRB of New York
Federal Reserve P.O. Station
New York, NY 10045

Oklahoma City
226 Dean A. McGee Avenue
Oklahoma City, OK
(405) 270-8652

Oklahoma City Branch
FRB of Kansas City
P.O. Box 25129
Oklahoma City, OK 73125

Omaha
2201 Farnam Street
Omaha, NE
(402) 221-5636

Omaha Branch
FRB of Kansas City
P.O. Box 3958
Omaha, NE 68102

Philadelphia
Ten Independence Mall
Philadelphia, PA
(215) 574-6675 or 6680

FRB of Philadelphia
P.O. Box 90
Philadelphia, PA 19105-0090

Pittsburgh
717 Grant Street
Pittsburgh, PA
(412) 261-7863
(412) 261-7988 (recording)

Pittsburgh Branch
FRB of Cleveland
P.O. Box 867
Pittsburgh, PA 15230-0867

Portland
915 S.W. Stark Street
Portland, OR
(503) 221-5932
(503) 221-5921 (recording)

Portland Branch
FRB of San Francisco
P.O. Box 3436
Portland, OR 97208-3436

Richmond
701 East Byrd Street
Richmond, VA
(804) 697-8372
(804) 697-8355 (recording)

FRB of Richmond
P.O. Box 27622
Richmond, VA 23261-7622

For In-Person Visits	*For Written Correspondence*

Salt Lake City
120 South State Street
Salt Lake City, UT
(801) 322-7944
(801) 322-7911 (recording)

Salt Lake City Branch
FRB of San Francisco
P.O. Box 30780
Salt Lake City, UT 84130

San Antonio
126 East Nueva Street
San Antonio, TX
(512) 978-1305 or 1309
(512) 978-1330 (recording)

San Antonio Branch
FRB of Dallas
P.O. Box 1471
San Antonio, TX 78295

San Francisco
101 Market Street
San Francisco, CA
(415) 974-2330
(415) 974-3491 (recording)

FRB of San Francisco
P.O. Box 7702
San Francisco, CA 94120-7702

Seattle
1015 Second Avenue
Seattle, WA
(206) 343-3605
(206) 343-3615 (recording)

Seattle Branch
FRB of San Francisco
P.O. Box 3567
Terminal Annex
Seattle, WA 98124

St. Louis
411 Locust Street
St. Louis, MO
(314) 444-8665 or 8666
(314) 444-8602 (recording)

FRB of St.Louis
P.O. Box 442
St. Louis, MO 63166

United States Treasury
Washington, D.C.

Bureau of the Public Debt
1300 C Street, S.W.
Washington, D.C.
(202) 287-4113

Mail inquiries to
Bureau of the Public Debt
Washington, D.C. 20239-1000

Device for hearing impaired:
(202) 287-4097

Mail tenders to:
Bureau of the Public Debt
Washington, D.C. 20239-1500

Appendix B

Sample Mutual Fund Account Application Form

The numbers below match those on the accompanying sample mutual fund "Account Application" form which I've selected as typical of its kind and not as any particular product recommendation. I've only commented on those areas most often queried or misunderstood by new investors:

Step 1. This area specifies how you want your mutual fund account to be registered for tax and legal purposes. If you want a spouse to have equal access to the fund, specify joint ownership. If you do not want your spouse to have automatic survivor's rights in case of your death, you must mention that here. If you're buying the fund as custodian for a minor child, the distributions from the fund will be taxable on the child's IRS return. Above all, be sure your social security number (SSN) is entered correctly. Although this particular form allows you to certify your social security or taxpayer's identification number with a signature on the form, some mutual fund companies require submittal of a separate IRS Form W-9. If so, that form will normally be included with your kit.

Step 3. This particular form lists in this section a number of funds within the investment company's fund family. This allows you to open several accounts at once merely by checking the name of the funds, entering the amount you want to invest in each, and paying with a single check for the total of all your choices. Make sure you observe any minimum investment amounts.

Step 5. Here's where you specify any additional features you may want for your account. All Frugal Investors should select the fund's DRP option on their initial investment. If you intend to make dollar-cost average (DCA) contributions, you can do so automatically as part of a payroll deduction (or Treasury or Government Direct) plan—a painless way to save provided you can afford the deduction you select. I discourage wire transfer or telephone redemption provisions since you'll withdraw cash very infrequently and the few days you'll save seldom justifies the added cost. If you're investing for current income, check the box that stipulates how you want to receive your Dividends/Capital Gains Distributions. The prospectus will tell you if other options, such as a systematic withdrawal program, are available. Remember, too, that any account option can be cancelled if it no longer suits your situation. (See Figure B-1.)

Figure B-1. New Account Application.

The Benham Group®

For personal service call: 1-800-472-3389
between 6 a.m. and 5 p.m. Pacific Time, Monday-Friday.

Account Application

Please call for a Tax-Free Funds, IRA or Pension/Profit Sharing (Keogh) account application.

All account owners must complete Steps 1,2,3 and 4. Please read the prospectus of the Fund(s) in which you plan to invest. Do not send cash.

STEP 1: OPEN YOUR ACCOUNT — *Tell us how you would like your account registered.*

☐ **Individual**
Complete line 1

1. First Name, Initial, Last Name — Social Security Number

☐ **Joint Registrant**
Complete lines 1 & 2

2. Social Security Number
Joint tenants with right of survivorship presumed, unless otherwise indicated:
For joint owners, the first name and Social Security Number listed will be used for IRS reporting unless alternate instructions are given.

☐ **Transfers to Minors**
Complete lines 3, 4 & 5. Only one minor and custodian can be registered on a single account.

3. Custodian's Name — Minor's State of Residence
4. Minor's Name — Minor's Social Security Number
5. Minor's Birthdate
Some states permit the nomination of a Successor Custodian and/or continuation of a custodianship beyond the beneficiary's age of majority. Consult your investment or legal advisor.
Successor Custodian — Age Custodianship Terminates

☐ **Trust,** ☐ **Estate or** ☐ **Conservatorship**
Check one and complete lines 6, 7 & 8. If grantor trust, provide grantor's/trustee's social security number. For all other entities, provide tax ID number.

6. Trustee, Executor, Guardian, Conservator — Social Security Number
7. Trustee, Executor, Guardian, Conservator — Social Security Number
8. Trust Name, Estate, Conservatorship - If no Tax I.D. Number is provided, the Social Security Number on line 6 will be used for IRS reporting — Trust Date (If applicable) — Tax Identification Number

☐ **Corporations & Other Organizations**
Complete line 9 and Step 7 on the reverse of this form.

9. Name of Corporation or Other Organization — Tax Identification Number

STEP 2: ADDRESS — *Please provide all information requested in this section.*

For Multiple Registrant Accounts, use the birthdate of the individual first named on the account.

Street or P.O. Box — Individual Owner's Birthdate — Daytime Telephone ( )

U.S. citizen: ☐ Yes ☐ No
If no, specify country of citizenship below.

City — State — Zip Code — Evening Telephone ( )

STEP 3: CHOOSE YOUR INVESTMENT(S) — *Indicate amount to invest in each Fund ($1,000 minimum).*

Please indicate amount to invest in each fund ($1,000 minimum). Make a separate check payable to each of the funds in which you plan to invest.

Money Market Funds *(Check writing included)*

☐ Capital Preservation (01) $
☐ Capital Preservation II (02) $
☐ Government Agency (71) $

Stock Funds

☐ Gold Equities Index (80) $
☐ Income & Growth (81) $
☐ Equity Growth (82) $
☐ Utilities Income (83) $

Bond Funds

☐ Adjust. Rate Govt. Securities
Check here for check writing ☐ (72) $
☐ GNMA Income
Check here for check writing ☐ (70) $
☐ Short-Term Treasury and Agency (73) $
☐ Treasury Note (50) $
☐ Long-Term Treasury and Agency (74) $

International Fund

☐ European Govt. Bond (92) $

Zero-Coupon Bond Funds

☐ Target Maturities Trust
1995 Portfolio (62) $
2000 Portfolio (63) $
2005 Portfolio (64) $
2010 Portfolio (65) $
2015 Portfolio (66) $
2020 Portfolio (67) $

Other Funds (be specific)

☐ $

STEP 4: SIGNATURE(S) & CERTIFICATION — *All account owners must read, sign and date this section.*

PLEASE DO NOT WRITE IN THIS SPACE

If you do not indicate the number of required signatures, *any one* account owner may sign checks and/or written redemption requests:
Please check number of signatures required to process checks and/or written redemption requests: ☐ **One** ☐ **Two** ☐ **Three** ☐ **Four**

I certify under penalties of perjury that the Tax Identification Number shown in this application is my (the payee's) correct number, or I am (the payee is) waiting for a number to be issued to me (the payee), AND I am (the payee is) not subject to backup withholding because: (a) I am (the payee is) exempt from backup withholding, or (b) I have (the payee has) not been notified by the Internal Revenue Service (IRS) that I am (the payee is) subject to backup withholding as a result of a failure to report all interest or dividends, or (c) the IRS has notified me (the payee) that I am (the payee is) no longer subject to backup withholding.

☐ Check this box ONLY if the IRS has informed you that you are subject to backup withholding.

I am of legal age. I have received and read the Prospectus(es) for the Fund(s) in which I intend to invest, and I agree to its (their) terms. I understand that neither the Funds nor Benham Distributors, Inc. are banks and that Fund shares are neither backed nor guaranteed by any bank nor insured by the FDIC. Further, I understand that by signing below: (1) instructions given in Step 5 will apply to any account opened with the proceeds of exchanges until or unless I give alternate instructions; (2) Benham Financial Services, Inc. may accept orders to exchange or redeem shares from my account(s) which are communicated via telephone; (3) neither the Fund(s) nor Benham Financial Services, Inc. will be liable for any loss, cost, or expense for acting on instructions believed by them to be genuine and in accordance with the procedures described in the Prospectus; (4) I agree that I will read the Prospectus for any Fund into which I intend to exchange before I place my exchange order.

ALL ACCOUNT OWNERS MUST SIGN BELOW. (Minors & Successor Custodians are not authorized signers.) Date

X X

X X

THE BENHAM GROUP, 1665 CHARLESTON ROAD, MOUNTAIN VIEW, CALIFORNIA 94043

(Form continued on back) 3/93

Figure B-1. New Account Application *(continued)*.

Benham Money Market, Stock and Bond Funds Account Application

Please call for a Tax-Free Funds or Retirement Account Application (1-800-472-3389).

PLEASE DO NOT REMOVE LABEL

STEP 5: ACCOUNT SERVICES DESIGNATION

All accounts opened with this application will have dividends/capital gains distributions reinvested unless you give us alternate instructions. To transfer money to or from your bank, please attach a voided check or complete bank information below.

Dividends/Capital Gains Distributions will be automatically reinvested unless you check one of the following boxes:

DIVIDENDS Pay to: ☐ my home address ☐ my bank account OR ☐ Direct to the following Benham account #

CAPITAL GAINS Pay to: ☐ my home address ☐ my bank account OR ☐ Direct to the following Benham account #

Automatic Investment Services – To establish a regular, automatic investment program from your bank, please fill in the information that applies. Your automatic investments may not begin until the following month.

☐ BANK DIRECT – Transfer $_____ ($25 minimum/account) from my bank on the: ☐ 1st of the month AND/OR ☐ 15th of the month to the following Benham account number(s):

Any co-owner of your bank account who is not a co-owner of your Benham account must sign here:

Bank Information

Bank Name

Bank Address

City   State   Zip Code

Name in Which Account is Registered

Bank Account Number

☐ Checking Account ☐ Savings Account

Bank Routing or ABA Number (If unknown, your bank can furnish this.)

For other automatic investments to your Benham account, check below to receive the forms you need to invest.

☐ PAYROLL DIRECT – to deposit any part of your paycheck.
☐ TREASURY DIRECT – to deposit interest and principal payments from Treasury securities.
☐ GOVERNMENT DIRECT – to deposit your entire government payment.

STEP 6: DUPLICATE/COMBINED STATEMENT REQUEST

If you want someone else to receive a copy of your statement and to access information on your account by phone, please complete this section.

Name   ☐ This is a broker/dealer or financial advisor.

Address

☐ Check here to authorize this person to transact on your account and we will send you a Limited Power of Attorney form.

To combine the quarterly statements you receive for your new account(s) with those of another identically registered Benham account, please provide the other account number here:

STEP 7: CORPORATIONS/ORGANIZATIONS/PARTNERSHIPS

Please specify type of entity here: ☐ Incorporated ☐ Nonprofit ☐ Sole Owner ☐ Partnership

I, _____ (NAME OF CERTIFYING PERSON OR OFFICER) _____ (CORPORATION/ORGANIZATION/PARTNERSHIP) hereinafter "Organization"), incorporated or organized under the laws of the state of _____ certify that the following is a true copy of a resolution now in full force and effect, adopted on _____, 19___

RESOLVED, that any ☐ one ☐ two ☐ three ☐ four of the persons whose names and signatures appear below are authorized to establish and maintain accounts with any Benham fund or trust and to effect purchases and redemptions of shares on behalf of this organization. I further certify that an authorized agent of the corporation has read, understands and agrees to the terms of the Prospectus for each Fund in which the corporation is investing.

Print Name	Title	Signature
Print Name	Title	Signature
Print Name	Title	Signature
Print Name	Title	Signature

☐ Check here if no corporate seal (corporations only)

CORPORATE SEAL

X _____
Signature of Certifying Person or Officer   Date

All required signers must also sign Step 4 (Signature(s) & Certification) on the front of this application.

228

Appendix C

Interpreting Investment Information

Data—an orderly set of facts—is cheap and plentiful. Good information based on that data is less plentiful and a lot more valuable. Knowledge gained through the interpretation of information is rarer and more valuable still. In fact, we call it *power*.

In Frugal Investing, knowledgeable decisions are made by applying insights and experience to information supplied by a variety of data analysts—virtually all of it obtained *free* from securities companies, brokerage firms, Uncle Sam, magazines, newspapers, and market newsletters carried at the nearest public or college library. In this appendix, I'll show you how to expand your Frugal Investing knowledge by offering my own insights and experience to the best of the commonly available investment information sources.

General Information Sources

The decade of the 1990s has been hailed as the first milestone on the new information "superhighway." While this sounds great and evokes images of high-tech schoolkids, scientists, and businesspeople zooming effortlessly through virtual reality, the *real* reality is that most of us will continue to depend on the tried and true methods of gaining information: reference books, specialty magazines, company and government brochures— and oh yes, don't forget the daily newspaper.

Good Books On Investing

You might want to check out one or a few of the following books from your local library for more detailed background information on specific markets and additional investing techniques:

• *Beating the Street*, Peter Lynch with John Rothchild (Simon & Schuster, New York). This entertaining bestseller by the mastermind of Fidelity's Magellan Fund presents a lot of useful information about picking stocks and understanding how mutual funds work.

• *Bogle on Mutual Funds*, John C. Bogle (Irwin, Burr Ridge, Ill). Vanguard's "Chairman Bogle" explains how indexing will, and perhaps already has, conquered the investing world. A natural Frugal Investor, Bogle's analysis of fund fees and annual reports are excellent.

• *How Mutual Funds Work*, Albert J. Fredman and Russ Wiles (New York Institute of Finance, New York). If you're the kind of investor who wants to know how a clock works in order to tell the time, this book is for you. Professor Fredman packs a lot of basic information about risk, return, and market timing into what amounts to a surprisingly readable textbook.

Investment Magazines and Newspapers

Most periodicals on investing seem torn between a desire to entertain (that is, to keep up with the latest financial trends and industry gossip) and inform: to give readers what they really need as well as what editors think they want. Here are a few that seem to do both successfully most of the time:

• *The Wall Street Journal:* Referenced frequently throughout this book, the WSJ is simply the best single source for general, economic, and investment news there is. Check especially the recurring column, "Your Money Matters."

• *Kiplinger's:* Formerly called *Changing Times*, this venerable magazine (launched in 1947) is as old as many of the Baby Boomers who read it. If you don't mind the rather pungent style, conservative outlook, and ventures into consumer issues unrelated to finance, it often contains useful nuggets of Frugal Investing information.

• *Smart Money:* Flamboyant and fun to read, this magazine is one of the few that actually keeps track of the performance of the investments it recommends. Despite the glitzy design and iconoclastic appeal, its editorial parents (*The Wall Street Journal* and Dow Jones) add substance to the contents.

Investment Newsletters and Research Sources

Most libraries will contain one or all of the biggest and most popular investment newsletters, including their research addendums (usually updated quarterly) and forecast issues. Each contains a wealth of data and information about securities, mostly domestic stocks:

The Value Line Investment Survey
711 Third Avenue
New York, NY 10017

Standard & Poor's The Outlook
25 Broadway
New York, NY 10004

United Business & Investment Report
210 Newbury Street
Boston, MA 02116

Of these big three, I like Value Line best (I'll come back to it shortly) because of its statistical comprehensiveness and objective evaluations—both of great value to long-term investors.

If you're interested in IPOs, I recommend *New Issues* as much for its calendar of upcoming offerings as its analysis and advice. Write:

Institute for Econometric Research
3471 N. Federal Highway
Fort Lauderdale, FL 33306

For S&P-style information (such as ten-year financial performance summaries, investment analysis, etc.) on over 700 (out of 900) specific foreign companies, Morningstar has launched a new publication—the first of its kind—available in some libraries, or by subscription. If you're interested, contact:

American Depositary Receipt
Morningstar Mutual Funds
1-800-876-5005

Why You Shouldn't Rely on Your Broker's Newsletter

Some novice investors think that the research publications of a big wire-house like Merrill Lynch, or even a discounter like Charles Schwab, are all they need because millions of dollars are pumped into them and they're offered free (or at a nominal cost) to clients. They say that if you look past the blatant ads for the brokerage firm's products, you can find lots of good information about the markets.

To this rational-sounding advice I reply, Well, maybe. Yes, broker-supplied information about economic trends can be useful, particularly when you compare it to what you hear or read from other sources. Unfortunately, broker-supplied information, or even information supplied by independent analysts specializing in a given product area, is *never* completely unbiased. Why? Because researchers, by definition, have a vested interest—even a great affection if not a passion—for their field. Such people have a tendency to always find something "important" to say (or at least important sounding) when they're asked their opinion on their favorite topic. As a result, specialists on growth stocks or emerging world markets or whatever almost *always* have something positive to tout, or a recommendation to make, about the beloved object of their time and attention. As asset allocators, Frugal Investors can never afford to "fall in love" with their investments and shouldn't seek advice from people who do.

Computerized Investing Assistance

The vehicle of choice on the new communications superhighway for many is the home computer. Armed with the right software and a modem, you can now conduct virtually all of the trades, and much of the analysis, people used to spend an arm and a leg to obtain from brokers and other sources. If you're such a techie, here are a few software candidates you might consider:

Schwab's Street Smart

For under $60, Big Three discounter Charles Schwab will equip its account holders with the Windows-oriented *Street Smart*, a software trading package that also offers access to the Dow Jones news service and over 5,000 Schwab research reports. For do-it-yourself trades, you'll save a further 10 percent on the Schwab commission. For securities research, you'll receive one hour of free access to Dow Jones and another for company reports and price updates. After that, you start paying a couple of dollars for each minute you're plugged into the network. A slightly smaller fee is charged for each thousand data characters you download after you're in the system. Unless you're a stock chaser who's willing to spend lots of money on your hobby, you probably won't want to use this software too often.

Fidelity's Online Xpress

The second-biggest discounter, Fidelity, offers similar software (and a similar trading discount) for $49.95 to its customers, called *Online Xpress*, but without the Windows format. If you don't mind working with DOS and like Fidelity as a broker, you might want to check it out.

E*TRADE

E*Trade, a Silicon Valley pioneer in electronic trading, has eliminated the human element altogether and allows consumers to trade by touch-tone phone and computer for only $25.

NATIONAL DISCOUNT BROKERS

Another discount house, National Discount Brokers, will whack 20 percent from its usual $25 trading charge if you use a touch-tone system and leave the broker out of the loop.

EVERGREEN'S *DIVIDEND REINVESTMENT PORTFOLIO TRACKER*

Serious DRP investors with IBM-DOS and compatibles might want to try Evergreen Enterprises (301-953-1861) no-frills, easy to use investment tracking package. This program has no graphics, but if you consistently enter the information from your DRP-OCP statements, it will handle one of the most tedious aspects of stock recordkeeping: identifying the cost basis of your shares—a godsend at tax time for liquidated shares.

OTHER TECHNICAL SOFTWARE

Mutual fund shoppers may appreciate the Business Week Mutual Fund Scoreboard for use on IBM-PC and compatibles. It offers data and performance results for over 2,185 equity and 2,183 bond funds, with

monthly updates for $299 per year. Its best feature, though, is a customiz-
able screening program that allows you to isolate funds based on twenty-
five different parameters you can set yourself, including the frugal investing criteria I've given you in this book. If you're interested, contact:

> Business Week Mutual Scoreboard
> P.O. Box 1597
> Ft. Lee, NJ 07024
> 1-800-553-3575

Another popular analytical program is *FundWise*, also for IBM-PC.
This software specializes in performance data for no-load funds and features many graphic bells and whistles, such as timeline comparison of
competing funds, and comparisons of actively managed funds against a
relevant index. One feature Frugal Investors may like is a subroutine that
allows you to generate a portfolio of funds whose historic performance, if
continued, would meet specific investment goals. If this sounds good to
you, contact:

> FundWise Financial Sciences
> 261 Hamilton Ave, Ste 215
> Palo Alto, CA 94301
> 1-800-323-9822

If you're thinking seriously about jumping into the electronic trading
pool, be sure to ask any potential vendor about options and procedures
that protect investor interests. What happens if you get confused by various telephone codes or forget the symbol for your shares? A human voice
shouldn't be far away or the firm shouldn't take so long to solve your
problem that you've forgotten about the question. Also, be sure adequate
records (such as hard-copy trade confirmations) are provided and that
account access is reasonably secure.

How to Interpret a Stock Price Quotation

Although it's old news before the ink is dry on the newsprint, securities
price quotations are published daily in most metropolitan papers and in
national financial publications like *The Wall Street Journal* and *Investor's
Business Daily*. As long as you view such data in its true "historical" perspective, you won't get into trouble. Open your local paper or a recent

issue of the WSJ to the financial pages and follow along from left to right as I interpret a typical entry:

- *High and Low:* These are the best and worst prices the stock has experienced during the past year. If the stock "split" (doubled its outstanding shares while halving its value) or declared a dividend bigger than 25 percent, the high and low period will begin from that event.
- *Stocks:* This is the abbreviation or trading symbol for the stock. The quotation always applies to common stock unless a "pf" after the symbol shows the stock is preferred.
- *Div:* This is the size of the most recent annualized dividend, in dollars and cents per share. The bigger this number is, the faster your portfolio will grow in the company's DRP program.
- *Yld %:* This is the annualized dividend return, or dividend yield, calculated by dividing the dividend by that day's closing price. Income-oriented investors like this number to be very big, but even growth-oriented investors want to see some dividend yield because it indicates a well-managed company. As this book is being written, any dividend yield over 3 to 3½ percent is considered reasonably high, although this varies with the industry and overall economic climate.
- *P/E Ratio:* This is the so-called price-to-earnings ratio, computed by dividing the current share price by the company's most recent annual per-share earnings. A P/E ratio of 10, for example, means that the price of the stock is ten times the dollar value that each share "earned" over the last reported period. Stocks with low P/E ratios are considered undervalued and are often sought by bargain hunters. Of course, these stocks may also simply reflect poorly run companies, although this supposition is already built into the stock's lower price, which is determined by market action. Thus earnings gain meaning mostly from their historical context: Has the company been able to boost or sustain them through good times and bad? Unfortunately, the stock quotations tell you nothing about this. For longer term information, you'll have to go to one of the industry's standard references, such as the *Value Line Investment Survey* or the company's annual report—both information sources presented later in this appendix.
- *Sales in 100s:* This is the number of shares that changed hands during the course of the day's trading. This information is used primarily by technical analysts who try to predict future price changes based on the "volume" and "momentum" (or rate of change in volume) of such sales. Since this matters mostly to market timers, Frugal Investors can safely ignore it.

• *High, Low, Close, Net Chg:* The remaining quotations show the day's trading results: best, worst, and last price of the stock, and the dollar value of any "net change." For example, a stock that began trading at $20 per share and closed at $22.50 would show a net change of "+2½." A net loss is preceded by a minus. This performance range gives stock market charts their distinctive appearance: the high/low/close range appears as a short vertical line for each time period plotted. As time along the horizontal axis increases, the collection of "daily ranges" forms a pattern from which the larger price cycles of the stock may be easily seen.

The meaning of a stock's price is relative: You're interested more in *changes* to that price after you purchase it than you are in the absolute dollar value of each share, since that's how capital gain is determined. However, very cheap stocks (those below $5 per share) are usually valued that low for a reason, and are considered highly speculative.

• *Footnotes:* Obviously, the standard quotation is more a sketch than a portrait of a stock's activity—even on a daily basis. On many issues, you'll see a variety of letters denoting footnotes printed (and sketchily defined) elsewhere in the listing. Footnote codes of special interest to Frugal Investors include:

a   *Also extra, or extras*—means an extra dividend was paid during the past year.

b   *Annual rate plus stock dividend*—means that stock was issued, as well as cash, as a dividend to shareholders.

j   *Paid this year, dividend omitted, deferred, or no action taken last meeting*—means that the dividend shown, for some reason, may not be continued.

x   *Ex-dividend or ex-rights*—means the ex-dividend occurred on this date.

How to Read a Data Page in Value Line

Altough the *Value Line Investment Survey* is one of the best sources of unbiased stock information around, its cavalcade of useful information first appears like an avalanche of useless facts to the uninitiated. Fortunately, Frugal Investors must inspect only a few entries to find out what they need. The numbers in Figure C-1 correspond to the numbers shown on the accompanying sample page:

1. *Check the stock's price volatility. Beta* is the measure of a particular stock's price volatility compared to other stocks in the market, with the

Figure C-1.

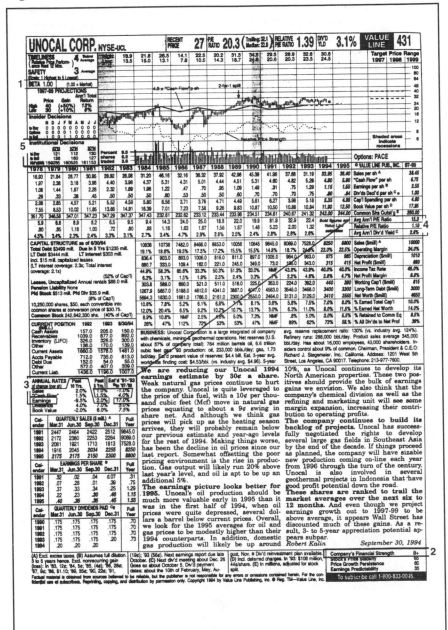

index beta as 1.0. More volatile stocks will have betas greater than 1.0 (that is, their prices will change *faster* than those of the index) and less volatile stocks will have a beta *less* than one, meaning their prices will change more slowly.

Value Line publishes the beta for each stock in the upper left-hand area of the page. Since Frugal Investors focus on long-term results, I recommend only those stocks with betas between 0.9 and 1.2, or stocks whose prices will vary within 10 to 20 percent of the market average. Extremely aggressive investors may want to skew their selections toward more volatile stocks (betas of 1.3 to 1.4) but they should be prepared to ride the volatility roller coaster throughout the life of their portfolio, including the adverse effect this can have on compounded returns. Conservative or income-oriented investors will be happiest with stocks at or slightly below the 1.0 index.

2. *Check the issuing firm's financial health.* In the lower right corner of the page, you'll find Value Line's "letter grade" for the company's overall financial strength. This grade is based on the application of generally accepted accounting tests and ratios. Since you plan to hold your shares a very long time, disqualify any firm that doesn't score an "A."

3. *Examine the company's earnings history.* If the company's financial strength is excellent, go to the box on the lower left-hand panel labeled "Annual Rates of Change Per Share." The entry you want is the third one down, marked "Earnings." If the percentage shown for the "Past 5 Years" is negative—meaning that the firm, regardless of its financial strength, has been unable to operate profitably over the last business cycle—forget it and go on to the next stock on your list.

4. *Match the stock's performance with your growth or income objectives.* Your final check ensures that the company can probably deliver the performance you need to meet your investment goals, all other things being equal.

If you're a growth-oriented investor, look at the column just to the right of the "Past 5 Year Earnings" you used in number 3. This gives the estimated growth rate for the next three years. Now, divide this number by the "Avg Ann'l P/E Ratio" stated in the box below "Beta" on the right-hand side of the page. The higher the resulting number, the better the prospects for growth. From among your finalists, choose only those stocks with the highest "growth-to-P/E" ratio.

If you're income-oriented, perform the same calculation as above but for stocks that show the highest average annual dividend yield ("Avg Ann'l Div'd Yield"—which is printed just below the average annual P/E ratio you just used). This will ensure that the high-yielding

stocks you chose for income will likely have the growth capability needed to sustain those dividends.

5. *When in doubt, go with the big institutions.* If you're a very conservative investor or just a person who feels better if a "respected authority"
endorses your choice, look just below the chart at the upper left of the page
to the box labeled "Institutional Decisions." Divide the last number in the
table by the number of "common shares outstanding" (use the last number for the most recent year in the table below the chart) to get the percentage of stock held by institutional investors. If all your other (now very
highly qualified) candidates seem pretty much the same, you may want to
choose those with the largest percentage of institutional ownership.

How to Read a Data Page from Morningstar Mutual Funds

Similar to Value Line, but serving group investors, is Morningstar—a
great source of independent information on mutual funds. The following
numbers correspond to the appropriate data location on Figure C-2.

1. *Historical profile:* This qualitative assessment is your preliminary
guide to the suitability of a particular fund for Frugal Investing. Check the
risk (it should be low) and the rating, which should be four or five stars.

2. *3-, 5- and 10-year rating:* This chart shows the risk/return history of
the fund for its first three, then five, then ten years of operation. Look for
an average historical rating of four or higher.

3. *Investment style:* Morningstar uses this clever cube for both equity
and fixed-income funds, so its scales will depend on the type of fund evaluated. For fixed-income funds, maturities are matched against quality so
you want the dark squares to be in the middle or to the left side of the box
(high rated bonds and shorter maturities). For equity funds, the "sweet
spot" of the grid is in the middle and upper squares.

4. *Portfolio breakdown:* Make a qualitative inspection of the securities
in the fund's portfolio. Most of the names should be well-known companies. In the Credit Analysis portion at the lower right, look for the 50 percent break point: At least half of the securities should be of a rating and
type that match your investment objectives. For example, a high-yield
bond fund shopper would want at least half the fund in lower-rated, or
noninstitutional junk bonds.

5. *Sales fees:* All Frugal Investors want no-load funds, the first item on
the list. Next, check the minimum initial purchase: make sure it's afford-

Figure C-2. Vanguard F/I Short-Term Corporate.

Volume 22, Issue Number 8. 6/24/94. Reprinted with permission.

Vanguard F/I Short-Term Corporate

Objective	Load	Yield	SEC Yield	Assets ($mil)	NAV
Corp Hi Qlty	None	5.5%	N/A	3370.9	10.53

Vanguard Fixed-Income Securities Short-Term Corporate Portfolio seeks income consistent with liquidity and minimum principal fluctuation.
The fund invests in short-term investment-grade bonds and other fixed-income securities. It is expected to maintain an average weighted maturity between one and three years. Not more than 30% of the fund's assets may be invested in debt securities rated BBB. The fund may also invest in U.S. government securities, bank obligations, commercial paper, repurchase agreements, and foreign securities.
Prior to Oct. 28, 1991, the fund was named Vanguard Fixed-Income Securities Short-Term Bond.

Historical Profile
Return Average
Risk   Low
Rating ★★★★★ Highest

Analysis by Kyleiane Purcell 06/10/94

Vanguard Fixed-Income Securities Short-Term Corporate Portfolio has a few risks up its sleeve, but they've only enhanced its magic.

Comanagers Bob Auwaerter and Ian MacKinnon also run two other Vanguard short-term portfolios: Short-Term Federal and the newer Short-Term U.S. Treasury. At each, the duo tries to wrangle the most income and capital gain out of the one- to four-year bond markets. They've had the most success with this fund: Over the past three years, this fund has posted better returns, higher yields, and a lower risk score than either of its siblings.

This fund's success results from Auwaerter and MacKinnon's making hay of a sunny market. The two take an active approach to all their funds; with this vehicle, they seek out uncommon spreads between sectors or credit qualities, and they augment income with a few high-paying issues from such less-trafficked markets as taxable municipal bonds, Yankee bonds, and some foreign issues. These choices are not available to them at their government-bond portfolios.

Often, seeking unusual opportunities incurs extra risks: Although this fund sticks to investment-grade debt, it is subject to more credit risk than are its government siblings. For example, the fund suffered its very first default last year on a small Towers Health Care position. So far in the 1990s, however, the bond markets have been interest-rate driven, and as a result less-rate-sensitive corporates have been steady performers. This explains why this fund has performed better than its siblings in good markets and bad.

If credit quality becomes more of a market concern, the fund's extra risks may nibble at a record that has also outdistanced most short-term corporate portfolios. Even so, this fund will still be a solid choice for those fearful of losing their principal—and, because of low expenses, it will offer as much or more yield than its competitors.

Address	Vanguard Financial Ctr. P.O. Box 2600 Valley Forge, PA 19482
Telephone	800-662-7447 / 215-669-1000
Portfolio Manager	I. MacKinnon (10/82)/R. Auwaerter (1/84)
Advisor	Vanguard's Fixed-Income Group
Subadvisor	None
Distributor	Vanguard Group
Ticker	VFSTX
States Available	All

Sales Fees	No-load
Management Fee	Provided at cost.
3-5-,10-yr Expense Projections	$8, $15, $33
Min Initial Purchase	$3000 (Add'l: $100)
Min IRA Purchase	$500 (Add'l: $100)
Min Auto Invest Plan	$3000 (Systematic Inv: $50)
Shareholder Report Grade	A-
Date of Inception	10/29/82

© 1994 Morningstar, Inc. All rights reserved. 225 W. Wacker Dr., Chicago, IL 60606. 312-696-6000
Although data are gathered from reliable sources, Morningstar cannot guarantee completeness and accuracy.

MORNINGSTAR Mutual Funds

able and appropriate for the investment or allocation you have in mind. Below that, check the shareholder report grade. This is Morningstar's qualitative assessment of the timeliness, completeness, and reliability of shareholder communications—accept only B+ or higher. Finally, check the date of inception, or the calendar date when the fund was established. Don't buy any fund that has not been around at least three years, although four to six (a complete business cycle) would be even better.

6. *Ticket symbol:* If the fund looks like a strong contender, note the market symbol so you'll be able to check its current quotation in the newspaper and track its performance over the years. Finally, make sure under states available that the fund is marketed to residents of your state—not all of them are.

How to Read a Data Page from Morningstar ADRs

Morningstar American Depositary Receipts does for ADRs what Value Line does for individual domestic stocks: gives you a combination qualitative and statistical evaluation in one easy-to-read, easy-to-digest format—provided you know what to look for. The numbers in Figure C-3 correspond to the following numbers:

1. *Price-to-earnings ratio:* Check the top of the page for the P/E ratio. This means the same for an ADR as it means for a U.S. stock, so your first test is: the P/E of a candidate ADR should be no worse than the P/E of its nearest, similar domestic competitor.

2. *Trailing P/E ratio:* This compares the most recent P/E to the P/Es of other listed firms in that same industry in the United States. Anything at or beneath 1.0 (which means the ADR performance is better) is acceptable.

3. *Forward P/E:* Now look directly below this number to see Morningstar's prognosis for this company's future performance. Since this is still a best guess, rather than a historical record, use it advisedly— but a forward P/E that's significantly higher than the trailing P/E should raise some flags of caution.

4. *Yield:* Now go back to the top line and check the yield, or the dividend as a percentage of share value. (Thus a 3 percent yield means that the dividend, if any, was 3 percent of the price of each share.) An ADR's yield should be comparable to the average yield of a good domestic index,

Figure C-3. Coca-Cola FEMSA.

Coca-Cola Femsa

	Price (US$)	P/E	P/B	P/Sales	Yield%	Industry	Country
	26.63	18.8	3.22	1.8	N/A	Beverages	Mexico

Coca-Cola FEMSA is a Mexican holding company. Through its subsidiaries it produces, markets, and distributes soft drinks in the Mexico City region (the Valley of Mexico territory) and southeastern Mexico (the Southeast territory). Together these territories are home to about 29% of the Mexican population. The company has the exclusive right to produce and market Coca-Cola, diet Coke, Sprite, diet Sprite, and Fanta in these territories under two bottler contracts with The Coca-Cola Company.

Profile
Size Medium Cap
Style Value
Risk N/A

Alpha N/A
Beta N/A
R² N/A

Chairman
Eugenio Garza Lagüera
CEO
Alfredo Martinez Urdal
Address
Paseo de la Reforma
No. 404, 3rd Floor
06600

Tel 525-325-0924
Fax 525-207-2211
US Tel N/A
US Fax N/A
US Exchange
NYSE (sponsored)
US Ticker KOF
Employees 11,996

Valuation Ratios

		Relative to US Industry
Trailing P/E	18.8	0.6
Forward P/E	22.0	1.6
Price/Book	3.22	1.04
Yield	N/A	N/A

Growth Rates

Avg annual %	3 Yr	5 Yr	10 Yr
Sales	N/A	N/A	N/A
Earnings	N/A	N/A	N/A
Net Worth	N/A	N/A	N/A
Dividends	N/A	N/A	N/A

Calculated per ADR in local currency.

US Accounting

	FY93 1Yr %Chg
Net Inc ($mil)	46.7 37.0
Earn/ADR ($)	1.26 21.2
Net Worth ($mil)	338.0 1,472.1

Region

Sales %	12/91	12/92	12/93
Valley of Mexico	73.2	73.5	74.9
Southeastern	26.8	26.3	25.1

Operating Margins %			
Valley of Mexico	13.1	13.3	16.1
Southeastern	15.6	11.9	10.7

Interim Result

Sales (US$mil)	3/31	6/30	9/30	12/31	Year
1992	N/A	N/A	N/A	N/A	517.4
1993	138.6	151.9	152.7	164.7	607.9
1994	149.8	—	—	—	651.6

Earnings/ADR					
1992	N/A	N/A	N/A	N/A	1.07
1993	N/A	N/A	N/A	N/A	1.42
1994	0.28	—	—	—	1.21

Dividend/ADR					
1992	N/A	N/A	N/A	N/A	0.37
1993	N/A	N/A	N/A	N/A	N/A
1994	N/A	—	—	—	0.18

Balance Sheet

Assets (US$mil)	12/92	12/93	Local Cur % Chg
Cash & Short-Term Inv	0.7	6.2	766.9
Accounts Receivable	18.2	24.8	36.5
Inventory	21.7	24.7	13.7
Other	18.6	13.3	-28.8
Current Assets	59.3	69.0	16.5
Tangible Assets	315.6	357.7	13.4
Net Investments	0.0	3.4	NMF
Other	3.8	17.4	352.7
Total	378.7	447.5	18.2

Liabilities (US$mil)			
Accounts Payable	4.1	6.6	60.3
Short-Term Debt	126.9	2.7	-97.9
Other	29.5	35.8	21.2
Current Liabilities	160.6	45.1	-71.9
Long-Term Debt	140.5	0.0	-100.0
Other	6.6	9.2	40.3
Shareholders' Equity	71.0	393.2	453.8
Total	378.7	447.5	18.2

Capital Structure as of 12/93
Equity/Capital % 87.9 Int Exp (US$mil) 35.3
Debt/Capital % 12.1 Int Coverage 3.3x
Equity consists of 242,250,000 series A shares (only owned by Mexican nationals, full voting rights), 142,500,000 series D shares (full voting rights, subject to transfer restrictions), and 90,250,000 series L shares (limited voting rights). 47.5 million equivalent ADRs.

Fiscal Year (Dec)

	1994	1985	1986	1987	1988	1989	1990	1991	1992	1993	1994	
Currency Change vs US$ %					-3.1	-15.0	-8.8	-3.8	-1.7	-0.1	-8.6	
Sales (US$mil)					424.4	421.9	420.4	487.1	517.4	607.9	651.6	
Operating Income					11.2	21.9	31.9	67.2	67.1	85.6	81.4	
Operating Margin %					2.6	5.2	7.6	13.8	13.0	14.1	12.5	
Tax Rate %					N/A	N/A	41.5	36.8	38.6	36.0		
Net Income					9.3	23.2	38.5	50.7	35.1	49.8	57.6	
Net Margin %					2.2	5.5	9.2	10.4	6.8	8.2	8.6	
Long-Term Debt					73.0	31.4	56.4	100.3	140.5	0.0	0.0	
Net Worth					245.3	224.7	206.0	97.6	71.0	393.2	406.7	
Return on Equity %					3.8	9.9	18.1	33.8	41.7	21.5	13.7	
Return on Assets %					N/A	N/A	N/A	23.9	21.8	17.3	12.2	
Equivalent ADRs (mil)					N/A	N/A	N/A	26.3	32.5	47.5	47.5	
Payout Ratio %					N/A	N/A	N/A	30.0	34.6	N/A	14.9	

Per ADR (10.0 Shares)

Sales (US$)					N/A	N/A	N/A	18.51	17.80	15.20	13.72	
Cash Flow					N/A	N/A	N/A	2.49	1.43	1.78	1.49	
Earnings					0.40	0.97	1.59	2.10	1.07	1.42	1.21	
Capital Expenditure					N/A	N/A	N/A	2.85	1.91	1.52	1.18	
Net Worth					N/A	N/A	N/A	3.71	2.19	8.28	8.56	
Dividend					N/A	N/A	N/A	0.63	0.37	N/A	0.18	

Calendar Year

		6/94
Average Price to Earnings	22.6	22.6
Average Price to Book	5.40	3.54
Average Price to Cash Flow	20.47	18.18
Average Yield %	1.33	0.00
Total Return %	37.90	-18.24
Market Capitalization (US$mil)	1,555.6	1,264.7

Analysis by Andrew Clarke 07/12/94

Coca-Cola FEMSA (CCF) is posting some refreshing numbers in the thirsty Mexican market.

In 1994's first quarter, the Mexican soft-drink bottler posted earnings of $12.6 million, a 77% gain on its performance in the first quarter of 1993. (Per-ADR profits remained unchanged, however, as CCF's 1993 equity issuance resulted in substantial dilution.) The strong performance is especially impressive in light of the Mexican economy's continued weakness. Although the nation's GDP grew at a rate of only 0.5%, CCF boosted revenues by more than 13% in the same period.

Until recently, this ADR reflected the good news, trading as high as 26 times trailing earnings in mid-February. Since then, however, the bottler's ADRs have gone flat, partly a result of political turmoil that has reverberated in Mexico's financial markets. CCF has shed about 30% of its value since the assassination of

presidential candidate Luis Donaldo Colosio. It now fetches a P/E of 18.8 —what one could expect to pay for some of the less-exciting stories in the U.S. beverage industry.

There is some basis for a bearish stance. For example, the company's operating margin narrowed in the first quarter, as the prices of sugar and Coca-Cola's concentrates rose. Hector Trevino, the company's CFO, expects this margin to remain below its 1993 level for the rest of the year. But net profits should rise, Trevino notes, thanks to stronger sales and the absence of financing expenses, which vanished when creditors agreed to swap debt for equity.

Earnings growth could proceed more quickly if CCF purchases a stake in Coca-Cola, S.A. Industrial, Comercial y Financiera. Details remain sketchy, but CCF is negotiating to buy a controlling stake in the Argentine bottler, which generated revenues of $306 million in 1993.

Ownership

Major Owners %
N/A

Mutual Funds (thous ADRs)
SteinRoe Special 440.0
Berger 101 100.0
Dean Witter Am Value 62.0
Legg Mason Spec Invmt 50.0
T Rowe Price Gr & Inc 43.0
Fidelity Sel Fd & Agrcltr 38.0
Dreyfus Growth & Incom 35.0

Insiders % N/A

Notes Italics = Morningstar estimates. The co reports according to Mexican accounting standards. In 1993, the co was incorporated on 10/31/91. Forecasts do not include acquisition of Coca-Cola, S.A. Net income and earnings/ADR include nonrecurring items of $2.3 mil (1993), -$1.2 mil (1992), and $4.9 mil (1991).

©1994 Morningstar, Inc. All rights reserved. 225 W. Wacker Dr., Chicago, IL 60606, 312-696-6000
Although data are gathered from reliable sources, Morningstar cannot guarantee completeness and accuracy.

MORNINGSTAR American Depository Receipts

Reprint

such as the S&P 500 or DOW, or a good domestic company in the same industry. If the yield is N/A or not available, call Morningstar for an update or contact the company directly.

5. *Earnings:* Reading to the left, check the ADR's earnings history: it should show a long-term, steady increase.

6. *Long-term debt:* Under liabilities in the lower left corner, ensure that the U.S. dollar-denominated long-term debt is less than the shareholder's equity, published two lines beneath it.

7. *Dividend:* Now go back to the Per ADR results midpage on the right side. The last entry is Dividend. Reading to the left, check the firm's dividend history. The absolute amount (percent) is less important than the fact that it should have been consistent, or increased steadily over time.

How to Evaluate a Mutual Fund Prospectus

Your first detailed encounter with a candidate mutual fund (or stock IPO) won't be through newspaper price quotations or Value Line, but in the investment company's *prospectus*: the legal description of the security being offered. No matter what a financial salesperson or brochure may have said, promised, or implied, the prospectus is always the last word on the investment. I recommend leaving all prospectuses in the envelope until all your candidates arrive. That way you can make head-to-head comparisons quickly and accurately and not be "charmed" by the first one you open or too fatigued with data overload to give the last one a fair reading.

Although each prospectus contains information unique to each fund or offering, they all follow generally the same format; so in that sense, if you can read and understand one, you can read and understand them all. Fortunately, Frugal Investors don't have to wade through the entire booklet (let the SEC's lawyers do that!), but deal only with the parts I'll mention here.

Step 1: Make Sure You've Received the Prospectus You Asked For

The cover of the prospectus will state the fund's "Investment Objective" and it should match your own—at least for this particular component of a particular asset class. For example, if you've decided to break your equity allocation into 50 percent for index, 25 percent for growth, and 25 percent for aggressive growth, be sure the fund objectives you inspect for these investments match the goals you have in mind. This may sound like an obvious precaution, but you'd be surprised how many novice investors misallocate (and have to switch within the first few months, incurring needless costs) simply because they got confused by some admittedly *very* similar sounding product names.

Part of this initial "quality control" check is to make sure the fund is no-load and open-end.

Step 2: Check the Fund's Track Record

The chart and text at the front of the prospectus will describe the fund's performance history—and sometimes forecast future performance, with lots of caveats, of course. Here is where you can apply what I told you earlier about the desirability of having weathered at least one market cycle, fund size, and how quickly the fund may have grown.

New SEC rules, including clearer presentation of annual gains and losses, will make these financial charts and tables easier to read—and more useful—than in the past. One big improvement will be a required comparison between the fund's *after expense* performance and a relevant index, such as the S&P 500 for an equity fund or the Lehman Corporate Bond Index for a fixed-income fund, and optional comparisons against their closest rivals. These features alone, I predict, will go a long way toward cutting down on the astounding growth in the number of actively managed funds and increase the number of investors who give up their starry-eyed hopes of beating the market consistently and see the wisdom of indexing for long-term growth.

Step 3: Check the Operating Expenses

Look up the cost elements you want to compare among your candidate funds in each prospectus's index. Apply the cost criteria I've given you earlier in this book for each type of fund.

The expense ratio is usually presented with the asset data, although you sometimes need a magnifying glass to see it. While you're there, check the "turnover rate," or the percentage of securities traded within the period stated. If significantly more than half of the portfolio is traded during the period, you may want a more decisive (or better qualified) asset manager to run the fund. Compare, too, the "contingent deferred sales charge," or back-end "stinger" or penalty sometimes charged for redeeming your shares before the expiration of a specified initial holding period, as well as the other fees I've mentioned. If you notice a wide divergence in the types and amounts of fees for very similar funds, make a list of those costs for each candidate and add them up. You don't want to select a low-expense ratio, no-load fund only to discover you'll be eaten alive by a lot of kooky, nonstandard fees the manager threw in to make up the difference.

Step 4: Check the Fund's Special Features

Frugal Investors are regular *re*investors, so you'll want to make sure the fund offers a good dividend reinvestment plan. If the fund is part of your IRA, check the index for any special information that may affect your plan, such as securities the fund holds that aren't recognized by the IRS for that function.

Step 5: Check the Management's Tenure

Some advisors will tell you to study the managers' resumes in great detail, but I think that's a waste of time. Unless you work in the investment industry, you probably won't recognize even the bigger "brand names" among fund managers and their former employers. The same is true for the fund's custodian bank, transfer agent, CPA, and all the rest. If the fund has been around for at least one business cycle and has generated some good returns, you can safely assume that the people in charge know what they're doing.

What *is* important is how long the management team has been in place. Even a good fund with too many new faces will suffer a learning curve of anywhere from a few months to several years while the "new guys" figure out what they want to do and how they're going to do it. If most of the key players have changed within the past year, go to the next candidate.

How to Evaluate an Annual Report

Among the venerable rituals of corporate life is the issuance—free—of the *annual report to shareholders*: a document purporting to inform investors (and anyone else who's interested) about the company's performance, accomplishments, problems, and financial condition over the preceding year. Although these (often very slick and colorful) booklets tend to come across as elaborate PR pieces, the trend in recent years has been to make their contents more meaningful—the intent of the SEC and Financial Accounting Standards Board (FASB) rules that dictate their format and, indeed, their very existence.

The following are the components of a typical corporate annual report I feel are most relevant to Frugal Investing:

Step 1: Check the Financial Highlights

At the beginning of a report, often on the inside front cover, the company presents an excerpt, or "highlights," of the more detailed financial statements inside. Naturally, these more often tell good news than bad, and are no substitute for the comprehensive statements from which they're drawn. My rule of thumb: If the highlights look great, be on guard. If they seem to tell a balanced tale that jibes with what you know from media reports, price quotations, and quarterly reports from the company, give the firm a couple of points for honesty and keep reading.

Step 2: Dissect the Top Excecutive's Letter

The first real mistake many investors make is to ignore the president's letter as so much propaganda. In truth, this is one of the most useful parts of the report because it's the first place where *knowledge*—the interpretation of information gleaned from facts—is presented in summary form. In my experience, most presidents (or CEOs or board chairmen or whoever authored the letter) have a high moral and personal stake in the letter and try to deal substantively with questions they believe investors and critics may raise about the year the company has had. In fact, a senior Wall Street executive, Benjamin Edwards (chairman of A.G. Edwards & Sons, an investment and brokerage firm) broke new ground in annual report candidness when he acknowledged, in his 1994 report's letter to shareholders, his abhorrence of "the proliferation of fees and charges our industry is imposing on investors." His example won't be lost on other brokerage chiefs and the heads of the companies whose securities these firms buy.

In short: note the two or three main points of self-criticism the letter makes, or hints at, then look for substantiating or explicating information in the other parts of the report—especially in the financial statements.

Step 3: Check Selected Parts of the Financial Statements

Unless, like me, you have an interest in photography, you'll skip over the pages and pages of glossy four-color photos of happy workers, imposing skyscrapers, and sparks flying above high-tech production machinery and go straight to the financial section—basically the last half of the report. (Since the staffers who put the report together think investors look mainly at pictures, here is where most of the annual report's budget has gone. Enjoy it, but don't depend on it for significant information.)

The most important thing to remember about financial statements is that each fact depends on another for accurate interpretation. Like a plate of spaghetti or house of cards, you can't move one part of it without affecting another. The key is to know which parts are worth bothering with; and fortunately, that's a lot fewer than most people think.

A: CHECK THE INCOME STATEMENT

Also called the *profit and loss statement*, this is like a newsreel, or video, showing the inflow and outflow of money during the year: where it came from and where it went. The proverbial bottom-line tells you whether all this resulted in a profit or loss. I think *profit before taxes* is a much more relevant measure of managerial success, since (depending on the industry) our mammoth and complex tax structure tends to distort virtually everything it touches. To compare one year's performance to another, however, look primarily at *net earnings*, or profit *after* tax, since this is the basis for dividends and virtually all the stocks I find acceptable for Frugal Investing have a long history, and stated policy, of paying competitive dividends. Obviously, you want to see net earnings that grow steadily, year after year, rather than one or two spectacular years followed by one or two years "in the red."

B: CHECK THE BALANCE SHEET

If the income statement is like a motion picture, the balance sheet is like a snapshot taken before, then after, the action started. Its whole purpose is to show you how the company's assets and liabilities changed during the year, and how those changes affected *owner's equity*, or shareholders' net worth—what you're left with when liabilities are subtracted from assets. This is also known as the *book value* of the company; a measure of what shareholders can claim if the company goes belly up. When you calculate the stock's price-to-book ratio, you're really looking at how well the company's management has acted as stewards of shareholder wealth.

One of the most important measures of balance sheet health is *liquidity*, and it means the same thing for companies as it does for individuals. Just divide the current assets by the current liabilities. Long-term liquidity, or *solvency*, is gaged by dividing the dollar value of fixed assets by the company's long-term debt. Most accountants agree that no healthy company should owe more than its net worth.

The last thing I look at on the balance sheet is *retained earnings:* the amount of money the company keeps to expand or self-finance new operations. If you're interested in growth, the retained earnings should be high. If you've invested for income, this value should be low, since a dollar of retained earnings is one less dollar available for dividends.

C: CHECK THE SOURCE AND APPLICATION OF FUNDS

Also called the *statement of changes in financial condition*, this portion of the financial section gives further explanations about why the income statement and balance sheet came out the way they did. The main things to check here are where the cash for operations came from: new debt, new equity issues, from normal day-to-day business, or from nonbusiness operations (such as royalties or income from the company's own portfolio of investments). Naturally, you don't want high income and a plump balance sheet financed by funds that have little or nothing to do with the company's reason for being here: its lines of business. It's interesting, but less useful, to know how such cash was "applied"—to build inventories, pay workers, construct new factories, purchase a new jet plane for the executives, or whatever. Again, too much money going for nonbusiness operations, egregiously high executive salaries and perks, or nonproductive acquisitions and mergers suggest the company's top management may have forgotten why they're in business.

D: CHECK THE FINANCIAL FOOTNOTES

Ignoring the financial fine print is the second big mistake many novice evaluators make. You don't have to read it all, but if you think there is a "smoking gun" lurking behind the financial facts, here's the most likely place to find it. The financial statement footnotes are where most companies "bury the bodies"— explain bad news that has otherwise been camouflaged in the data. That's why the footnotes are sometimes longer than the financial statements themselves! Thank the SEC and FASB for this; most companies certainly wouldn't volunteer such information on their own. If anything you've seen so far looks too good or too bad to be true, check it out in the footnotes.

Step 4: Check the Auditor's Statement

The independent *auditor's opinion* is usually a short paragraph at the end of the financials affirming that the statements were prepared according to generally accepted accounting practice and represent a fair appraisal of the firm's condition. If the auditor's statement fails to say this, or runs half a page or more in length, then some skeletons may have been discovered in the firm's accounting closet and you should know about them.

Step 5: Check the Company's Long-Term Track Record

Most annual reports compile five- and ten-year summaries of previous results taken from past financial statements. Although, as a Frugal Investor, you plan to stick with your investment and make OCP/DCA contributions through good times and bad, a company headed for bankruptcy or liquidation (or, more likely, acquisiton by or merger with some industry sharpshooter) sometimes tips its hand in these historical charts. Because Frugal Investors put money almost exclusively in blue chips, I rarely advise dumping a stock because of an adverse trend. However, if the firm is *not* a dividend-paying blue chip and shows more than three or four consecutive years of net losses *and* the qualitative evaluations and explanations in the president's letter, financial statements, and the media are bleak, it may be time to dust-off Value Line and think about jumping ship before the waves roll over the deck.

To sum up: One annual report is seldom a reliable guide to a company's performance, and hence its prospects for delivering continued growth or dividends. By comparing a series of annual reports, however, then comparing these sequential changes to similar changes in competing firms in the same industry, you *can* get a pretty fair picture of a firm's, and a stock's, prospects for delivering the results you need. Here are a few that tend to mean the most over time:

- *Earnings:* Earnings should steadily increase from year to year.
- *Profit margin:* The profit margin should be constant or slightly increase over the years.
- *Return:* Return on equity, or the amount of investor money used to capitalize the company, should remain competitive with alternative investments—not just other stocks, but the prevailing return of securities in other asset categories, like bonds.

Above all, the best stock prospects adhere to one of the fundamental Frugal Investing criteria I gave you at the beginning of this book: *they must engage in business operations that enhance the quality of life in America.*

If they don't, such success as they may have enjoyed to date will likely not continue too far into the future.

Appendix D

Sample Treasury Direct Tender Forms

Figure D-1. Sample Treasury Direct Tender Forms.

FORM PD F 5176-1
(February 1990)

OMB No. 1535-0069
Expires: 09-30-92

TREASURY DIRECT®

TENDER FOR 13-WEEK TREASURY BILL

TENDER INFORMATION

AMOUNT OF TENDER: $ _____

FOR DEPARTMENT USE

BID TYPE (Check One) ☐ NONCOMPETITIVE ☐ COMPETITIVE AT ▊▊ . ▊▊ %

ACCOUNT NUMBER ▊▊▊ - ▊▊▊ - ▊▊▊▊

TENDER NUMBER
912794

INVESTOR INFORMATION

CUSIP

ACCOUNT NAME

ISSUE DATE

RECEIVED BY

DATE RECEIVED

ADDRESS

EXT REG ☐

FOREIGN ☐

BACKUP ☐

CITY   STATE   ZIP CODE

REVIEW ☐

TAXPAYER IDENTIFICATION NUMBER

CLASS ▢

1ST NAMED OWNER ▊▊▊ - ▊▊ - ▊▊▊▊ **OR** ▊▊ - ▊▊▊▊▊▊▊
SOCIAL SECURITY NUMBER   EMPLOYER IDENTIFICATION NUMBER

TELEPHONE NUMBERS

WORK (▊▊▊) ▊▊▊ - ▊▊▊▊   HOME (▊▊▊) ▊▊▊ - ▊▊▊▊

PAYMENT ATTACHED

TOTAL PAYMENT: $ _____

NUMBERS

CASH (01): $ _____   CHECKS (02/03): $ _____

SECURITIES (05): $ _____ $ _____

OTHER (06): $ _____ $ _____

DIRECT DEPOSIT INFORMATION

ROUTING NUMBER

FINANCIAL INSTITUTION NAME

ACCOUNT NUMBER

ACCOUNT TYPE ☐ CHECKING
(Check One)

ACCOUNT NAME ☐ SAVINGS

AUTOMATIC REINVESTMENT

1 2 3 4 5 6 7 8 Circle the number of sequential 13-week reinvestments you want to schedule at this time

AUTHORIZATION

For the notice required under the Privacy and Paperwork Reduction Acts, see the accompanying instructions.

I submit this tender pursuant to the provisions of Department of the Treasury Circulars, Public Debt Series Nos. 1-86 and 2-86 and the public announcement issued by the Department of the Treasury.

Under penalties of perjury, I certify that the number shown on this form is my correct taxpayer identification number and that I am not subject to backup withholding because (1) I have not been notified that I am subject to backup withholding as a result of a failure to report all interest or dividends, or (2) the Internal Revenue Service has notified me that I am no longer subject to backup withholding. I further certify that all other information provided on this form is true, correct and complete.

_____ SIGNATURE   _____ DATE

SEE INSTRUCTIONS FOR PRIVACY ACT AND PAPERWORK REDUCTION ACT NOTICE

☆ U.S. GPO: 1991 – 291-492

Figure D-1. Sample Treasury Direct Tender Forms *(continued)*.

PD F 5174-1
Department of the Treasury
Bureau of the Public Debt
(Revised May 1994)

OMB NO. 1535-0069

TREASURY DIRECT

2-3 YEAR TREASURY NOTE TENDER

TENDER INFORMATION   AMOUNT OF TENDER: $ _____   FOR DEPARTMENT USE

TERM _____

BID TYPE (Check One) ☐ NONCOMPETITIVE ☐ COMPETITIVE AT ▉▉ . ▉▉ %

TENDER NUMBER

912827

TREASURY DIRECT ACCOUNT NUMBER   ▉▉▉▉-▉▉▉-▉▉▉▉

CUSIP

INVESTOR INFORMATION

ISSUE DATE

ACCOUNT NAME

RECEIVED BY

DATE RECEIVED

EXT REG ☐
ADDRESS (FOR NEW ACCOUNT ONLY)

FOREIGN ☐

BACKUP ☐

REVIEW ☐

CITY   STATE   ZIP CODE

TAXPAYER IDENTIFICATION NUMBER

1ST NAMED OWNER ▉▉▉-▉▉-▉▉▉▉   OR   ▉▉-▉▉▉▉▉▉▉   CLASS ☐

SOCIAL SECURITY NUMBER   EMPLOYER IDENTIFICATION NUMBER

TELEPHONE NUMBERS   (FOR NEW ACCOUNT ONLY)

WORK (▉▉▉) ▉▉▉-▉▉▉▉   HOME (▉▉▉) ▉▉▉-▉▉▉▉

PAYMENT ATTACHED   TOTAL PAYMENT: $ _____   NUMBERS

CASH (01): $ _____   CHECKS (02/03): $ _____

SECURITIES (05/06): $ _____ $ _____

OTHER (07): $ _____ $ _____

DIRECT DEPOSIT INFORMATION   (FOR NEW ACCOUNT ONLY)

ROUTING NUMBER ▉▉▉▉▉▉▉▉▉

FINANCIAL INSTITUTION NAME ▉▉▉▉▉▉▉▉▉▉▉▉▉▉▉▉▉▉▉▉▉▉▉▉▉▉▉▉▉

ACCOUNT NUMBER ▉▉▉▉▉▉▉▉▉▉▉▉▉▉▉▉▉▉▉▉▉   ACCOUNT TYPE ☐ CHECKING

ACCOUNT NAME ▉▉▉▉▉▉▉▉▉▉▉▉▉▉▉▉▉▉▉▉▉▉▉   (Check One)   ☐ SAVINGS

AUTHORIZATION

I submit this tender pursuant to the provisions of Department of the Treasury Circulars, Public Debt Series Nos. 2-86 (31 CFR Part 357) and 1-93 (31 CFR Part 356), and the applicable offering announcement.
Under penalties of perjury, I certify that the number shown on this form is my correct taxpayer identification number and that I am not subject to backup withholding because (1) I have not been notified that I am subject to backup withholding as a result of a failure to report all interest or dividends, or (2) the Internal Revenue Service has notified me that I am no longer subject to backup withholding. I further certify that all other information provided on this form is true, correct and complete.

_____   _____
SIGNATURE   DATE

*U.S.GPO:1994-378-760/00319   SEE INSTRUCTIONS FOR PRIVACY ACT AND PAPERWORK REDUCTION ACT NOTICE

Figure D-1. Sample Treasury Direct Tender Forms *(continued)*.

PD F 5174-3
Department of the Treasury
Bureau of the Public Debt
(Revised April 1994)

OMB NO. 1535-0069

TREASURY DIRECT®

5-10 YEAR TREASURY NOTE TENDER

TENDER INFORMATION

AMOUNT OF TENDER: $ _____

FOR DEPARTMENT USE

TERM _____

BID TYPE (Check One) ☐ NONCOMPETITIVE ☐ COMPETITIVE AT ███ . ███ %

TENDER NUMBER
912827

TREASURY DIRECT ACCOUNT NUMBER ████ – ███ – ████

CUSIP

INVESTOR INFORMATION

ISSUE DATE

ACCOUNT NAME

RECEIVED BY

DATE RECEIVED

EXT REG ☐

ADDRESS (FOR NEW ACCOUNT ONLY)

FOREIGN ☐

BACKUP ☐

REVIEW ☐

CITY   STATE   ZIP CODE

TAXPAYER IDENTIFICATION NUMBER

1ST NAMED OWNER ███ – ███ – ████ OR ███ – █████████

SOCIAL SECURITY NUMBER   EMPLOYER IDENTIFICATION NUMBER

CLASS ☐

TELEPHONE NUMBERS (FOR NEW ACCOUNT ONLY)

WORK (███) ███ – ████ HOME (███) ███ – ████

PAYMENT ATTACHED

TOTAL PAYMENT: $ _____

NUMBERS

CASH (01): $ _____ CHECKS (02/03): $ _____

SECURITIES (05/06): $ _____ $ _____

OTHER (07): $ _____ $ _____

DIRECT DEPOSIT INFORMATION (FOR NEW ACCOUNT ONLY)

ROUTING NUMBER ██████████

FINANCIAL INSTITUTION NAME ████████████████████████████████

ACCOUNT NUMBER ████████████████████ ACCOUNT TYPE ☐ CHECKING

ACCOUNT NAME ████████████████████ (Check One) ☐ SAVINGS

AUTHORIZATION

I submit this tender pursuant to the provisions of Department of the Treasury Circulars, Public Debt Series Nos. 2-86 (31 CFR Part 357) and 1-93 (31 CFR Part 356), and the applicable offering announcement.

Under penalties of perjury, I certify that the number shown on this form is my correct taxpayer identification number and that I am not subject to backup withholding because (1) I have not been notified that I am subject to backup withholding as a result of a failure to report all interest or dividends, or (2) the Internal Revenue Service has notified me that I am no longer subject to backup withholding. I further certify that all other information provided on this form is true, correct and complete.

_____ _____
SIGNATURE   DATE

SEE INSTRUCTIONS FOR PRIVACY ACT AND PAPERWORK REDUCTION ACT NOTICE

*U.S.GPO 1994-301 685/01176

Index